GLOBAL ECONOMICS
AND RELIGION

GLOBAL ECONOMICS
AND RELIGION

Edited by

JAMES FINN

Transaction Books
New Brunswick (U.S.A.) and London (U.K.)

© 1983 by Council on Religion and International Affairs
170 East 64th Street, New York, NY 10021

Library of Congress Catalog Number: 83–421
ISBN: 0–87855–477–7(cloth)
Printed in the United States of America

HB
72
G56
1983

Library of Congress Cataloging in Publication Data
Main entry under title:

Global economics and religion.

    Includes index.
    1. Religion and economics—Addresses, essays, lectures.
2. Economic development—Religious aspects—Addresses, essays, lectures.   I. Finn, James, 1924-
HB72.G56   1983   261.8'5   83–421
ISBN 0–87855–477–7

Contents

Acknowledgments vii

Introduction 1
    James Finn

PART I INDIA 11

Introductory Essay 13

  1. India: Values, Visions, and Economic Development 17
      Ralph Buultjens

  2. Religio-Cultural Values, Political Gradualism, and Economic
     Development in India 35
      Francine R. Frankel

PART II IRAN 67

Introductory Essay 69

  3. Patterns of Religion and Economic Development in Iran
     from the Qajar Era to the Islamic Revolution of 1978–79 73
      William O. Beeman

  4. Iran, Islam, and the United States 105
      R.K. Ramazani

PART III MEXICO 119

Introductory Essay 121

  5. Catholicism, Capitalism, and the State in the Development
     of Mexico 125
      Douglas C. Bennett

  6. Religion and Values in the Formation of Modern Mexico:
     Some Economic and Political Considerations 143
      Claude Pomerleau

PART IV JAPAN 161

Introductory Essay 163

  7. Religion and Economic Development in Japan: An
     Exploration Focusing on the Institution of *Ie* 167
      Koichi Shinohara

8. Interrelationships of the Economic and Social Systems in
   Japan 179
   Ron Napier
PART V NIGERIA 195
Introductory Essay 197
9. Religion and Economic Change in Nigeria 201
   Henry S. Bienen
10. Economic Values and Traditional Religion among the
    Yoruba of Nigeria 229
    Benjamin C. Ray
About the Contributors 241
Study Group Participants 245
Index 249

Acknowledgments

As project director of this study I express gratitude for all who participated, particularly those whose papers constitute this volume. I would also like to thank those many people who gave encouragement, advice, and particular suggestions, but who were unable to participate otherwise. A particular word of thanks to Theresa Mancuso who compiled the index, typed and assisted in proofreading the manuscript, and handled all the correspondence for the project. It remains only to say that these efforts and this collection would not have been possible without a grant from the Exxon Education Fund.

James Finn

Introduction

James Finn

The sorrows and hopes of our time undoubtedly stem from material causes, economic and technical factors which play an essential role in the course of human history, but even more profoundly they stem from the ideas, the drama in which the spirit is involved, the invisible forces which arise and develop in our minds and hearts.

—Jacques Maritain

It is imperative in our times to review and reconsider the relationship between religion and economics. On both the popular and scholarly levels, our understanding lags behind our perception of the significance of religion in a socially, politically, and economically complex world, and of changes in the relationship between religion and economics.

On the popular level, it is not unusual to find editorials in leading newspapers praising religion but consigning it to the private, personal realm, while news stories in the same issues report the important, occasionally startling role religion has had in some current event. Perceived as politically and economically irrelevant, religion is frequently shunted aside while attention is focused on the admittedly major political and economic factors. But in recent years and months a number of events have revealed the inadequacy of such an approach. The revolution in Iran, which took most of the world by surprise, not only forced people to ask about the role of Islam in the revolution, but to ponder its role in whatever political and economic paths Iran will take in the future. In Poland the Catholic Church

1

was a powerful force as Polish workers united in solidarity against entrenched government policies, and their opposition was and may again be strengthened by the presence of a Polish pope. In Latin America that same church is intensely involved in struggles for social and economic rights. In Africa insurgents appeal to and obtain economic aid from worldwide Christian communities, including the World Council of Churches. All the candidates in the election that established Black rule in Zimbabwe were Christians. Traditional Hindu values have been invoked and criticized by leading statesmen and politicians in India when speaking of needed economic changes. And in the politics of Sri Lanka and Southeast Asia, Buddhism plays a notable role.

In various countries not only religious majorities but religious minorities play key roles in international, commercial, and political ventures. The Christian banking community in Lebanon, the Chinese in Southeast Asia, Hindus in Africa and the Caribbean are important beyond their numbers and often influence economic policies of the countries in which they reside. These are all obvious examples to which others could be added. Less obvious, are the manifold ways in which those religions create and sustain values in terms of which people make decisions and shape their lives.

One of the pioneers in the effort to assess the impact of religion on the social and economic values of different cultures, including those of India, China, and the Protestant West, was Max Weber. Although recent scholarship has treated a number of his contributions with less than complete sympathy, his subtle and complex work remains a central reference point. The framework he established provides questions that are still pertinent. Was there, he asked, a connection between the rise of capitalism in the West and religion? If so, what was that connection? What were the conditions during this particular historical period that allowed or encouraged this new form of economic development to take place?

Economic conditions, taken by themselves, could not account for this extraordinary growth. Weber located some noneconomic conditions in the particular qualities of Calvinism—thrift, orderliness, prudence, hard work —qualities required by this new pattern of economic behavior. Some critics of Weber have attempted to turn his theory on its head, finding in the development of capitalism elements that placed a high value on certain human attitudes and forms of behavior which, in turn, helped shape the Protestant ethic that responded to these values. Other social analysts have asserted that there is a strong relationship between a religious ethic and capitalism but that the influences are reciprocal.

The study of the relationship between religion and economics has thus continued to focus on a number of concerns central to Weber's thesis, and some contemporary debates are prefigured, if underdeveloped, in the earlier discussions. Since the end of World War II (to short-circuit decades of scholarship and experimentation) there have been various attempts not only to understand better the forces behind religion and economic growth, but also to extend the benefits of economic growth to those countries that, during the 1960s, were commonly referred to as underdeveloped. Among the experts who worked in this field, a significant number assumed a rough correlation between economic growth and development: if an under-developed country could increase its per capita gross national product, it would be on the road to self-sustaining development. Western technical experts in particular favored models that introduced modern technology, industrialism, rationalized work procedures, and the values of individual-ism and entrepreneurship. Some analysts were content to focus on the economic aspects of these matters, assuming that other aspects, however interesting, were dependent variables that would, in due course, align them-selves with the new economic processes. The path of development was expected to be historically marked out by Western countries.

This narrow approach was never satisfactory to all the experts. In his three-volume study on poverty, *Asian Drama,* Gunnar Myrdal expressed a number of reservations that, to a greater or lesser degree, many others shared. He initiated his study with the conviction that economic problems could not be studied profitably in abstraction from their social, political, and demographic setting. Only a broad, institutional approach, he felt, would allow him to understand the economic development in the region. He also felt that to apply to South Asia theories and concepts that derived from and were appropriate to Western societies was to introduce a distort-ing bias. That is, general propositions derived from the study of particular countries at particular times cannot readily be universalized and applied to other cultures, countries, or times.

Like a number of other "experts in development," Myrdal concluded that he knew of "no instance in present-day South Asia where religion has induced social change." And again, "by characterizing popular religion as a force of inertia and irrationality that sanctifies the whole system of life and work, attitudes and institutions, we are, in fact, stressing an important aspect of underdevelopment, namely, the resistance of that system to planned induced changes along the lines of the modernization ideals."[1]

Views such as these are still current and strong. For a number of people who hold them it follows quite naturally that those attitudes, beliefs, cus-toms, and institutions that are obstacles to the desirable goals of economic growth and modernization should be overcome—destroyed, if necessary. But since resistance to change is profound, the success of this model de-pends on a forceful imposition from above. It would be unrealistic to expect its democratic implementation. Short of the imposition of measures appropriate to such a model—not always a realistic prospect—it might still be possible to encourage the privatization of religion, to limit or exclude the participation of religion and the sacred from social decision making. In brief, society could and should be secularized.

The Revolt

Development models based on these diverse assumptions have been employed for years in different areas of the world with varying degrees of success, measured in terms of GNP or per capita GNP. There has also been a growing disenchantment with dominant development models and concepts. It is not because noticeable—in some instances, remarkable—improvements have not been realized in the decades since World War II. But unease and dissatisfaction with methods and results are extensive; a reevaluation is underway.

It is possible to list, without attempting to mediate, some central points of concern. The concept that growth defined as increase in per capita GNP is in itself a sufficient or even desirable goal is being critically assessed. Although some development economists still equate growth with development, others question it on various grounds. First, it is possible for a country to achieve remarkable growth but in such a way that the increase is unevenly distributed. The gap between the rich and poor increases, the poor sometimes falling back not only in relative but in absolute terms. According to this view, the equation between growth and development must be broken. The concept of growth should be limited to the increase of GNP. It can be measured with a fair degree of accuracy. Development, however, is an evaluative term suggesting criteria by which growth can be judged as more or less desirable, helpful.

Another criticism of the view that growth equals development has been couched in terms that support a rejection of development itself. In 1967, Pope Paul VI issued an encyclical that said that "development is the new name for peace." Enthusiastically adopted for some years, particularly by many Latin Americans, it later came under attack and was rephrased to read "development is the new name for exploitation." The charge was that the development that took place in Latin American countries was growth that did not benefit the people of Latin America. What was being criticized was a kind of growth judged unbeneficial. What was being demanded was change in accordance with certain standards.

A concept closely associated with economic growth and one now subjected to critical evaluation is that of modernization. Marked economic growth today is usually dependent on technology and its rationalized procedures. These are powerful forces which, when introduced into a developing country, have a disturbing effect on the culture, institutions, and traditions. Old patterns of life are shaken, new ones are encouraged. For some time this process was generally regarded as both desirable and irreversible. For a variety of historical reasons both assumptions are being reexamined. Modernization is now being regarded as a mixed package, some elements of which are more valuable than others. In the early 1980s this question is pertinent to societies as different as Iran and Poland. Religious leaders in Iran have insisted, for example, that they are not opposed to "genuine modernization" but only to the uncritical acceptance of measures that erode their own religious, moral, and cultural values. The assumed irreversibility of modernization, with the many complex factors involved in that process, is also challenged. Present emphasis on limits and the calls for zero growth run counter to plans and expectations that long fueled development and modernization efforts. The resistance is sufficiently extensive to have been labeled a "revolt against modernity."

Still another related concept is secularization. Myrdal, in the work cited previously, said that important research could be done on "whether, to what extent, and how fast, secularization is diminishing the force of this source [religion] of social inertia and irrationality, as a result of the spread of the modernization ideals and planning and other social economic changes." This suggestion is couched in the cautious terms of a careful scholar. Others, less cautious, have assumed that secularization was a desirable and likely, if not inevitable, corollary of modernization planning. This group includes Christians who observed that secularization had increased the measure of religious liberty in the West and favored its extension to other areas of the world. Now, however, in different parts of the world and for various reasons, secularization is being challenged. In Latin America, for example, religion has become a support and unifying force for those struggling against what they see as forces of oppression. For the people involved in this struggle, religion—not secularization—is the liberating force.

Accommodations

All these reservations, reviews, criticisms, reevaluations, do not add up to a coherent, unified view. They indicate that the deficiencies of past and present patterns of economic change are forcing people to look in different and new ways at the relation of economics to religion and cultural values. Robert Bellah, a sociologist who has deeply studied these questions, has conjectured that even those who are critical of the overwhelming dominance of modern technical culture are themselves sufficiently in thrall that they find it difficult to hear what traditional religious wisdom might tell us about our present condition. What traditional religions have in common, he suggests, is a general skepticism that modern ideology will provide an adequate response to that condition. "The traditional religions, however variously they may express it, hold forth an ideal of human fulfillment, both personal and interpersonal, that goes far beyond the search for wealth and power, comfort and control, because it promises to bring human life into some kind of harmony with the Holy or the Good that infinitely transcends it."[2]

Some theorists of development have attempted to be more specific about what such an insight, pressed into service, might yield. One evolving position is that every freely functioning society operates from a moral base; that is, the society has a generally accepted set of standards and norms which provide criteria and guidance for both individual and collective acts. Economic growth and development that run counter to or are indifferent to this moral base will, in time, founder and provoke contradictory impulses in the society. Those economic plans and activities that are sensitive to and take sympathetic account of this moral base, these societal norms, are most likely to have long-range possibilities of success.

In most parts of the world societal norms will not be comprehended apart from the dominant religions of the region. A participant in a recent symposium on religious values and development stated it thus: "A view which sees religion as a major factor in the moral base of society and consequently as a social limit on development is likely to provide a more fruitful view of how religion and development intertwine."[3] One of the most eloquent spokesmen for this view is the Indonesian philosopher Soedjatmoko. He has said: "The religio-cultural substratum in which prevailing value configurations are rooted constitutes the inescapable baseline from which modernization will have to start if it is to have any permanent effect at all and if it is not to become a superficial and temporary aberration in a long process of historical continuity or stagnation. . . . The search for solutions in keeping with religio-cultural norms initially may retard the development process and the rate of growth. On the other hand, history has shown the magnitude of the political costs incurred when the traditional sectors are allowed to fall behind in the development process."[4]

To take such views seriously is to recognize that it is not sufficient to say that development plans must be sensitive to religious values, as if religious traditions were static and unchanging. The religious communities must themselves seek in their traditions the resources to cope with contemporary conditions. "The great natural religions, as well as the prophetic religions of Islam and Christianity," says Soedjatmoko, "must come to terms with societies whose historical dynamics have turned out to be stubbornly autonomous and which have drawn people outside the social and individual morality of these religions."[5]

Viewed from this perspective, religious communities and economic planners are more likely to achieve goals agreeable to both if they work not in opposition but in ways that make acceptable accommodations to each other. Historically, religious faiths have not only provided standards for judging the world but have developed new forms of participation. Today economic planners are increasingly attentive to the noneconomic aspects of rapid material progress, the religio-cultural values that are not to be measured in quantitative terms.

This is the arena in which the significant and rich relations between economics and religion are being reexamined today. Applied to the United States, this reexamination has produced in recent years a small but growing body of literature that challenges long-standing conventional views of industrialization, modernization, capitalism, corporate practices, and multinational enterprises. The ways in which these processes and entities have been evaluated by major religious communities are also being reexamined. The result is lively discussion and debate on issues that are central to global economics. It is too early to predict the outcome of this ferment; but it will become increasingly difficult to remain content with long-standing views, pervasive in this country, about the relation of religion and religious values to economic issues.

The project which is the substance of this book was undertaken with the perspective provided by this general understanding. The particular mode of examination was determined by a small group made up of Robert Myers, president of the Council on Religion and International Affairs; Kenneth W. Thompson and Ralph Buultjens, both trustees of CRIA; and myself as project director. We explored a number of alternative procedures before we decided to adopt an approach that had been successfully employed in an earlier CRIA project. Instead of focusing on a single region, religion, or economy—all legitimate avenues of investigation—we decided to examine countries with significant economies and different major religions in various parts of the globe. As the table of contents evinces, our choices narrowed down to a selection of India, Iran, Mexico, Japan, and Nigeria. Each has an economy that is significant in terms of its region—it has a measurable impact on neighboring countries—and in terms of U.S. interests. The major religions of these countries include Hinduism, Islam, Christianity, Shinto, Buddhism, Confucianism, and what are generally termed traditional (folk) religions.

After these countries had been selected, I asked a handful of acknowledged authorities to address various aspects of these large but circumscribed issues. For each country I asked two experts to focus on related but different portions of our overall examination. At the risk of oversimplifying the procedure, I will say that one person was asked to concentrate on the relation of religious practices and beliefs to the informing values of the society, those values which are an assumed part of societal life and which cannot be challenged without setting up internal contradictions. The other person was asked to relate these informing values to observable patterns of economic activity. These differing tasks were not meant to exist in watertight compartments but to complement each other, and this they did in the intense discussion of which they were the focus.

The group to which each of these experts presented his or her paper was made up of political scientists, economists, theologians, businessmen, missionaries, anthropologists, and regional experts. It has been said that regional experts tend to see the aspects of a region that distinguish it from others, while authorities in cross-cultural disciplines see the similarities. Whatever the validity of this observation, we attempted to cope with it by ensuring that each paper was subjected to different disciplines and approaches. The inquiry became cross-cultural and international. The composition of each discussion group provided a broad spectrum of knowledge and angles of vision. The discussions were both wide-ranging and incisive, focusing at different times on relevant concepts such as tradition versus modernism; the family and societal structures analogous to the family; central authority and the periphery; hierarchy, status, and equality; the entrepreneurial role of the state; public morality and public policy; religion, political variables, and economic policy. But whatever the concept and whatever the region being examined the attempt was always to discern what have been termed "patterns of plausibility," to describe the underlying core values which permeate and support the institutions and activities of a particular society and to perceive how they relate both to the major religion(s) and the economies of that country. In the light of discussion, questions, additional information, and insights, the papers were then revised. This volume is the result.

An additional word about this volume and its intentions is in order. Everyone who participated in the project understood both its scope and self-acknowledged limitations. Each set of essays here is illuminating and self-contained. Each set reveals much about the delicate and profound relations between economics and religion in the selected country. But these essays also point beyond themselves, for those relations take different shape as one looks from one geographic area to another, one religion to another, one economy to another. The same sets of questions will provoke different responses as one moves, for example, from Japan to Mexico to India to Africa. To be more specific: in the following pages, Douglas Bennett brings a particular approach to his analysis of Catholicism and development in Mexico. Were he to apply the same method to an analysis of the same issues in another largely Catholic country, say Argentina or Chile, his findings would be different and the comparison would be instructive. Or were William Beeman to investigate the relation between Islam and economic issues in Indonesia using the anthropological method he brings to bear on his analysis of Islam in Iran, his findings would also be different and the comparison of the effects of Islam in different countries would be illuminating.

These comparative studies should help answer one of the most difficult questions that face scholars, businessmen, political analysts, economic planners, and all who are seriously concerned with the relationships between religion and development: Why does a particular religion seem to have different economic consequences in different settings? In seeking answers to this question—or to make general and valid statements about the relation between religion and economics—one must start with the particulars. The following pages provide many of those particulars.

Notes

1. Gunnar Myrdal, *An Approach to the Asian Drama* (Selections from *Asian Drama: An Inquiry into the Poverty of Nations*) (New York: Random House, 1970), pp. 109-10.
2. Robert Bellah, "Faith and a New World Order," *International Development Review* 22 (no.1, 1980-81):35.
3. *Religious Values and Development* (Notre Dame, Ind.: University of Notre Dame Press, 1979), p. 26.
4. "Development and Human Growth." In Development and Freedom, Ishizaka Lectures, no. 3 (unpublished).
5. Ibid.

Part One

INDIA

Introductory Essay

Any hypothesis examining the relationship between religion, economics, and national development, will sooner or later focus on India. The lineaments of Indian society have been and continue to be deeply marked by religion. Perhaps even more significant than the intensity of this belief is the multilayered nature of the Indian religious experience.

Over the past several centuries there has been on the subcontinent an interaction between most of the major faiths of mankind—Hindu, Buddhist, Moslem, Sikh, and Christian. While each has largely preserved its own identity and integrity, the presence, coexistence, and continuity of these religious traditions have made India unique as a spiritual meeting-place. This in turn creates a strong social role for religion in that it affects almost every segment of society.

In the twentieth century these spiritual traditions have affected the evolution and development of public policy. In varying degrees, elements of these beliefs have converged into and inspired the making of the great modern secular "religion" that is Indian nationalism. Since the creation of the Republic of India in 1947, the ideas of the great faiths have had a considerable impact on a society in the process of nation building.

During the thirty-five years of India's existence as an independent nation, a substantial transformation has taken place. This transformation is little realized outside India, yet it is of global significance since it concerns 15 percent of the Earth's population. From being primarily a rural economy, India is now the ninth largest industrial producer in the world, having available major human resources in this area. Agriculture has expanded so that India can now feed itself from domestic food sources—a condition which neither the Soviet Union nor China has achieved. This progress has been constrained and skewed by several severe problems, but the gains have been real.

The concurrent existence of these two conditions—deep religious imprints and considerable economic development—raises a number of issues. Among the most intriguing, in the context of the relationship between religion and economic development, are five interrelated questions:

1. Is there any connection between religion and recent economic development in India?
2. If there is, has the relationship enhanced or allowed for the economic progress that has taken place?
3. Have religious traditions retarded economic growth or contributed to the economic problems besetting the nation?
4. Does the relationship between religion and politics affect economic development?
5. What is the prospect for religious influence on economic policy in the future?

In succeeding chapters, two eminent scholars with many years of field experience in India, examine these questions from different perspectives. Francine Frankel reviews India's economic development and discusses the idea that noneconomic factors are the major explanation for many of its economic problems. Refuting the widely held notion that the rural economy has stagnated, Frankel suggests that a more correct picture indicates overall growth with wide regional variations. These variations, she asserts, are largely due to noneconomic elements, and improvement can only come about through a change in religio-cultural attitudes; a change best engineered through democratic politics practiced over time.

This economic gradualism could perhaps be accelerated by a decline in some of the social manifestations evolving from India's religious traditions, such as caste. In developing this theme, Frankel analyzes the contribution which the ethics of modern Hinduism, seen in the ideas of Mahatma Gandhi, has made to Indian economic development. Her conclusions suggest that democratic politics could be the great economic mobilizer of the future.

Ralph Buultjens approaches these issues from a more political and philosophic dimension. He argues that concepts and ideas have long had a central importance for Indian society. This "ideological" pattern continues into our time. Buultjens perceives India as an arena in which two broad sets of ideas, two overarching visions about what India is and what it should be in the future, have clashed in recent generations.

One set of ideas, embodying a more traditional and religious content, is represented by the visions of Mahatma Gandhi. These embrace a series of values and thoughts in which religion is a major factor, and a major portion of that religious dynamic is derived from Hinduism. The other set of ideas, embodying a more modernizing content, is represented by the visions of

Jawaharlal Nehru and Indira Gandhi. These embrace a distinctly secular approach to public policy, among other more modern features. Buultjens sees Indian elections as often providing a referendum on ideas—with the modernizers having defeated the traditionalists for the most part. To summarize a complex and multifaceted argument, he believes that religion will be even less influential in determining economic development in the future.

While addressing the central concerns about religion and economic development, both Frankel and Buultjens also provide a variety of other insights about India. In doing this, they remind us of an underlying reality: to understand even the most basic questions about traditional societies, it is essential to perceive them from many different angles. India, more than most nations, requires this prismatic analysis.

J.F.

1

India: Values, Visions, and Economic Development

Ralph Buultjens

There are many ways of perceiving the quest for political power. Among the more compelling sources of inspiration which move individuals in this quest are the thirst for personal glory; a sense of class, community, or family obligation; loyalty to an organization; or belief in a complex of ideas. The political record of modern times suggests that, of these wellsprings, many of which overlap and interconnect, the most dynamic component is that of ideas. These create the visions which enable personalities to view themselves as agencies of higher purpose and to view public life as the arena on which this higher purpose has to be enacted.

Indian history, to a greater extent than that of most other nations, demonstrates this link between personal belief and public action. Through centuries cultural traditions, all profoundly penetrated by religion, have imprinted deep psychological and social patterns on the people of the subcontinent. Central to these patterns is the concept of the individual serving ends that transcend his or her particular personal situation, a theme which infuses all the major traditions of India. The internal visions, values, and beliefs of those who hold political power take on a larger significance. These flow powerfully into public policy, which then frequently becomes an extension of personal visions—individual values guiding the ethical choices made in society.

Examined within this focus, the Indian subcontinent becomes a vast historical and geographic stage on which contrasting sets of ideas about the nature of society, its purpose and organization, have clashed as powerful

17

personalities have sought to enact, market, or impose their visions on the people of the area. These clashes, frequently inspired by religious and cultural visions, reach back almost four thousand years to the roots of Indian history.

At that time, when the Aryans migrated into Northern India from Central Asia, they brought with them defined concepts of society and of man's role in the universe. Conjecture suggests that these concepts were as much a cause of conflict with the indigenous peoples as the physical invasion itself. The gods of the Aryans—Agni, Indra, Rudra, Surya, and others —were not only deities to be worshipped and manifestations of nature; they were also progenitors of a new society. And when the Aryans prayed, as the hymns of their Rig Veda tell us, they prayed for the establishment of a new world: "We will with Indra and all gods to aid us, bring these existing worlds into subjection."[1]

Centuries later, when the Islamic Moghuls also assaulted Northern India from Central Asia, they too saw their mission in the context of ideas rather than of physical conquest alone. The forerunner of the Moghuls was the fearsome warrior Timur, also known as Tamerlane, who with greater justification than more recent aspirants was proclaimed Conqueror of the World. In his memoirs Timur describes his attack on the sultanate of Delhi in the 1390s as a type of holy war to create a new society, or perhaps to demolish an ideologically uncongenial older one.[2] While the veracity of his statements is suspect, it is interesting that he felt obliged to cloak his search for booty in these terms.

Timur's assaults were sporadic, but his descendants established the Moghul dynasty in Northern India in the mid–sixteenth century and ruled a major portion of the country for about three hundred years thereafter. The Moghul emperors were diligent recorders of contemporary history and many of them left testaments, memoirs, or fragments of autobiography.[3] Once again, the desire to attribute their public policies to ideas beyond personal enhancement is evident. As Emperor Babur expresses it: "If God bring it right, we shall take Samarkand. . . . God showed right; we did take it in exactly fourteen days. . . . God has allotted to us such happiness and has created for us such good fortune that we die as martyrs, we kill as avengers of His cause."[4] Timur, in his autobiography, narrates incidents where soldiers under his orders killed thousands of men, women, and children: "The pen of fate had written down this destiny for the people of this city. I was desirous of sparing them; I could not succeed, for it was the will of God that this calamity fall upon the city."[5]

This same tendency persists in the self-perception of other Indian rulers —Hindu and Moslem, Sikh and Buddhist. The variety of historical and cultural conditions under which they ruled seems to have changed very little the way in which personal visions, often shaped by religious belief, were fused into civic policy. There was and continues to be, it is true, a coexisting belief which theoretically contrasts with the concept of the ruler as agent of ideas and visions. The concept of the Great King implied that the ruler's greatness sprang from himself and that ideas and concepts served him and were his tools, to be used or discarded as he wished.

In theory, the potential for friction between these two approaches to governance was considerable; in practice it was minimal. Even the greatest of the Great Kings, certainly most of them, readily acknowledged that their majesty derived from the ideas they served. While they may or may not have believed this themselves, their public presentation generally reflected this theme. The persistence of this feature in public life tends to support the conclusion that visions have had a momentum of their own through most of Indian history and, whether rooted in the thinking of individuals or not, have been a consistent and powerful element in the traditional culture of the subcontinent.

While the perception of the vision for and of society has often changed with time and with its protagonists, the stage has also been transformed. The early Aryans thought in cosmic dimensions, their visions embracing galactic systems and a universe far beyond the comprehension of their contemporaries in other parts of the world. However, the immediate theater of their mundane activities was only a portion of India. And so it was with most of the other ruling groups in Indian history.

The coming of the British to India in the late 1500s began to change and expand the arena. British penetration began as a commercial enterprise and the early British conquests were administered by the British East India Company, an ancestor of the modern multinational corporation. These territories were folded into the British Empire and came under direct control of the government in 1858. Eventually, the British accumulated disparate parts of India by military conquest or by negotiation with a multitude of local rulers from the last Moghul king of Delhi to local maharajas. Larger and smaller kingdoms were grafted on to the core of their territorial holdings.

The British did more than accumulate territory. They instituted an imperial regime which imposed an administrative and political unity on India, governing 60 percent of the land directly with their own officials and supervising 562 local rulers whose principalities constituted the rest of India. To do this, they developed the tools of cohesion—a centralized bureaucracy headed by the viceroy with his seat in Calcutta and later in New Delhi, an Indian civil service, an Indian army, a national communications network.

This produced an integrated opposition to colonial rule. The idea of liberating "India," a historically new construct, began to emerge. Initially, the idea was expressed through a series of military resistances and uprisings. Later, especially from the early twentieth century when Mahatma Gandhi became the leading figure of the independence movement, it was expressed through nonviolence, passive resistance, boycotts, and other peaceful means. The concept of a *national* freedom effort to liberate a *national* entity was born. Powerful personalities, often at odds with each other, led this movement. Whatever their divergencies, they all adhered to the idea of independence for India as a whole. As a result, the stage on which any political, social, or economic concept would be enacted was broadened. Any contest of ideas would hereafter be national in scope. National political power was now the key to advancing ideas and visions.

A land as large and diverse as India breeds a variety of ideas and visions about society and what it should be. The fertility of the Indian intellectual tradition enhances this proliferation. In the twentieth century there have been two distinct ways of thinking about India and its future in terms of broad sociopolitical visions—one associated with the ideas of Mahatma Gandhi and the other governed by the concepts advocated by India's first prime minister Jawaharlal Nehru and his daughter Indira Gandhi.

Each of these visions has an umbrella-like quality; under them cluster various subspecies of thought. While overarching in nature and broad enough to accommodate these subspecies, each vision embraces a distinct set of approaches toward India's problems and its future. It can be argued that the final objectives of both visions coincide: a better standard of living and equality of opportunities for all Indians. However, these are only superficial similarities which conceal deeply different notions about the nature of Indian society and the ultimate destiny of India and Indians in the world.

In one sense, these visions symbolize an untidy congealing of Indian socioeconomic and political thought into two groupings during the past eight decades. Although they have their intellectual roots in the minds of Mahatma Gandhi and Jawaharlal Nehru respectively, they are visions still subscribed to by a major portion of the opinion makers of modern India. While the two visions have sometimes come together, as in their opposition to colonialism and economic monopoly, contests between them have been at the heart of Indian politics for the larger part of the past eighty years.

The earlier vision flows from the thinking of Mahatma Gandhi and was dominant in the first half of the twentieth century. Its values were the leitmotif of the liberation struggle, and national independence was largely obtained as a result of the inspiration generated by these values. Gandhi had shaped and installed these at the center of the freedom movement, especially after it had become a mass effort in the 1920s.

The Gandhian vision blended elements of Hindu ideas, Jeffersonian economics, Greek city-state politics, and Puritan social ethics. It was both demanding and liberating, traditional and reformist. Socially it denounced sexuality and advocated prohibition, vegetarianism, extreme simplicity of dress, and rigid codes of personal behavior. It also denounced social discrimination, whether against women or underprivileged castes, and it developed vigorous action programs to combat these wrongs. Its cultural and artistic values were highly traditional, often excluding foreign influences as such. Its educational model had a traditional and highly moral content.

In economics, Gandhi believed in self-reliance to the point of autarky. People should downscale their wants and satisfy their needs through their own economic activities. Agriculture, particularly small-scale farming, was important, and a daily regimen of spinning was both morally and economically valuable for the individual. Land reform could be accomplished through persuasion and change of heart rather than through law and its enforcement. Industry and technology were suspect, for they made people dependent and caused a weakening of family and community ties. Gandhi said: "Control gives rise to fraud, suppression of truth, intensification of the black market and to artificial scarcity. Above all, it unmans the people and deprives them of initiative."[6] Manual labor was an integral part of Gandhian economics. It developed a sense of the dignity of work and contributed to self-reliance. Rejecting both Western-style socialism and capitalism, Gandhi envisaged a decentralized, village-based, self-sufficient economy functioning in harmony with nature and providing only the necessities of existence.

The decentralized village unit was also the bedrock of the Gandhian political vision. Largely autonomous villages would govern themselves and provide the essential administrative services required for a community. Modern political parties would have little place in this world, and a rural democracy, drawing its representational character as much from consensus as from election, would prevail. Gandhi even suggested the dismantling of the Indian National Congress once independence was attained. A national movement should not be converted into a political party. The centralized, bureaucratic instruments of state would be minimized and no national military forces would exist. In foreign policy, India would be a major moral power but would seek little beyond that.

The modern consecration of bigness was highly suspect in Gandhi's thinking. He resisted ideas which would create or perpetuate large industry, large cities, large institutions, and the concentration of economic and political power. "The seven deadly sins are: politics without principles; wealth without work; pleasure without conscience; knowledge without character; commerce without morality; worship without sacrifice; and science or technology without humanity."[7]

This vision was infused with religious and moral ideas. Although primarily lodged in Hinduism, these ideas reflected the sentiments of several major world religions and the ecumenical angularities of Gandhi's spiritual perspectives.[8] Work had an almost sacred quality and, combined with the collective impact of small private initiatives, could support a national development effort directed toward India's economic self-sufficiency. Employment was not primarily a matter for state planning, but could be procured through individual effort. Improvement in the condition of the poor could come through a combination of self-help and supportive measures by the privileged, who would voluntarily contribute to these activities if their spiritual conscience was aroused. Population control was unnecessary in such a society, but where required could be achieved by personal restraint. Religious and moral imputs would underwrite the Gandhian vision and become energizing commodities in themselves. In economic terminology, macroeconomic development would be sacrificed to a system based on microeconomic solutions; nonmaterial incentives would substitute for personal enrichment as a means of mobilizing human creativity.

The inherent clarity of this vision, its easy comprehension, and its egalitarian and spiritual themes made it a formidable political force in the thirty years before Indian independence was achieved in 1947. Its economic viability, however, was not and has not been tested on any scale beyond the small experimental communities which Gandhi and his followers established. While Gandhi's vision achieved wide popular acceptance, it did not go unchallenged and at its very moment of triumph it receded.

The patriotic credentials of those who resisted all or part of the Gandhian vision were exemplary. In the early 1920s, the Bengali sage Rabindranath Tagore questioned the introverted nature of Gandhi's programs. Tagore, as dedicated to national freedom as Gandhi, suggested that India's future should not be mortgaged to its past. The implementation of Gandhi's ideas might deny India the benefits of advancement and lock it into culture-bound hypotheses. Proposing a more universalist approach, Tagore suggested the discriminating use of Western ideas and systems and their modification in the Indian context. India as a synthesis of the highest of the East and West was his aspiration. However, Tagore was a cultural rather than a mass leader, and his political and ideological impact was limited.

The next major opposition to the Gandhian vision came from Subbas Chandra Bose, one of his own close followers. Bose was a dynamic younger luminary of the Congress movement who was attracted to the organizational and apparent economic success of European Fascism in the late 1930s. Application of these robust disciplines would produce a more vitalized Indian future than any Gandhian prescription. The nonviolent and evolutionary ideas of Gandhi appeared incompatible with the urgencies Bose espoused. After a short struggle Bose was ousted from the Congress hierarchy in 1939 and eventually left the country to join the Axis in fighting against the British in World War II. Although Gandhi prevailed and Bose died a fugitive from the victorious Allies in 1945, Netaji Subbas Chandra is honored throughout India for his contribution to the anticolonial struggle and his unyielding nationalism.

The third and most serious challenge to the Gandhian vision was contained in the ideas of his political heir, Jawaharlal Nehru. A sophisticated internationalist, Nehru was a modern intellectual of the highest order who was deeply influenced by the humanistic ideals of the European Enlightenment and by the democratic socialism of more contemporary times. Unlike Tagore, Nehru was a charismatic popular leader with an extraordinary following. When the Gandhian vision finally procured India's independence in August 1947, Nehru naturally became the first prime minister and principal director of the public conscience. For seventeen years, until he died in office in 1964, Nehru's vision infused state policy and his values were implanted in most major national endeavors.

Toward the end of his life, Gandhi began to doubt the stamina of his vision and despaired of its influencing the future of India. On his seventy-eighth birthday in October 1947, he declared: "There was a time when whatever I said the masses followed. Today, mine is a lonely voice." Again, at this time, came another lament: "I find myself alone. Even Patel [deputy prime minister] and Nehru think I am wrong. They wonder whether I have not deteriorated with age. Maybe they are right and I alone am foundering in darkness." Shortly before his assassination in January 1949, Gandhi said: "All my labors have come to an inglorious end."9

The Gandhi charisma has outlasted the Gandhi vision. No significant Indian political leader fails to invoke his name and tap the reservoir of affection his memory evokes. Yet as a guideline for public policy the Gandhian vision has been long buried beneath the vision of Nehru. However, its idealism and simplicity still have a residual appeal capable of occasionally igniting political tempests.

Contained within Nehru's reverence for Gandhi and his ideas were the components of a different and more modern vision for India. It is a vision which has been, with brief exceptions during the governments of Premier Lal Bahadur Shastri (1964–66) and the Janata-Lok Dal administration (1977–79), the dominant force in Indian public life in the second half of the twentieth century. As Gandhi was not the sole originator of the constructs which constitute the Gandhian vision but was its most forceful and popular articulator, so also Nehru was not the only source of the ideas which form the Nehru vision. He did draw into his thinking a number of discrete elements which he refined into a cohesive conspectus. Indira Gandhi has in her time accepted, with some modification and redefinition, the general themes of her father's vision. The dominant political influence of Nehru and Indira Gandhi has made these ideas the cornerstone of state policy in the past three decades.

The Nehru vision, as it has endured in these years, has excited the imagination of a generation of younger Indians. Gandhi found his verities in the past. Nehru, while not rejecting tradition, saw India's future in the context of modern progress. He did not fear bigness or the concentration of power, but sought to harness large forces toward socialistic objectives and to mobilize them in national economic development efforts. Like Gandhi, Nehru was appalled by the excesses of Marxism and the predatory nature of capitalism. His answer was a compound of democratic socialism, some-what along the lines of Western European parliamentary liberalism. When Gandhi said he was against socialism, Nehru said Gandhi did not under-stand it.

Nehru's vision is grounded in four fundamental ideas, each of which have very different definitions from the Gandhian conception of these terms. For Nehru these were:

- *Democracy:* There would be large-scale representative democracy with maximum popular participation, an acceptance of dissent, and constitu-tional protection for the underprivileged and minorities. An emphasis on individual rights, rather than Gandhi's emphasis on obligations.
- *Secularism:* The state would give no preference to any particular reli-gion, nor be governed by religious principles. There would be moral hopes and perhaps moral targets, but the separation of church and state was to be clear and fundamental. Religious freedom was a personal right and would be protected by law, but religion was not a matter of public policy.
- *Nonalignment:* India would be a major force in international politics, but would position itself midway between the Western bloc and the Marxist group. It would balance and bridge the differences between these two hostile camps. More important, it would help create a new center in world affairs—a locus for new nations of the Third World who did not want entanglement in the global struggles of the superpowers.
- *Economic Planning:* There would be a mixed economy with government controlling critical sectors of capital and production and private enter-prise coexisting in many fields. In this way, the direction of the economy would be set by the state, and central planning processes would enable the public interest to be maximized. Yet there would be ample opportu-nity for the personal profit incentive to operate in the free enterprise sector. Thus, national economic considerations and objectives could be promoted without dampening individual enthusiasm. Necessary but

low-profit public interest projects would not be underfinanced or neglected.

Socially, the Nehru vision embraced Gandhi's antidiscrimination ideas but it was in general more permissive. Social regulation was less rigid and more accommodating of human frailty. While suggesting an austere lifestyle, Nehru believed that personal choice should govern matters of food, drink, dress, and social relationships. Culturally, his perspectives were more cosmopolitan than Gandhi's. While tradition was important and valued, world culture should not be denied to Indians. Public education would be secular with a modern content. While Gandhi did separate the roles of the sexes, Nehru stressed equal opportunity according to talent. Gandhi underscored the need for social regulation and economic decontrol; Nehru tended toward the opposite.

In economics, Nehru perceived the advantages of international trade and the creation of a mixed economy. If India was both to improve the standard of living of its people and attain a degree of economic independence, the building of modern industry and the application of new technology was a high priority. A new and expanding public enterprise sector had to be created, either through the erection of state-owned corporations or the nationalization of private companies in the critical and highly capital-intensive industrial sector. International finance and foreign investment were welcome under controlled conditions. The Gandhian manifesto was rejected as uneconomic and inappropriate for the goal of modern national development. Thus, for instance, the textile factory was preferred, on quality, cost, and personal income-generating criteria, to the homespun production of cloth. Population control was a matter in which the state would intervene through education and incentive programs.

In this vision agriculture was important but industry was vital, a priority which has become more balanced as Prime Minister Indira Gandhi has shaped the Nehru legacy. Agricultural modernization would come from large capital investment by the government and land reform enforced by law. A Central Planning Commission would assist and monitor the allocation of capital by the government. The overall goal was a strong national economy which would distribute income equitably and reach for three objectives through modernized means: (1) full or adequate employment; (2) reduction of inequality through economic adjustment and legal measures; (3) elimination of absolute poverty.

The political portion of Nehru's vision coincided with the idea of the modern federal nation-state—a nationalistic entity with a strong central government and a decentralized, subordinate, federated system of provincial or local state administrations. India's 600,000 villages would fit into this structure in which modernizing impulses would flow from the center outward and downward. Electoral processes would produce a multilayered representational form of democracy from the Lok Sabha or federal legislative assembly to the Panchayat or village councils. Political parties would be the operational engines of the system on its electoral front, while a centralized national bureaucracy would conduct the administrative mechanisms of the state. National military forces were necessary to protect the country. In foreign policy, India would be a major power seeking to influence and involve itself in world events.

Although Nehru understood the religious nature of Indian society, little if anything in this vision was directly related to religious faith. His own view of religion was agnostic: "I have always hesitated to read books of religion. The totalitarian claims made on their behalf did not appeal to me. . . . Mythology affected me in much the same way. If people believed in the factual content of these stories, the whole thing was absurd and ridiculous. But as soon as one ceased believing in them, they appeared in a new light, a new beauty, a wonderful flowering of a richly endowed imagination, full of human lessons."[10]

While dismissing much of Indian religiosity as unrealistic and superstitious, Nehru did have a profound appreciation for the great cultural traditions of his nation. He had, in earlier days, written extensively about the formative and conditioning influences they had on the Indian personality—producing fatalistic, accepting, and supernaturally oriented attitudes toward life and therefore toward socioeconomic development.[11] He also saw the retardant effect which the more negative elements could have on economic development and it was his hope that with modern education these features would gradually disappear. An ethical humanism, a belief in science and technology, and a socialistic liberalism were the philosophic impulses behind the Nehru vision. Many others who have supported these ideas have accepted the statement of philosophic values underlying them, at least in terms of public profession. In that sense, the Nehru vision constitutes the modernist and secularist response to the problem of India—a macroeconomic approach offering material improvement as a means of mobilizing human creativity.

Although there has been rigorous resistance to this vision by the more conservative segments in Indian society, its essential features have been translated into a series of five-year plans and government programs. This is largely the personal achievement of Nehru himself and of Indira Gandhi, and it reflects their own position in the political scene. Although challenged by groups within the Congress Party and, more recently, by forces from outside, the modernist vision has prevailed and endures today.

In many ways, this vision has served India well. Policies derived from it have produced an economy which has the world's ninth largest industrial output, and has also finally achieved sufficiency in agriculture. Social improvements have been sustained and a variety of cultural expression has been promoted. A vital political democracy exists. India is a major and respected participant in the international political system. Considering the diversity and contending pressures in India, and prolonged unfavorable external conditions, this is a highly creditable performance.

Yet there are serious flaws in the conditions created by the Nehru vision. Endemic poverty persists and distributive justice has not matched gains in output. Modern education has not dispelled many of the more retrograde inheritances of tradition, such as caste. A strong Indian military establishment has not deterred costly conflicts. And the structure of government has inflicted a lethargic bureaucracy on society. The sophisticated nature of modern social and economic management has also tended to produce an elitist approach to the tasks of nation building. The grass-roots acceptance of the Nehru–Indira Gandhi vision has derived more from faith in their leadership than from an understanding of their ideals. Nehru and, even more, Mrs. Gandhi have had an extraordinary charismatic relationship with the Indian people. This, despite the fact that the sophisticated character of their vision makes it difficult to communicate its details to the masses except in broad general terms. However, these generalities have been understood by and inspired a generation of Indians, as nobody who has witnessed the electrifying mass response to Mrs. Gandhi's cry "Garibi Hatao" (eliminate poverty) can doubt.

Gandhi and Nehru saw India's problems in similar ways, and both shaped their visions in answer to these problems. Both drew on the traditions of the past to help frame these answers. But in interpretation, method, and approach, they differed sharply on issues such as continuity versus change. In the society of the past these differences would have been debated among small groups of traditional leaders. In modern India, the forum has been popular politics.

From this perspective, one can look at Indian general elections as referendums on visions of what India should be in the future and how to realize them. As political leaders campaign at the polls, they not only present themselves to the public, but they also articulate the visions they believe in. There are constraints on the expression of visions: populism has to be balanced against the influential local notables, regional and group tensions have to be accommodated, the behavior of frequently undisciplined party workers has to be explained, important personalities demand special attention, and appropriate obeisance has to be made to tradition. However, on the whole, there is a referendal quality in the national electoral process.

If this hypothesis is accepted, there have been seven referendums in the

seven general elections between 1951 and 1980. In each of them, the Gandhian vision and the Nehru–Indira Gandhi vision were the two principal
competing conceptions of society. At first, the dividing line between these
different sets of ideas was blurred. Many traditionalist Gandhians paid a
reluctant lipservice to the Nehru vision, sometimes for electoral reasons and
sometimes because of personal deference to the immensely popular prime
minister. Nehru himself, as Gandhi's closest associate and political legatee,
often presented his ideas as an extension of the Mahatma's concepts.

As years passed and the Nehru vision flowed into public policy, those
who interpreted Gandhi's vision in the strictest sense became increasingly
disenchanted. In some leaders, like Morarji Desai, this disenchantment was
spurred by fierce personal ambition. In others it was a genuine philosophic
disagreement. Several older leaders left the Congress Party. On Nehru's
death in 1964 the differences within the Congress Party were temporarily
resolved by the appointment of Lal Bahadur Shastri as prime minister.
Shastri seemed to give more weight to the Gandhian vision and, in several
instances, began reversing Nehru's policies. With Shastri's death in 1966
and the accession of Mrs. Gandhi to the premiership, the conflict of visions
became too acute to contain. Mrs. Gandhi was and is a firm advocate of
the Nehru vision, and she decisively pursued his ideas, adapting them to
present conditions. In 1969, another and more important group of leaders
left the Congress Party. The 1970s saw more splits. In each instance, the
defectors sought electoral endorsement of their actions and philosophy, and
in almost every instance the voters rejected their claims and opted for the
Nehru–Indira Gandhi vision.

The conflict was most powerfully joined at the 1977 elections. A number
of self-proclaimed upholders of the Gandhian vision coalesced into the
Janata Party. Its geriatric leadership consisted of Morarji Desai, Jayaprakash Narayan, Charan Singh, Acharya Kripalani, and Jagjivan Ram—
all former followers of Gandhi, all former luminaries of the Congress Party,
all in their seventies or older. Below them were the younger echelons of the
Lok Dal and Jan Sangh, who had long opposed Nehru's ideas, and several
disgruntled ex–Congress figures. It was the last political opportunity for
many of these leaders. And it was the last chance for the Gandhian vision
to claim the levers of power. The demographic profile of the Indian population, the long-term emplacement of the Nehru vision in the government
structure, and the increasing political stature of Mrs. Gandhi suggested that
the constituency for the Gandhian vision was dwindling.

The election campaign was bitterly fought. The Janata used religious
symbolism and personal invective to attack the programs and policies of
Indira Gandhi. Invoking the vision and the memory of Mahatma Gandhi,
they accused her of advocating an inappropriate, modern set of ideas for

Indian society and of imposing them in an arbitrary way. Above all, they promised to restore the Gandhian vision and dismantle many elements of the Nehru–Indira Gandhi policies. Her approach to family planning was among the most controversial issues, as was the declaration of emergency which had enabled her government to acquire strong enforcement powers between 1975 and early 1977. Mrs. Gandhi, campaigning virtually single-handed against the Janata alliance, vigorously defended her policies and constantly referred to the Nehru vision and its achievements in building modern India. At the most visible level, this election was a hotly contested struggle for power. At another and more meaningful level, it was a clash of visions and a referendum on the direction of Indian society.

In one of the most discussed elections of modern times, the Janata defeated Mrs. Gandhi's Congress Party. However, it was a victory of a particularly regional character. The Janata scored heavily in the Hindi heartland of the North, where their religious invocations and Gandhian rhetoric provoked significant response. In the South, Mrs. Gandhi increased her already strong position. In some ways, the regional polarization reflected a reaction to the conflict of visions. Across Northern India, where economic development has been spotty, the charge that Mrs. Gandhi was destroying the Hindu character of society through modern secularist approaches seemed to touch a sensitive political nerve. In Southern India, a non–Hindi-speaking area where economic development has been generally broader-based, the Nehru vision has provided protection against Hindi hegemonism, which Southern Indians have long seen as a threat.

The Janata soon set about realizing the vision they had evoked in the election campaign. Major efforts were made to include segments of Gandhi's ideas in administrative policy and a number of the Nehru–Indira Gandhi programs were aborted. Family planning was virtually abandoned, successive budgets tended to favor agrarian smallholders, small industries appeared to obtain preferential treatment, science and technology were considered less relevant for economic development, and a strong bias towards Hindi culture became evident. "Small is beautiful" was an often proclaimed theme, as Janata policymakers constantly referred to the book by that title written by the English economist E.F. Schumacher.[12]

Articulating a vision is easier than operating a government. The Janata was riven by vicious infighting, differences over policy, and divisions resulting from the vaulting ambitions of its principal leaders. Ineffective administration and massive corruption lowered public esteem of the government. Defections weakened its parliamentary majority. Above all, its charter vision appeared increasingly ineffective as it was translated into public policy. By August 1979, the Janata alliance had ruptured fatally, Prime Minister Morarji Desai had been displaced, and Lok Dal leader Charan

Singh (Desai's deputy and latterly finance minister) had succeeded him. But a government could not be sustained, and elections were scheduled for early January 1980.

Almost three years of the Janata in office had destroyed the Gandhian vision as an electoral instrument. Those who advocated it increasingly appeared as a greedy, venal coterie of aged powerseekers. Their political instrument, the Janata Party, splintered into impotent and warring factions. A vicious and prolonged vendetta against Mrs. Gandhi suggested a lack of any serious moral criteria in government. Above all, the Gandhian vision had failed to arouse the masses beyond the brief election campaign of 1977. It was unable to produce any positive impact on economic development. One can argue that the fault was not in the vision, but in those who claimed to be its guardians and implementors. But the odium of discredit was evenly spread.

In January 1980 Mrs. Gandhi returned to power with a large parliamentary majority. Her policy and public statements again expressed the concepts and approaches derived from her father's visions and which have increasingly come to be associated with her. In the year since her election, Mrs. Gandhi has continued to apply these broad guidelines to the key elements of her policies. However, she has varied their consistency to incorporate a moderate liberalization in the private business sector and some added incentives for agriculture. Whether this mix in the Nehru–Indira Gandhi vision will be able to support enhanced economic development remains the key question for India's future.

There are a series of early warning signals that suggest a turbulent period ahead. The demographic message has an economic urgency. India's population of 700 million is growing at close to 2 percent each year and 40 percent of all Indians are below fifteen years of age. They are also the beneficiaries of the first generation of mass public education, which now contains significantly less religious elements than in the past. The decline in religious education makes it likely that the fatalistic and accommodating impact of traditional beliefs will also be reduced. India's youth will not only have to be fed, clothed, housed, and employed, but their threshold of patience and endurance will probably be lowered by their schooling. This is a potentially incendiary situation.

Industrial growth has been slow in recent years and not especially oriented to high employment. Publicly owned businesses provide over four million jobs, hold almost three-fourths of the nation's industrial assets, and produce about one-third of the total industrial output. Opportunities for expansion at a rate adequate to absorb unemployment appear unlikely. Agriculture has performed effectively, but improvement in production has largely come from techniques that are also labor-saving. With 75 percent of the population living in the countryside, the introduction of more labor-intensive techniques, the dispersal of smaller industries to rural areas, and the initiation of massive job creation, public works programs appear to be essential if economic development and political stability are to be attained in the future.

The next three to five years will test the continued viability of the Nehru–Indira Gandhi vision. Three possibilities suggest themselves:

1. That the now dominant vision will be the locomotive which enables the Indian economy to move ahead with a powerful thrust and that it has prepared the economy for entering a period of dynamism which will reach impressive proportions shortly. There are signs that given relative political calm and strong leadership, this could happen in the mid-years of the decade ahead.
2. The failure of policies based on this vision may cause a resurrection of Gandhian ideas about national development. However, in the modern social and political climate of India, this course seems remote.
3. That the Nehru–Indira Gandhi vision will dissipate and that its fading will provide a transitional phase between its vigorous past and the emergence of some more vital visions of the political Left or Right.

If the Nehru–Indira Gandhi vision begins to lose vitality—what alternative ideas and forces could provide the visionary content apparently so essential a part of Indian politics? Objectively examined, India should be the proving ground for one of several Marxist theories about the relationship between poverty and revolution. Yet, two local factors have intercepted the validity of this analysis. Since Mahatma Gandhi and Jawaharlal Nehru preempted the anticolonial and nationalist positions in Indian politics, the Communist parties have had difficulty in developing an image acceptable to the Indian electorate. They are still often perceived as local agents of outside powers, embracing an alien ideology. A second reason has been the prevalence of religion. The values of Indian religion are antithetical to those implicit in Marxism and its godless nature is a liability at the polls. In thirty years of national electoral contests, the combined Marxist share of the popular vote has not exceeded 11-12 percent. Marxist doctrine has had limited acceptance among the masses or by the present and potential manipulators of the levers of power—the intellectual and financial elites, the prominent political cadres in national or state politics, organized labor, student leaders, the military, and of course, religious and moral notables. Opportunities for the orthodox Marxist to inherit or develop a primary role in the political milieu seems inauspicious, at least for the next decade or so.

The establishment conservatives also seem unable to attain the element of intellectual and emotional credibility which provides the opportunity for access to governmental power. Their activities àre beset by an inherent and irresolvable paradox. To maintain a stance as defenders of orthodoxy, they have to propound a sociopolitical prescription which embraces traditional Hinduism and the Hindi language. This immediately secures a formidable position in the Hindu-Hindi heartland of Northern India; it also immediately alienates all minority groups and the large number of non–Hindi-speaking Hindus of Southern and other parts of India. Thus, the conservatives have been and are denied the character of a national force. As modern education advances, there is a growing segment of opinion which believes that economic development cannot be based on the injunctions of religion. The multiplicity of religions in India also works against national acceptance of a politico-religious leader of the type of Ayatollah Khomeini. Taken together, these factors reduce the possibility of a sustained political resurgence of the older conservatives and traditional religious-oriented groups.

Another potential force is the nonparty elements which could reach for power in the Indian polity—mass movements of youth or peasants, the military, or even groups of alienated workers acting outside the existing trade union structure. Recent agitation by farmers' organizations in several states indicate some potential for disrupting the existing order, but little capacity to initiate a large-scale transformation of national goals and purposes. Much the same can be said of youth movements and worker activism. The military has remained politically neutral and its tradition makes politicization a remote prospect under relatively normal socioeconomic conditions. However, if any of these groups is to be politically energized, the underlying motivations are likely to be political ideologies of either Left or Right, or a rural populism, rather than religious wellsprings.

Given these counterbalancing or nonstarting considerations, the articulators of alternate visions to the Nehru–Indira Gandhi vision appear to have limited likelihood of access to power in the immediate future. Should this analysis be sustained by events, and should the Nehru–Indira Gandhi vision begin to falter seriously, one possibility emerges. Mrs. Gandhi is a flexible and resourceful political leader, who has the capacity to move beyond the policies associated with her father's and her own governments. If the imperatives of the national condition make it necessary for her to recast her own visions, she could be an effective and dynamic proponent of a new order. Under normal circumstances in Indian politics, Mrs. Gandhi would have at least ten more years of active public life, a period in which considerable readjustment could take place in Indian society.

Should such a readjustment take place, there is little evidence to suggest that it will be based on a resurgence of religious values as applied to economic development. Religious revivals and declines may well be a constant and reactive feature of modern personal and social life, but traditional Indian faiths have yet to evolve strategies for guiding modern development and influencing current public economic policy in any significant way. As the most potent part of Indian tradition, religion contains a vast potential for energizing any task it espouses, but it appears unable to respond to critical questions concerning its capacity for influencing major issues. Those issues include questions of how to extend its mass support in village communities to the increasingly important urban centers, whether to adopt an eclectic or ecumenical stance to obtain wider acceptance in contemporary society, how to weave the concepts and ethics of technology into the fabric of religious myth without diluting its content, how secular education can be prevented from undermining traditions, whether caste differences inherent in the Hindu religious structure are to be deemphasized, what the role of religion should be in the context of developmental politics.

Until these challenges are met, whatever future patterns evolve, the influence of religion as a central element in the economic progress of India appears to be clearly circumscribed. While religion will have a major role in the sociocultural sphere and its capacity to move individuals must never be underrated, its contribution to the larger spectrum of national policies has been consistently less significant in each of the three decades since the creation of the Republic in 1947. It is difficult to believe that the decade of the 1980s will reverse this trend. The vision which in so many ways brought forth the political birth of India has receded before the more secular approaches and concerns of contemporary economic circumstances.

Notes

1. *Hymns of the Rig Veda,* ed. J.L. Shastri (New Delhi: Motilal Banarsi Dass, 1976), hymn 157, book 10, p. 644.
2. *Memoirs of Timur,* trans. Charles Stewart (London: Oriental Translation Committee, 1830).
3. Memoirs or records of notable Moghul emperors include those of Akbar, Babur, and Jahangir. Some of these were directly dictated by them and some composed by writers in their courts. For a typical example, see *Tuzuk-i-Jahangir,* trans. Alexander Rogers (New Delhi: Munshiram Maroharlal Publishers, 1978).
4. *Babur-Nama* (Memoirs of Babur), trans. Annette S. Beveridge (New Delhi: Oriental Book Reprint Corporation, 1979), pp. 132, 557.
5. *Memoirs of Timur.*
6. Gandhi quoted in *The Economist* (28 March 1981): 32 (India Survey).
7. For elaboration of Gandhi's social-political-economic ideas, see his autobiography. *The Story of My Experiments with Truth* (Boston: Beacon, 1957). Also his several other writings on this subject.
8. Gandhi told the Federation of International Fellowships in January 1928:

"After long study and experience, I have come to these conclusions: (1) all religions are true; (2) all religions have some errors in them; (3) all religions are almost as dear to me as my own Hinduism. My veneration for other faiths is the same as for my own faith."

9. William L. Shirer, *Gandhi: A Memoir* (New York: Simon & Schuster, 1979), pp. 221-22.
10. Jawaharlal Nehru, *The Discovery of India* (Garden City, N.Y.: Anchor Books, 1960), pp. 40-41.
11. See Nehru's *Autobiography* (New Delhi: Oxford University Press, 1980); and other works, including *The Discovery of India.*
12. E.F. Schumacher, *Small Is Beautiful: Economics as If People Mattered* (New York: Harper & Row, 1973).

Selected Readings

Mohandas K. Gandhi, *The Story of My Experiments with Truth* (Boston: Beacon, 1957).

Jawaharlal Nehru, *Mahatma Gandhi* (New York: Asia, 1976).

Jawaharlal Nehru, *The Discovery of India* (Garden City, N.Y.: Anchor, 1960).

Donald Eugene Smith, *India as a Secular State* (Princeton, N.J.: Princeton University Press, 1963).

Indira Gandhi, *India: The Speeches and Reminiscences of Indira Gandhi* (London: Hodder & Stoughton, 1975).

Savepalli Radhakrishnan, *The Hindu View of Life* (New York: Macmillan, 1963).

M.N. Srinivas, *Social Changes in Modern India* (Berkeley: University of California Press, 1971).

Gunnar Myrdal, *Asian Drama*, vol. 1 (New York: Pantheon, 1968).

Ralph Buultjens, *Rebuilding the Temple: Tradition and Change in Modern Asia* (New York: Orbis, 1974).

B. Madhok, *Stormy Decade* (New Delhi: Indian Book Gallery, 1980).

2

Religio-Cultural Values, Political Gradualism, and Economic Development in India

Francine R. Frankel

India's experiment has compelled the interest of both the humanist and the social scientist. Perhaps in no other developing country has the political leadership so long debated the question: how can the economic gains of modernization be secured without attacking the religio-cultural foundations of the traditional social structure? Almost from the time when Mahatma Gandhi assumed command of the nationalist movement in 1920, those goals of independence defined only in terms of political freedom and economic development were questioned for having nothing to say about the moral content of modern life. On one level, Gandhi's religious lifestyle, his personal austerity, and voluminous writings assigned highest priority to removal of rural poverty. He dramatized the plight of "those toiling and unemployed millions who do not even get a square meal a day and have to scratch along with a piece of stale bread and a pinch of salt."[1] Under his leadership, Congress workers were required to alternate political tasks with "constructive work" in the villages, and to play an active part in the establishment of hand spinning and supplementary cottage industries; in basic education; and in welfare activities on behalf of untouchables to whom he gave the name of *Harijans* (children of God).

Yet Gandhi's impact on the nationalist intelligentsia went beyond his identification of the freedom movement with the social uplift of the rural masses. His inspiration as a reformer came from the popular Hindu religious movement of *bhakti*,[2] rather than the secular humanism that guided

35

liberals and socialists among the Western-educated middle classes. His zeal in working for the removal of untouchability was aimed at "purifying" Hinduism of an ugly deformity to preserve the healthy body of the ancient social order. Gandhi never altered his view that the teachings of *varna-shramadharma* and belief in the sacred obligation to observe caste duties embodied a higher moral principle of social organization than the individualism of advanced capitalist countries. He argued that the original fourfold *varna* classification of Brahmin, Kshatriya, Vaishya, and Sudra made no judgment of superiority or inferiority among the major divisions of society. All were complementary to the other and "each as necessary for the whole body of Hinduism as any other."[3] Rather, Hinduism, in its uncorrupted form, had offered a unique solution to the problem of the division of labor. It protected the organic unity of the social system from the inroads of individualism, acquisitiveness, and competition that were sapping the sources of spiritual vitality in modern civilization.

Gandhi went further. He was convinced that the ancient moral glory still survived in India in its hundreds of thousands of village communities that had endured over the milennia despite foreign invasions and colonial rule. He wrote of the peasants that "the moment you talk to them and they begin to speak . . . wisdom drops from their lips. Behind the crude exterior, you will find a deep reservoir of spirituality. . . . In the case of an Indian villager, an age-old culture is hidden under an encrustment of crudeness. Take away the encrustation, remove his chronic poverty and his illiteracy and you have the finest specimen of what a cultured and free citizen should be."[4]

According to Gandhi and those who became his devoted disciples, India's mission after Independence was to restore and rebuild the villages, to cleanse them of the impurities that had corroded but not destroyed the spiritual genius of the ancient civilization. The reconstructed village, organized around caste purged of its hierarchical content, would sharply limit individualism and competition, reconciling differences in ability with a functional division of labor. Simultaneously, the revival of small industries based on hand technologies and the application of cooperation to ownership of land, tools, and animals in agriculture, would reduce economic inequalities while restricting the scope for accumulation of wealth. Such a society was the India of Gandhi's dreams, an India that would preserve its traditional spiritual identity and offer a model of redemption from the modern illusion that life's meaning could be found in the relentless pursuit of machinery, material goods, and bodily pleasures.

The majority of the middle-class intelligentsia rejected Gandhi's vision of free India's future. Secular humanists never accepted his argument that the egalitarian reconstruction of society could be accomplished solely through an attack on untouchability within the framework of *varna-*

shramadharma. These teachings not only sanctioned ritual, occupational, and political privileges for the small number of "twice-born" castes in the Brahmin, Kshatriya, and Vaisha *varnas,* they also categorized the majority of castes as *Sudra* or servant, by definition placing them in a position of subordination to the upper castes. Modernists also rejected the idea that India should remain primarily an agrarian society. They were convinced that free India could become a strong, unified, and prosperous nation only if it carried out large-scale scientific, technical, and economic development.

Nevertheless, Gandhi's glorification of the ancient social order altered the intelligentsia's orientation to the moral content of the modern society they were trying to build. Under Gandhi's tutelage, they thought they saw in the surviving structures of traditional society—no matter how decayed or corrupted they had become—evidence of a system of social morality superior to any in advanced capitalist countries. They discovered in the institutions of the joint family, caste, and the village community, an entire society based on the "security, stability, and the continuance of the group." Men like Nehru identified the vital and enduring element in Indian society, the "worthwhile something" that had preserved India's cultural integrity over the ages of political division and disorder in the system of social organization firmly rooted in the "group ideal."[5]

During the late 1920s and early 1930s, many intellectuals who could not accept the restrictions on industries that Gandhism demanded, were attracted to Marxist theory and the practical example of the Soviet Union as an alternative socialist pattern more congenial to the Indian genius than capitalism. Socialism also appealed to Congress modernists because of its association with economic planning. It offered a "scientific" approach to the allocation of investment that seemed intrinsically superior to capitalism's dependence on unpredictable market forces.

Yet under Gandhi's influence, Indian socialists conceded that public ownership and control of the means of production would still not avoid the alienation created by the very process of modernization, although it might eliminate the economic exploitation associated with capitalism. This was particularly the case with respect to the breakdown of the extended family and local communities, either through large shifts of population to the cities, or the amalgamation of villages into huge, state-owned collective farms. Concentration of all economic resources in the hands of the state constituted an ever-present threat of political abuse and government regimentation.

Indian socialists, in an attempt to avoid the pitfalls of the Soviet model, decided on two major modifications: a mixture in industry of private enterprise and public ownership so that new units in industries of basic and strategic importance would be set up only in the public sector; and preservation of the village, reorganized around cottage and small-scale enterprises in industry, and cooperative forms of organization in agriculture, as the primary unit of economic development in the countryside. In making these revisions, the socialists held out the hope of achieving a more humanistic version of modern society than any yet realized by building on the foundations of the old group values and social units without sacrificing individual freedoms. Nehru, in a famous formulation, spoke of India's approach to national development as "a third way which takes the best from all existing systems—the Russian, the American and others—and seeks to create something suited to one's history and philosophy."[6]

The question remained of how such a transformation could be achieved. At Independence, India was still stamped with the inequalities of the most sharply stratified society in history. Despite the introduction by the British of such new principles of justice and administration as equality before the law, and recruitment on the basis of merit to the few coveted places in English medium schools and the Indian Civil Service, new opportunities for mobility in caste-free occupations were disproportionately concentrated in coastal towns and cities. In the countryside, the traditional coincidence of caste, occupation, economic rank, and power was hardly disturbed.

Gandhi had always insisted on the necessity of nonviolent techniques of social transformation. He couched his pronouncements on this issue in religious terms, celebrating the Hindu ideal of *ahimsa* (noninjury), which precluded the use of violence as a moral method of resistance to evil. Related cultural attitudes reinforced the religious motivation in his thinking. The traditional approach to conflict management, which emphasized the moral superiority of arbitration and compromise in the settlement of disputes, was linked to religious ideals of self-control and provided further justification for conciliation methods. Gandhi's personal attraction to a consensual style of conflict resolution was also consistent with his glorification of ancient village life. In his view, the village councils had protected community values by relying on arbitrational techniques in settling disputes. Judges had always been more concerned with finding a compromise solution acceptable to both sides than with strict enforcement of justice based on the merits of the case. In this way, the village community was spared the factional polarization and decline in social cohesion associated with a direct confrontation between opponents under adversary procedures.

Nevertheless, starting in the mid-1930s, socialists inside the Congress Party argued that if independence was to serve the interests of the peasant masses and workers, the privileged groups would have to be divested of their privileges. History showed, according to Nehru, that some measure of coercion would have to be applied. The most militant socialists, who formed a separate group inside Congress in 1934, and founded a new party in 1948, formally adopted a program endorsing class struggle and revolution.

Socialists both within and outside Congress underwent a profound transformation in political outlook after Independence in 1947. At Partition, India was torn by ferocious communal riots, followed within a little more than five months by the trauma of Gandhi's assassination. The noncommunist Left was badly shaken by these events. Jayaprakash Narayan, the most heroic leader of the radical socialists, took the dramatic step of announcing his conversion to Gandhi's teaching that "nothing but good means will enable us to reach the goal of a good society, which is socialism."[7] Nehru also made a firm commitment to nonviolence as the only valid means of approaching social reform in India.

The conversion of socialists to peaceful methods of change was also rooted in political realism. A myriad linguistic, religious, and caste cleavages divided the subcontinent and overlapped with economic inequalities. The poor tended to define their identity in terms of relationships based on religion, caste, kinship, and patron-client ties. They displayed, by contrast, a very weak sense of class solidarity. Under these conditions, a frontal attack on the existing social hierarchy would only delay or abort desired egalitarian changes, fragmenting large numbers of the rural poor among more potent allegiances to language, religion, and caste. Worse still, economic conflict might easily spill over into caste or religious confrontations that could eventually threaten national integration.

Such constraints placed a premium on preserving the Congress Party as an instrument of national political consensus while the leadership compromised on social issues that could provoke polarization and precipitate civil disorder. The post-Independence government tried to find a balance between the ideal of removing social, educational, and economic inequalities, and the facts of the existing situation, described by Nehru: "For a variety of causes for which the present generation is not to blame, the past has the responsibility, there are groups, classes, individuals, communities who are backward." The government had to move in the direction of the ideal without violating the fundamental rights of individuals guaranteed by the Constitution. This overarching constraint led inevitably to a strategy of social change that emphasized "pull[ing] people up and not pull[ing] them down." Such an approach could only proceed by a "step by step" advance to a state "where there is less and less inequality and more and more equality,"[8] in a process Nehru once characterized as a gradual revolution.

There could be no frontal attack on Hinduism or the caste structure of society. The framers of the Constitution, invoking Gandhi, limited themselves to abolition of untouchability, subject to legal penalties for discrimination. They also enacted special provisions for "protective discrimination" to improve the position of low castes within the framework of the existing social hierarchy. Seats were reserved in the Lok Sabha and state legislative assemblies for members of untouchable castes and tribes in proportion to their percentage in the population, and also for their appointment to reserved posts in the state and union services. The principle of reservation was extended under the First Amendment to give states discretionary power to make provisions for the advancement of any other socially and educationally backward classes of citizens (known as Other Backward Classes).

Most instrumental in weakening religious beliefs and cultural attitudes sanctifying hereditary inequalities was the liberating effect of modern science and technology under the impact of the five-year plans. A great impetus to change was expected from the process of industrialization, both in accelerating spatial and social mobility, and undermining parochial loyalties by speeding up formation of new economic classes cross-cutting communal and caste lines. The adoption of a Gandhi-style community development program in the rural areas envisaged institutional changes that amounted to a complete reorganization of village society on egalitarian and cooperative lines. The introduction of primary schools, cooperatives, and elected *panchayats* (councils) appeared to have the potential to simultaneously strengthen the economic independence of the weaker sections and create the political awareness required to transform superior numbers into cohesive electoral blocs capable of applying a nonviolent sanction from below for peaceful reform. All this was expected to occur at a time of rapidly increasing productivity that would facilitate readjustments in the distribution of economic and political power with a minimum of class conflict.

The optimism of that early period has long since dimmed. At the time of Nehru's death in 1964, it was already clear that the spread effects from industrialization were much narrower than anticipated, and that the overall growth rate had only modestly exceeded that of population. The most glaring failures occurred in the agricultural sector. Institutional changes, including land reforms and the rapid expansion of the cooperative sector, were never effectively implemented under the community development program. As a result, the energies of the mass of small cultivators and agricultural laborers could not be harnessed for development work. Prosperity was confined to favored regions and the larger farmers, bypassing the majority of the peasantry. Chronic shortfalls in agricultural production, glaring shortages of essential commodities, and a rising spiral of prices created an atmosphere of economic crisis.

Gunnar Myrdal, in his 1968 *Asian Drama,* an exhaustive three-volume study of poverty in India and South Asia, argued that it was the "overgradualist" approach and the avoidance of a frontal attack on religious beliefs, cultural attitudes, and inequalities of existing institutions that was responsible for these failures. Raising anew the question of revolution versus evolution as a policy choice, he stated his own strengthened belief, on the basis of his investigations, in the hypothesis that *"often it is not more difficult but easier to cause a big change rapidly than a small change peacefully.* The bigger and more rapid change must be attained by resolutely altering the institutions within which people live and work, instead of trying by direct or indirect means to induce changes in attitudes while leaving institutions to adjust themselves to the changed attitudes. But institutions can ordinarily be changed only by resort to what in the region is called compulsion—putting obligations on people and supporting them by force."[9]

Over the last several years, this policy question has lost much of the academic quality it once may have had. The inability of post-Nehru governments to solve India's problems of low agricultural productivity, unemployment, and mass poverty has lead to increasing lack of confidence in the democratic system—and the first spell of Emergency Rule, imposed by Mrs. Gandhi between June 1975 and March 1977. Although parliamentary government has been restored, doubts about the efficacy of the democratic process persist. Jayaprakash Narayan, though stopping short of repudiating his thirty-year commitment to Gandhism, appeared to echo Myrdal in the years before his death (in 1978), calling for a "total revolution," that is, "an all around revolution, political, economic, social, educational, moral and cultural."[10] The remainder of this chapter will review India's development experience, while considering the thesis that noneconomic factors are the major explanation for its underdevelopment. It will conclude with a discussion of Myrdal's hypothesis that unfavorable institutions have to be altered through compulsion to produce attitudes more favorable to development.

The three five-year plans launched in the 1950s and early 1960s under the national leadership of Jawaharlal Nehru are widely credited for creating "the other India" of modern science, technology, and industry. The industrial growth strategy, emphasizing import substitution, was successful in achieving a dramatic increase in the economy's productive capacity. India in the 1980s is completely self-reliant in the manufacture of plants and equipment needed for major consumer industries (e.g. cotton textiles, jute, sugar, chemicals, paper, and cement) and key capital and intermediate sectors (like steel, fertilizer, oil refinement, and heavy machinery). The engineering industries, started only after Independence, are producing equipment for steel plants, coal mines, the manufacture of chemicals and pharmaceuticals, power generation, and the production of machine tools. India currently provides the largest number of consultants and turnkey projects to other countries in the Third World. There are over one hundred universities and technical institutes, and the third largest pool of scientific and technical manpower next only to the United States and the Soviet Union. University enrollment, which was 300,000 in 1950, stood at 2.5 million in 1977-78.[11]

The versatility of India's scientific and technical establishment has been displayed in fields ranging from basic agricultural research to nuclear energy. Agricultural scientists, following up the breakthrough pioneered by the Rockefeller Foundation in the mid-1960s for wheat in Mexico and rice in the Philippines, developed new generations of high-yielding and disease-resistant hybrid varieties of wheat, paddy, and maize better adapted to Indian growing conditions. Similarly, India's own nuclear scientists carried out the research that led to the May 1974 peaceful nuclear explosion, providing future governments with the option of acquiring nuclear weapons. At present India has the largest nuclear power program among non-communist developing nations. The Department of Atomic Energy is building a commercial breeder reactor which will become operational at the end of the decade, using plutonium fuel reprocessed from spent fuel in India's own power plants.

The achievements do not end there. Compared to the last decades of colonial rule, when food grains production was virtually stagnant, since 1952 the rate of increase of food grains output has averaged about 2.7 percent per year.[12] Stepped-up irrigation and the spread of the green revolution technology since the late 1960s have resulted in large agricultural surpluses in good weather years. Despite a severe drought in 1979, India easily managed to meet the growing demand on the public distribution system from its own large food stocks, banishing the specter of famine that had stalked the countryside in previous years when had monsoons failed.

Since the mid-1970s, India has become less dependent on foreign aid to provide a major proportion of the savings needed for investment. Whereas the ratio of gross savings to GDP seemed to stagnate at 12 percent during the 1960s and early 1970s, it has shown a steady increase since 1973, reaching 23.9 percent in 1978-79, almost exactly the same as the gross investment ratio of 24.1 percent in the same year.[13] The balance of payments has also showed an improvement over the large deficits of the 1960s and early 1970s. Export growth rates reached 10 percent annually from 1974 to 1978, with the dynamic element provided by engineering products and durable consumer goods. The rate of growth has since slipped, and India faces the largest trade imbalance since Independence because of the sharp increase in oil prices—oil imports now amounting to 70 percent of export earnings. Even so, rising revenues from invisibles, especially private remittances of foreign exchange from Indian nationals working abroad, have allowed the economy to maintain reserves in 1980 of about $6 billion.[14]

India has a high international credit rating and could choose to enter the commercial market for loans to finance development projects.

Despite all these accomplishments in diversifying and expanding the industrial base, and in almost tripling agricultural production over the last thirty years to maintain per capita agricultural output, "the most important objectives of planning have not been achieved, the most cherished goals seem to be almost as distant today"[15] as they were thirty years ago. Failures in implementation have been most marked in the social goals of planning as measured by progress toward full employment, reduction in disparities, and eradication of absolute poverty. Expectations that large investments in basic and heavy industry would have widespread effects, stimulating the development of small and ancillary industries, as well as the production of food and raw materials, and that the benefits of rapid growth would trickle down in the form of growing opportunities for additional farm and nonfarm employment were disappointed.

Gains in industrial output were achieved through the application of capital-intensive techniques designed to enhance labor productivity. During 1960-77 the proportion of the labor force employed in industry remained stationary at 11 percent.[16] Industrial advances were accomplished at the cost of substantial economic concentration. Although the share of the public sector in the net domestic product of organized industry increased from 8 percent in 1960-61 to almost 31 percent in 1976, the total assets owned by the twenty top business groups in the private sector increased by about 148 percent during roughly the same period, 1963-76.[17] Small industries also experienced a relative decline in growth compared to the medium and large sector. As a whole, industrial development was concentrated in a few states and districts "where the infrastructure is strong, markets are close and various services are readily available."[18]

The momentum of the industrialization process under these conditions was too weak to transform the basic economic structure. Eighty percent of the population continues to live in rural areas. The share of agriculture in the work force has remained virtually unchanged, at about 73 percent, since 1921. Agriculture still accounts for the largest proportion of net national product, about 45 percent, followed by an enlarged tertiary sector of over 33 percent, and at some distance behind, a manufacturing sector of some 22 percent.[19]

There is a permanent and growing labor surplus relative to demand. The backlog of unemployed is believed to be approximately 20 million.[20] In 1978, planners estimated that the annual addition to the work force was about 5 million persons, although only some 830,000 jobs were created in the organized sector in that year. More than 80 percent of the annual increase to the labor force drifts into part-time employment in rural areas or the informal sector of urban industry or trade, or becomes chronically unemployed.[21]

Although most entrants to the labor force will have to find employment in agriculture for decades to come, a pattern of regional and economic concentration of gains in productivity and income has limited the diffusion of new job opportunities. Data collected for the trienniums 1962-63 to 1964-65 and 1970-71 to 1972-73 give some sense of the growth of regional disparities. The upper 29 percent of districts achieved compound growth rates of more than 3 percent annually. The bottom 37 percent of districts, by contrast, recorded either negative growth rates or gains of less than 1 percent per annum. The middle one-third of districts registered annual gains of between 1 and 2.9 percent.[22]

There has also been growing concentration of economic assets among agricultural households. The dramatic improvement in the level of gross domestic savings registered in the economy after 1975 was accounted for mainly by increases in household savings which reached almost 63 percent of savings in the economy. (In 1977-78, a year when gross domestic savings reached 22.8 percent of GDP, household savings accounted for almost 17 percent, while the public and private sectors accounted for 4.4 percent and 1.5 percent respectively.)[23] Such high figures represented a sharp increase in the purchase of physical assets by large and medium farmers, with the help of loans from cooperative and commercial institutions. Most of this credit was transformed into irrigation structures and equipment, livestock, and equipment for fisheries, village industries, and transport enterprises.

At the bottom of the rural economic ladder, agricultural laborers and small farmers had the greatest difficulty in finding employment opportunities sufficient to meet their basic needs. Data on agricultural laborers as a percentage of the total work force, although not strictly comparable from the 1961 to the 1971 census, nevertheless suggest that their numbers were on the rise.[24] This trend was confirmed in the Labor Ministry's 1974-75 Rural Labor Enquiry showing an overall increase in the proportion and number of agricultural labor households; an overall decrease in the number of days of remunerated employment for men, women, and children, at least since 1965; and evidence of deterioration in the overall financial situation of this class as measured by growing average indebtedness to moneylenders for household consumption loans.[25]

India's first agricultural census in 1970-71 also revealed that the numbers of very small holdings had recorded a significant increase over 1961-62 levels. By the late 1970s the majority of rural households, about 57 percent, either owned no land or very small and marginal holdings of less than one hectare. Together they owned only 9 percent of the land.[26] This was the population chronically underemployed, the millions of rural poor subsisting at the border of or slipping below the line of absolute poverty. It is doubtful that any significant reduction in the proportion of the poor has occurred over the last two decades. Calculations made by the Planning Commission for the Sixth Five-Year Plan, 1980-85, estimate that 48 percent of the population, approximately the same as the estimate in 1960-61, are subsisting below the poverty line.[27]

Apart from the serious moral, social, and political issues raised by the growing concentration of assets, income, and wealth, the economic consequences were also severe. Once the major gains from the import-substitution strategy were exhausted by the early 1970s, the logic of industrial expansion demanded a substantial diversification of output in the direction of mass consumer goods. Yet the skewed flow of benefits from investments and institutional lending to a small minority of industrialists and traders in the cities and medium and large landowners in the countryside deprived the industrial sector of the most powerful stimulus to rapid development: production for an expanding home market. Planners flatly acknowledged that "the further expansion of industry is limited by the narrowness of the market." As a result, "an unduly large share of resources is absorbed by production which relates directly or indirectly to maintaining or improving the living standards of the higher income groups. The demand of this relatively small class not only for a few visible items of conspicuous consumption but for the outlay on high quality housing and urban amenities, aviation and superior travel facilities, telephone services, etc., sustains a large part of the existing industrial structure."[28]

In the private sector, weak demand was reflected in stagnant rates of investment in 1977-80;[29] greater emphasis on expanding existing units than building new ones; an increase of "sickness" in industry, especially cotton textiles, jute, sugar, and engineering; and a black money economy estimated at 25 to 30 percent of GNP,[30] geared to real estate speculation, hoarding of essential commodities, and smuggling of gold and luxury import articles. In the public sector, the momentum of public outlays on new industrial projects slowed. The central government had experienced serious political difficulties in raising additional resources from direct taxation of the agricultural sector that could tap the rising incomes of the most prosperous agriculturalists. Declining public outlays, dating from 1966, were a major factor in the decade-long recession of 1965-75 that saw rates of industrial growth fall back to about 4 percent per annum from about 9 percent between 1961-62 and 1964-65. An erratic pattern of recovery in the following years kept average growth levels below 6 percent. A serious setback in 1979-80, when industry registered a negative growth rate, dramatized the weaknesses of neglected infrastructure, already apparent in chronic power shortages, stagnant coal production, and the inability of railways to move a sufficient volume of freight.[31]

Regional disparities and the uneven distribution of assets and income in the rural sector also presented obstacles to the effective implementation of the "new economics of growth" embraced in the 1970s to make the agricultural sector into the most dynamic element of advance. Elements of this approach, dubbed a "trickle up" model of development by the international aid community, were endorsed by Mrs. Gandhi after her massive electoral victory in 1971 on the slogan of *garibi hatao* (abolish poverty). Under her leadership, the central government launched a large number of special schemes for a direct attack on rural poverty. These included the establishment of Small Farmer Development Agencies (SFDA) to advance subsidized loans to small and marginal farmers for investment on improved practices and ancillary farm enterprises; and a crash scheme in rural employment to create supplemental jobs for agricultural laborers on rural works projects.

The lynchpin of the approach was higher outlays on agriculture and irrigation to accelerate expansion of acreage under high-yielding seed and fertilizer technology to reap maximum gains in agricultural productivity. A rapidly expanding agriculture, it was believed, would raise rural incomes, increase demand for nonagricultural commodities and consumer services, and speed up a shift of marginal farmers and agricultural laborers into nonagricultural employment in labor-intensive small industries supplying the consumption needs of affluent peasants. Beyond this, the overall increase in rural purchasing power would expand the internal market for India's depressed manufacturing industries.

All these programs were taken up on a much larger scale by the Janata Party after its landslide victory in the 1977 national election fought on the issue of Mrs. Gandhi's unpopular Emergency Rule. Charan Singh, the architect of the Janata's economic policies, claimed that all the problems of the dual economy had arisen from neglect of agriculture and the villages in the "Westernized, centralized, trickle-down-from-the-top" model followed by Nehru and his successors. The country could only be saved, he asserted, by "return[ing] to Gandhi for redemption."[32]

The revised Draft Sixth Five-Year Plan, 1978-83, prepared on the lines set down by Charan Singh, allocated over 43 percent of plan outlay to agriculture. It placed highest priority on expanding the area under irrigation; increasing power for rural electrification to permit accelerated installation of tubewells; and providing modern inputs, especially fertilizers, pesticides, and high-yielding varieties to raise yield levels. Special programs for small and marginal farmers were expanded. A new Food for Work Program was introduced to provide additional employment to the unemployed and underemployed men and women in rural areas, utilizing surplus food grains for wage payments. A variety of measures were also adopted to facilitate the growth of small industries, including the creation of 460 district industry centers with access to substantial institutional credit.

Although the draft plan was not formally adopted before the fall of the Janata government in June 1979, the new policies had been set in motion. Despite the fact that Mrs. Gandhi ordered the Planning Commission to scrap the Janata's revised plan once she returned to power in January 1980, the new Sixth Five-Year Plan, 1980-85, adopted by her cabinet in March 1981, did not alter essential elements of the agricultural strategy.[33]

So far, the stimulus from greatly stepped-up investments in agriculture and irrigation has been too weak to spearhead an increase in agricultural productivity at levels required for rapid expansion of new employment in the rural economy. On the contrary, long-term production trends for food grains, despite dramatic improvement in yields of one major crop, show a failure to raise the aggregate growth rate using the new technology. Only a marginal increase, from 2.5 percent to 2.7 percent per annum, was achieved in the growth rate of food grains between 1952-65 and 1967-79. Growth rates of nonfood grains declined between these two periods, from 3.8 percent to 2.8 percent.[34] These growth rates can be contrasted with the estimated requirements for the success of the strategy of at least 3.5 percent for food grains and 6 percent for nonfood grains to support a growth rate of about 10 percent in industrial production.[35] The overall economic progress has also stayed at the same average rate of about 3.5 percent per annum (with wide swings in both directions), in comparison to the minimum of 5-6 percent considered necessary for significant progress toward the goals of full employment and eradication of abject poverty.[36]

Regional disparities have deepened. Rapid agricultural transformation has been confined to the irrigated wheat areas, primarily in three Northern states (Punjab, Haryana, and western Uttar Pradesh), with the growth rate and output more than doubling and the yields almost tripling in these areas. By contrast, only small pockets of growth could be created in the much larger area under paddy. Rice production recorded a lower growth rate in the later period (1967-79) of 2.6 percent than in the earlier period (1952-65), when it was 3.1 percent.[37] Paradoxically, rice production achieved its most rapid gains in the traditional wheat-growing states, especially in Punjab and Haryana where it was taken as a second crop.

The failure of the new agriculture-oriented growth policies to diffuse productivity gains, thereby creating a self-sustaining growth cycle of higher incomes, demand, and employment within the rural sector, has left virtually the entire burden of creating additional employment on the rural works projects mounted by the government. Yet given the magnitude of the problem, these have helped the agricultural laborer population only marginally.

The nationwide Food for Work Program launched in 1977 by the Ministry of Rural Reconstruction has been the most effective scheme to date in reaching workers living below the poverty line. During 1977-79, the state governments received, free of cost, surplus food-grains from the center's buffer stocks to pay the wages of laborers engaged in the construction of community works and rural infrastructure projects. According to the planning commission's evaluation study in ten states, the beneficiaries, as intended, were mainly agricultural laborers and small cultivators, a large proportion of whom belonged to the Scheduled Castes and Scheduled Tribes. At the peak of the program in 1978-79, these workers were able to increase their opportunities for additional employment by 10 percent and raise household income by almost 18 percent. More than one-third were able to increase their consumption as a direct result of the program. Yet these benefits, welcome as they were, occurred only on a short-term seasonal basis. By contrast, as the workers pointed out, they needed a continuing source of employment and income to permanently improve their living standards.[38]

It is difficult to imagine how resources might be found to take up a continuing program for all those who need additional employment to increase their consumption above the poverty line. The closest any state has come in attempting this goal is Maharashtra, which launched the Employment Guarantee Scheme in 1975. The EGS, at its height, provided employment to about 410,000 persons or about three-fourths of those believed to require additional work for 160 days a year at a minimum wage of 3 rupees a day. A study of sixty projects revealed that EGS "was successful in preventing further deterioration of the conditions of weaker sections in Maharashtra." Notwithstanding the income increases by two-thirds of the participants at about 33 percent, 90 percent of the individuals working on EGS schemes at the low cash wage offered were still living below the poverty line.[39]

Worse still, although Maharashtra raised its own resources to pay for EGS, the national Food for Work Program and its successor, renamed National Rural Employment Program, are dependent for implementation on supplies of surplus food grains sent by the center to the states. Once grain stocks were depleted by the 1979 drought, the Food for Work Program was drastically cut back, and as of 1981 was not restored to earlier levels.

Special programs for small and marginal farmers have also had only slight success in lifting the participants above the poverty level. Data from a recent field study of sixty-four villages in Tamil Nadu suggest reasons for this failure. Benefits under the program were diverted to the nonpoor, accounting for 15 to 25 percent of beneficiaries. Within the target group, a larger share of benefits flowed to the relatively better off and influential, so that small farmers were distinctly favored over marginal farmers and the latter were favored over agricultural laborers. When loans were extended to poorer beneficiaries, they were often unable to withstand the initial deficit incurred on a new enterprise, and the "benefit" became a debt trap from which they could extricate themselves only by resorting to further loans from moneylenders to repay institutional loans.[40] Over most of the country, the employment potential of district development corporations also remains unrealized. Handicaps include poor transportation facilities, inadequate power and/or very high rates for electricity; ineffective communications; absence of entrepreneurial skills; and lack of effective demand.

How can the failure of policies to overcome economic dualism be explained? One obvious reason can be put forward to account for this pattern characteristic of many developing countries. Population, which increased by more than 50 percent in the first half of this century at annual growth rates of about 1 percent, almost doubled during the next twenty-five years, reaching a peak of 2.5 percent per annum and remaining at that level. India's current population is almost 150 million higher than economic planners were able to anticipate.[41] In addition, the ability of heavy or capital-intensive industry to achieve high productivity with a small labor force has short-circuited the steady employment expansion necessary to absorb significant numbers of the rural unemployed. This tendency went unchecked because planners did not pay serious attention to the employment implications of the industrial technologies chosen.

Yet India's problems of employment and poverty are more deeply rooted. They cannot be fully explained without accounting for the chronic inability of the vast agricultural sector to achieve higher output well within the potential of existing technology. Such a constraint has been evident since the early days of planning. It is mistaken to argue as critics of the "Nehruvian strategy" of rapid industrialization now do, that the first three five-year plans neglected the importance of rapid increases in agricultural productivity and rural employment as the keystone of self-sustaining growth. On the contrary, planners fully realized the need to build up linkages between the modern industrial sector and the potentially vast internal market of the rural hinterland, and to do this by giving the poor peasantry higher purchasing power from gains in output on the land and employment in small industries. Nehru stated this development logic very clearly in arguing for the effective implementation of land reform and cooperative reorganization to create larger numbers of viable farms: "We cannot go on increasing our production unless we increase our consumption. We cannot increase our consumption unless there is the wherewithal to buy among large numbers of people. . . . Once this wheel of purchasing power got going, there is no end to it. This applies, not only to land but even more to industry. It applies especially to small industries which should produce many of the articles needed in the villages."[42]

During the 1950s and early 1960s, planners acted on the premise that agricultural output could be substantially increased through more efficient utilization of land and underemployed labor within the traditional framework of production. Optimism about the potentiality for rapid agricultural progress, with only organizational changes based on land reform and the introduction of cooperatives, appeared justified by the obvious gap between actual yields and known technical possibilities. Experts were convinced that expansion of 50 to 100 percent in yields per acre with only small changes in production techniques and using mainly indigenous inputs was feasible over a fifteen- to twenty-year period. Yet these potentialities were only partially realized. Despite large investments on major and medium irrigation projects, the compound rate of production increase for all crops between 1949-50 and 1968-69 was somewhat less than 3 percent per annum, while gains from productivity averaged 1.3 percent annually.[43]

India's inability to realize its agricultural production potential emerged in even sharper relief after introduction of the high-yielding seed and fertilizer technology in the mid-1960s, and the decision to adopt a new agricultural strategy providing financial incentives to the bigger farmers for investment on modern methods. Overall, the optimal rate of increase in agricultural output projected from technical yardsticks for the productivity of modern inputs was about twice the level of previous achievements—approximately 6–7 percent per annum. By contrast, average annual growth rates have remained under 3 percent, falling short of the scaled down targets of 4-5 percent per annum in recent plans.

It is primarily because of India's persistent failure to achieve existing production potential in agriculture that the explanation for underdevelopment has been sought in noneconomic conditions that induce resistance to change. One possibility, as Myrdal argued, is that irrational religious beliefs sanction cultural patterns, institutions, and modes and levels of living unfavorable to development. Charan Singh himself appeared to endorse something like this theory when he included in his "Gandhian blueprint" for development the following key prescription: "A transformation of our national psychology in the sense that Hindus, in particular, give up the belief that this world is not a mere illusion and as individuals and also as a nation we develop an urge to improve our economic condition and to that end our people learn to work better and harder."[44]

Yet the evidence suggests a more complex reality. The picture that rural India presents is not one of stagnation but of modest overall growth with wide regional variations. During 1961-71, output in the primary sector grew at approximately 2 percent per annum at the all-India level, yet ranged from 4.89 and 4.72 percent in Haryana and Punjab to -1.69 and -0.34 percent in Maharashtra and Bihar.[45] This pattern of uneven and encapsulated development persisted under "trickle up" and "trickle down" models of development and whether the agricultural strategy emphasized more efficient utilization of traditional labor-intensive techniques or modern inputs of high-yielding seeds and fertilizer. Other data for 1961-71 show a small positive shift of workers into the primary sector but a neglible all-India growth rate of male productivity at 0.16 percent. Such trends "certainly constitute ground for believing self-limiting factors are at work."[46]

Are these self-limiting factors, as Myrdal argued, primarily to be found in noneconomic conditions? More careful attention to regional variations suggests that Myrdal's "broad institutional approach" is indeed too broad as a general theory of India's underdevelopment. Its explanatory power is greater, however, applied to the setting of one important area, that of the "Hindu heartland" in the Gangetic Plain. In this region—especially in the most populous states of Bihar and Uttar Pradesh (exclusive of western Uttar Pradesh), the largest holdings and the largest proportion of agricultural land are still owned by wealthier members of the "twice-born" castes. Among them, the Brahmins are ritually proscribed from touching the plough. They cultivate mainly through managers and agricultural laborers or sharecroppers. Some members of other elite castes are equally reluctant to risk their prestige by participating in manual labor. Although in these two states a significant proportion of the crop land is under surface irrigation, and there are plentiful underground water resources waiting to be tapped for the installation of tubewells, the level of adoption of new technology (with the exception of western Uttar Pradesh) remains very low. This is especially striking in Bihar, an overwhelmingly agricultural state well endowed with alluvium soils and water resources, but where yield rates for almost all major crops, including the most important rice crop, are lower than all-India levels. According to one study of the major Kosi irrigation project in north Bihar, where utilization of water reached only 25 percent of potential in the early 1970s, landowners were "not overly concerned about annual returns."[47] They did not display much interest in agricultural modernization, whether through consolidation of holdings, mechanization and double cropping, or even by sharing the costs of modern inputs with their sharecroppers. They were less interested in the economic gains than apprehensive of the social costs of expanding economic opportunities. At stake was their economic hold over large numbers of land-poor and landless agriculturists who depended on their patronage for some leased land to cultivate, or for farm work and loans, and the legitimacy of their social and political privileges rooted in their ranking as "twice-born" castes. The close congruence between the *varna* hierarchy and the stratification system according to occupation and income has barely been disturbed in Bihar as a whole. The much more numerous low-caste or Sudra households have small holdings and although the majority are engaged in cultivation, by 1969 about one-quarter had been pushed down into the ranks of agricultural laborers. The groups at the bottom of the ritual hierarchy, those belonging to the Scheduled Castes and Tribes, rarely own or lease land and are predominately employed in agriculture as laborers.[48]

Still, even in Bihar, any explanation for rural poverty is not exhausted by an analysis of religious and cultural inhibitions on innovation. In fact, agricultural dynamism is not entirely absent. Lower-caste landowners have no ritual or status restraints in taking advantage of new economic opportunities. Some small farmers, moreover, have added to their holdings from land transfers stimulated both by implementation of Zamindari Abolition and efforts by larger landowners to evade further land redistribution under ceilings laws by selling "surplus" acreage.[49] This lower-caste and lower-middle-class peasantry are well aware of the importance of high-yielding seeds and fertilizers. Despite their meager surpluses, they have become sufficiently entrepreneurial in recent years to attract the label of "rising kulaks."[50]

The impulse toward economic improvement perceptible under the relatively pristine caste hierarchy of Bihar is pronounced outside the Hindu heartland where the dominant proprietor castes usually do not enjoy "twice-born" status. The claim of the Jats—concentrated in the Punjab, Haryana, and western Uttar Pradesh—to Kshatriya rank is disputed by the area's "twice-born" Rajputs. In the Southern states, where the Brahmins historically constituted no more than 3 percent of the population and other "twice-born" castes were even fewer in number or entirely absent, the dominant landed castes were drawn from among local proprietor communities (e.g. Kammas and Reddys in Andhra Pradesh, Mudaliars in Tamil Nadu, Nairs in Kerala, Okkaligas and Lingayats in Karnataka). Although the small Brahmin elite characterized these castes as "Sudra," in practice they were accepted as ritually ranking just below the Brahmins. In any case, none of these castes were under ritual or status compulsions to refrain from manual labor. What Miller says of the Jats in Badipur (Haryana) is generally true of the wealthier members of all these castes: "Jats are by tradition landowners, economically and politically dominant over most of the other castes; therefore, being born a Jat is a definite advantage for being able to respond to opportunities."[51] The desire of landowning castes for greater economic gains has found political expression. Since the 1977 elections, the "farm lobby," spearheaded by agriculturists in the most prosperous states and regions—Punjab, Haryana, western Uttar Pradesh, northern Rajasthan, Gujerat, pockets of Tamil Nadu, Andhra, and Karnataka—has become the most important new force in Indian politics. Franda writes: "Rural politicians have found they can get elected only if they appeal to farmers who typically have rights to holdings between five and thirty acres."[52]

The more prosperous farmers are themselves sitting in the national parliament; in 1978, 40 percent of the members described their occupation as "agriculturist."[53] These agriculturists have not hesitated to make their demands heard both inside and outside of government. In several states, agriculturalist associations have sprung up, headed by "nonpolitical" leaders who have organized rallies, demonstrations, and "long marches" to put forward various demands for higher government procurement prices of agricultural products; subsidies on inputs; postponement of collection of electricity dues for tubewell power pumps; and outright cancellation of payments on loans to small farmers.

All this suggests that the major self-limiting factor in closing the chronic gap between the potential for productivity and actual output in India is not found in religious ideas which prevent rational economic behavior. Rather, more direct obstacles to solving problems of underdevelopment can be found in the patterns of land distribution and tenure that prevent efficient allocation of land, labor, and capital. Even if the "twice-born" castes of the Hindu heartland were suddenly inspired to embrace the Protestant ethic, in the absence of prior institutional changes they would not have the economic incentive to carry out agricultural modernization.

Existing patterns of land distribution and tenure put major obstacles in the way of increasing per-acre yields, either through the more efficient application of traditional labor-intensive techniques or the introduction of modern methods. Large numbers of agricultural laborers and cultivators operating uneconomic or marginal holdings remain unemployed or underemployed for long periods during the year. They have neither the incentive nor the capacity to carry out labor-intensive production schemes that could increase yields within the traditional framework of production. The most obvious case is that of sharecroppers who pay 50 percent of their output in rent. They invest very little in fertilizer and do not lavish extra attention on leased land. Nor is there much scope for carrying out overhead labor-investment projects—construction and maintenance of field courses, field channels, wells, tanks, and drainage systems—which are critical for increasing productivity through traditional techniques. Individual agriculturists are unable to undertake such land improvement schemes, and groups of underemployed agriculturists have no interest in doing so. The government's effort after Independence to establish village councils with statutory authority to carry out construction of capital projects foundered on the inequalities of the land-tenure system. It proved politically impossible to mobilize "surplus" or underemployed labor on a voluntary basis when expected gains in productivity would increase economic concentration still further in favor of larger landowners.

The patterns of land distribution and tenure also present intractable obstacles to carrying out the productivity revolution in rice promised by the capital-intensive technologies. The high density of population in the most fertile paddy-growing areas, the small size of agricultural holdings, the subdivision of holdings into several small parcels scattered within and between villages, and the high incidence of sharecropping, are all inimical to agricultural modernization. The upper 15 percent or so of all households having medium and large holdings of ten acres or more commonly operate small farms. Yet the efficient cultivation of high-yielding paddy varieties, even in areas with canal irrigation, requires supplementary supplies of water from the installation of costly minor irrigation works (percolation wells, pumpsets, and tubewells), whose minimum command area is five to ten acres.[54] Similarly, the agrarian pattern of small and fragmented holdings inhibits investment on machinery for land leveling, construction of drainage systems to prevent water logging, and even a coordinated effort at pest control.

It is acknowledged by even the most enthusiastic advocates of technocratic development that changes in agrarian organization are necessary to achieve the full production potential of modern methods. Charan Singh has written that greater equality in land distribution would lead to greater growth in the countryside, and that "landlordism has to be abolished lock, stock and barrel," holdings consolidated and service cooperatives formed for more efficient use of land, labor, and capital, and pooling of resources for nonfarm activities.[55] James Grant, when he was president of the Overseas Development Council, went even further in taking his model of agrarian transformation from Northeast Asia and China. He argued for a pattern of 2.5-acre farms based on a cooperative structure in which "the individuals's return depends primarily on the extent of his output," as well as more labor-intensive agriculture linked to decentralized small industries.[56]

Such prescriptions gain credibility from a closer look at the atypical agroeconomic structure of the green revolution heartland.[57] The state of undivided Punjab and the bordering districts of western Uttar Pradesh provided an unusually favorable environment for rapid agricultural growth once modern techniques became available. As early as the 1920s, the construction of an extensive canal network had converted the area into one of the most prosperous regions of British India. The Sikh Jat and Hindu Jat cultivating castes were enterprising and eager to experiment with improved methods of cultivation. After Independence, once the Community Development program was introduced, the Punjab outdistanced other Indian states in the adoption of chemical fertilizer, improved farm implements, and installation of tubewells. Between 1952-53 and 1964-65, the Punjab had the highest growth rate in agricultural production in India, averaging 5.5 percent per annum, mostly from the extension of area under crops.

The region benefited not only from good water resources and enterprising agricultural castes. The pattern of land distribution and tenure was also unusually favorable to investment in modern methods. Owner-cultivated land had been steadily increasing since the early 1950s, and on the eve of the green revolution less than 20 percent of the cultivated area was under tenancy. Although the majority of *cultivators* were operating holdings less than the minimum area required for viability using the new techniques—some 8-10 acres—the largest proportion of the *area* was cultivated in holdings of 10 acres or more. Surplus producers responded enthusiastically to state programs of land consolidation which offered economies of scale necessary for investment in tubewells and agricultural machinery, and subsequently used this technology to expand the area under double cropping. Shortly after Punjab was divided in 1966, Punjab and Haryana led the country in an immediate response to the introduction of the new technology. Within a few years, virtually all the subsoil water had been tapped by the installation of private tubewells, and within the short period between 1965-66 and 1971-72, wheat output doubled, with major gains from yield increases.

An analysis attributing India's low agricultural productivity primarily to inefficient patterns of land distribution and tenure does not mean that religious and cultural patterns can be dismissed as important factors in explaining the slow progress toward goals of reducing disparities and removing abject poverty. Although religion and the caste hierarchy do not seem to inhibit rational *economic* behavior to maximize productivity and income by wealthier members of the landowning castes (except perhaps in the "Hindu heartland"), caste values and structures do retard rational *political* behavior to maximize power by the most numerous disadvantaged groups. It is the failure of the rural poor to organize on the basis of their common interests that has prevented electoral politics from becoming an effective instrument for peaceful agrarian reform.

The features of caste forestalling the emergence of class consciousness and organizational unity among the rural poor are extremely powerful. They have both economic and political dimensions. In areas undergoing agricultural development caste exerts a mediating effect on economic differentiation which is patterned less on the unequal abilities of individuals to take advantage of new opportunities than on the uneven economic resources of caste groups. The peculiarity of the Indian social setting is that economic and political hierarchies have not rested simply on control of assets or a monopoly of force, but have been interpenetrated by *varna* and caste status. Even in areas outside the Hindu heartland where the politico-economic hierarchy deviates from the classic *varna* model, caste and class have been so closely intertwined that it is virtually impossible to speak of one without the other—hence the category of dominant agricultural castes, not classes.

There are considerable differences of landholding, wealth, and education among the lineages of these dominant proprietor castes. Yet the largest number of persons able to respond to opportunities for investment on irrigation, agricultural machinery, or ancillary enterprises come from traditional landowning communities. As Miller points out, many persons cannot take advantage of new economic opportunities (in Badipur), because of "the educational and economic limitations imposed on certain members of particular castes by their traditional relationships to the means of production, by the share of economic production accorded them within the agricultural system." Despite the breakdown of traditional master/servant relationships between high-caste landowning patrons and Sudra and untouchable service and laboring castes, endogamous groups are still associated with specific types of activity and "the relative ranking of these castes." Even when villagers manage to establish their economic independence and enter the wider market economy, they tend to engage in occupations that are modern equivalents or extensions of their traditional occupations.[58]

Modernization under Indian conditions, even assuming widespread effects, can only partially duplicate the Western process which created economic differentiation among individuals to establish a new stratification system based on class. Since at the outset land and other assets are differentially distributed according to community, modernization initially accentuates class and caste differences. This tendency has inevitably been exacerbated under a process of modernization which is not widespread but self-limiting and encapsulated. The impact of social change on caste consciousness is as a result considerably blunted. A process of modernization that widens disparities among groups at the upper and lower levels of the ritual hierarchy may not only fail to create class consciousness but may heighten caste consciousness.

The persistence of caste identities has seriously undermined efforts to forge political solidarity among the rural poor. Those lineages and subcastes that have made the greatest gains from new economic opportunities can still appeal to traditional caste status in claiming power and authority within the modern political system. Throughout most of the period since Independence politics at the village level has revolved around intracaste competition for local leadership, with rival members of dominant castes manipulating multicaste factional alignments constructed of kin, caste fellows, and low-caste economic dependents. Similarly, national political parties have been built up by pyramiding vertical district and state factional alliances to mobilize grass-roots support during general elections.

This situation has shown signs of change only since the 1969 split of the ruling Congress Party when Mrs. Gandhi made a direct appeal for popular support with her promise to abolish poverty. Yet while recent elections give convincing evidence of a "critical level of political awareness" among the rural masses,[59] this has not found expression in political organization which can mount sustained pressure on elected governments to carry out promises of economic reform. Rather, in some parts of the country, heightened political consciousness has triggered caste conflict that ironically perpetuates the political fragmentation of the poor.

A manifestation of this phenomenon is the emergence of conflict between the Forward ("twice-born") Castes and the Backward Classes (predominately upper Sudra castes) throughout much of the Hindu heartland. On one level, it appears that the two sides are engaged in an economic struggle about access to education and jobs. In a society where the organized economy can absorb only a small fraction of new entrants into the labor force every year, and where the government is the single largest employer, it is not surprising that the Backward Classes should demand protective discrimination from their state governments in fixing higher quotas for reserved places in universities, professional schools, and the administrative services. It is equally unremarkable that the Forwards, who are much better equipped to meet regular admission standards, should insist on recruitment based on merit or reservations tied to low income, not caste.

Yet the leaders of the upper Sudra peasantry spearheading the Backward Classes movement perceive the struggle as predominately a caste conflict. Some of them have begun to experience modest economic improvement as a result of Zamindari Abolition and the introduction of modern agricultural methods, but they have been unable to overcome educational and social disabilities in competing successfully for the most lucrative and prestigious positions at the top rung of the administration, the professions, business, or the universities. Most argue that economic inequalities are not the cause of the underrepresentation of the Backward Classes in these fields. On the contrary, they are convinced that economic, educational, and social inequities are rooted in the disabilities historically imposed on the caste groups of the Sudra *varna* as a whole.

Paradoxically, the Backward Classes movement has not evolved an egalitarian ideology or seriously attempted to mobilize the most underprivileged groups. Although the leaders are emphatic that they want to break the hegemony of "twice-born" castes, and a few of the radicals among them even talk of "smashing the caste system," their constituency as a whole refuses to give up its own claims to caste dominance over those beneath them on the ritual scale, most particularly the Scheduled Castes who are also the bulk of the agricultural labor force. The outcome has been caste conflict, between Forwards and Backwards, and between Backwards and the younger Harijans who are themselves becoming politicized and conscious of their civil rights. The rural poor who represent the largest segment in all these contending groups remain divided according to caste loyalties.

Caste is also an important factor in politics even in areas outside the Hindu heartland where in the early part of the century dominant agricultural castes had themselves claimed to be "backward," relative to the Brahmins, to win concessions on reservations policy from the British government. After Independence, the leaders of this movement succeeded in becoming the political elite. By and large, they remained undisturbed in their position until the 1969 split in the Congress Party. Yet while Mrs. Gandhi's promise was to protect the interests of the "poor," the new Congress Party in practice reorganized around separate cells for Backward Classes, Scheduled Castes and Scheduled Tribes, and religious minorities. State leaders stressed reservations policy in their appeals for popular support, although they coupled this with assurances of economic reform. This challenge to the position of the dominant landed castes has stimulated growing political awareness among members of the "weaker sections" of the population. Yet this political awakening has still to be translated into organized forms of political cooperation among the various elements of the rural poor. Not only are they divided by economic interest—some being marginal farmers or sharecroppers, and others agricultural laborers—but they are separated by even stronger cultural barriers that prevent cooperation across the pollution line or even between Hindus and Muslims. The most striking example is provided by the agricultural laborers who in objective terms can be considered an economic class. Divided between caste Hindus on the one side, and Scheduled Castes, Scheduled Tribes, and some Muslims on the other, these poorest of the poor, with the exceptions noted below, have yet to be organized either in a common agricultural labor union or a political party.

The amorphous political participation of the "rural poor" which evaporates the day after elections, explains why all national governments since Independence, including those which had massive parliamentary mandates to abolish poverty, have been defeated at state and local levels in implementing their commitments to agrarian reform. The basic premise of all governments since the mid-1970s, including Mrs. Gandhi's Emergency Regime, the Janata interregnum, and the current Congress-I government once again headed by Mrs. Gandhi, is that land reform is politically impossible given the power structure at the village level. The result is that in trying to raise the income and employment of the poor, the most effective way has had to be ruled out, that is, providing a "basic asset that can yield a basic income" through redistribution of land.[60] Instead, benefits to the poor have to be delivered without upsetting the existing power structure by programs to "unscramble technology," including the use of subsidized loans to marginal farmers as a substitute for economies of scale, and the artificial creation of additional employment through rural works schemes. This marginalist approach can at most ameliorate the condition of the abjectly poor, without fundamentally altering the agrarian structure that limits their opportunities.

Was Myrdal right after all? Certainly, the architects of the development strategy made a number of sanguine assumptions about the role of economic modernization in promoting social change that were not correct under Indian conditions. Basic industrialization occurred in the context of a stationary industrial labor force, circumscribed urbanization, and in the absence of strong linkages to the agricultural sector. These limiting factors undermined its catalytic role in speeding up the formation of economic classes cross-cutting caste and communal lines. The deteriorating situation in the countryside, where the pressure of the working population on the land is increasing, has strengthened the power of the wealthier agriculturalists (who belong disproportionately to the traditionally dominant landed castes) in preventing implementation of institutional reforms.

It is true that some sections of the prospering upper Sudra peasantry have shown skill in using the political process to press for reservations in educational institutions and government services with the hope of challenging the hegemony of the upper castes. Such developments suggest that traditional caste relationships of interdependence and hierarchy (under which patrons provided security and clients returned deference and political support) are being transformed into ones of competition amid claims of equal opportunity. Yet far from dissipating caste feeling, this type of system change can initially imbue caste with a new intensity, derived from fears induced among dominant groups of loss of age-old privileges and anger unleashed among the Backward Classes by expression of long-stifled resentments at the historic disabilities imposed on their castes.

Unless, like Gandhi, one believes in the sacred character of *varna-shramadharma*, there seems little doubt that the disappearance of caste divisions would greatly enhance the political possibilities of carrying out institutional changes benefiting the rural lower classes. The Communist parties scored their greatest successes outside the Hindu heartland and in two states, Kerala and West Bengal, each of which experienced strong social reform movements early in the century that made it possible to almost completely root out the practice of untouchability. In Kerala, where the Communists have alternated in office since 1957, their ability to organize permanent *kisan* or peasant associations of tenant cultivators and unions of agricultural laborers has resulted in land redistribution to "significantly [alter] the structure of ownership" and provide a "remarkably high real wage rate [in terms of level as well as rate of increase],"[61] for agricultural laborers relative to that in other states. In West Bengal, where a quarreling left front gained office a decade later and the more radical CPI (Marxists) won a majority in their own right only in 1977, peasant mobilization based on strong *kisan* associations at the village level took just three years to give at least 50 percent of the sharecroppers in the state permanent rights to their holdings.[62]

Even so, it is difficult to concur in Myrdal's hypothesis that more rapid overall change can be achieved through a resolute effort to alter existing institutions by compulsion. There is no evidence, for example, that Mrs. Gandhi's Emergency Regime of 1975-77, which placed unlimited authority in the hands of the central government, suspending both the federal provisions of the Constitution and guarantees for fundamental rights, enjoyed markedly more power in carrying out its stated purpose of enforcing agricultural reforms than its democratic predecessors. This was not surprising since the Congress Party's populist rhetoric of social justice for the "weaker sections" was not matched by an organizational apparatus among the rural poor that could challenge the institutionalized power of the wealthier peasantry in the villages.

There is an even more fundamental objection. The different regions and states of India, divided by language and characterized by disparate configurations of caste structure, patterns of land distribution and tenure, social reform movements, communal composition, extent of commercialization, and degree of politicization of lower castes and poorer classes, defy the application of a uniform strategy of social transformation imposed from above and aimed at altering the institutions in which people live and work "all at once." Under Indian conditions, it is not easier to "cause a big change rapidly": even modest institutional changes require painstaking organizational effort, state by state, adapted to specific local relationships between castes, classes, and political parties. The foremost theorist of the CPI (Marxists), E.M.S. Namboodiripad, reflecting on the conflict between the Forward communities and the Backward Castes on the one hand, and the other Backward communities and the Scheduled Castes and Tribes on the other, had to concede that even "the party of the working class with its advanced ideology has also to take account of this factor"[63] of strong consciousness of caste, subcaste, and religious community in selecting candidates for election and making appointments to ministries.

The prospect for restructuring local party and government organizations to institutionalize the power of the rural poor seems much better under a decentralized and competitive political process in which socialist and reformist parties retain their stake in making numbers count. By contrast, an authoritarian political system is likely to create even more unfavorable conditions for social reform by freezing existing power relationships at the local level while the dominant landowning castes have the upper hand.

This kind of reasoning should not be used to gloss over the problem of finding an ultimate solution for mass poverty in India without the use of compulsion. More is required to lift large numbers of the rural poor above the poverty line than moderate land reforms providing security of tenure to sharecroppers, or even redistribution of some land to tenants and higher wages for agricultural workers, as the experience of Kerala and West Bengal is demonstrating. Small and inefficient farms cultivated by an impoverished peasantry are incapable of achieving higher increases in agricultural productivity and employment. Yet agrarian reorganization, which at a minimum requires consolidation of holdings and a strong cooperative service sector to provide economies of scale for small and marginal farmers, may provoke political opposition which cannot be reconciled through the democratic process.

It would be a mistake to underestimate the potential for peasant mobilization inherent in electoral politics. The introduction of modern participatory politics has already achieved the political redefinition of caste to create new categories of Forward Castes, Other Backward Classes, and Scheduled Castes and Tribes, each of which embraces large numbers of endogamous groups, for purposes of electoral cooperation. It was only in the 1920s and 1930s, after the British introduced a very narrow suffrage, that the nonelite Hindu proprietor castes began to make political demands by appealing to a new secular standard of legitimacy based on numbers (relative to those of the Brahman minority) and not birth. Although the introduction of universal suffrage at Independence did not immediately affect the dominance of the landed castes, the level of political awareness has progressively risen, especially since the 1969 Congress Party split and Mrs. Gandhi's *garibi hatao* campaigns. Ambitious politicians seeking to make up for desertions by leading members of the dominant castes have realized the need to appeal to a broader social and economic constituency of previously ignored groups. The most sophisticated of this new breed, such as Devaraj Urs in Karnataka, attempted to straddle traditional divisions among Other Backward Classes, Scheduled Castes, Scheduled Tribes, and Muslims by harnessing the resentment of all these groups against upper-caste dominance, while promising a mixture of reservations in educational institutions and government services for socially and economically disadvantaged groups, tenancy reforms, and antipoverty programs. Even in Bihar, where an ideological formula to rally all the Backward Classes and Scheduled Castes has yet to be found, the most astute of the upper Backwards realize they do not have the numbers, status, or economic resources needed to defeat the Forwards on their own. The most adventurous are beginning to argue that the reservations policy is meant to benefit all the poor, not just the Backward Classes, and that reservations are the entering wedge of a social and economic revolution. Moreover, whether in concert or as adversaries, the Backward Classes and Scheduled Castes are increasingly making situational distinctions that allow them to shift as appropriate between a two-pronged caste and class consciousness.

India's leadership appears to have correctly judged that under Indian conditions, a change in religio-cultural attitudes is the necessary precondition to altering social institutions and that such a fundamental shift in world view could only be accomplished gradually. They were mistaken, however, in pinning so much importance on economic modernization as an instrument of this transformation. Historically, changes in consciousness which spurred nonelite Hindu communities to carry out political organization transcending narrow caste boundaries were initiated by the introduction of modern politics, not economic modernization. The best hope for speeding social change over the long term is that the logic of electoral politics, which raises political awareness and creates the attitudinal conditions for a new political formation of excluded castes (and classes), should be allowed to work itself out.

Notes

1. M.K. Gandhi, *Socialism of My Conception* (Bombay, 1957), p. 255.
2. The devotional Hindu movement of *bhakti* dated from medieval times. The *bhakti* saints taught that salvation is available to all who seek God in the spirit of love and surrender, regardless of caste rank.
3. M.K. Gandhi, *The India of My Dreams* (Bombay, 1947), p. 72.
4. M.K. Gandhi, *Hind Swaraj or Indian Home Rule* (Ahmedabad, 1938), p. 44.
5. Jawaharlal Nehru, *The Discovery of India* (New York, 1946), p. 253.
6. R.K. Karanjia, *The Mind of Mr. Nehru: An Interview* (London, 1960), pp. 100-101.
7. Socialist Party (India), Report of the Sixth Annual Conference, 19-21 March 1948 (Bombay, 1948), p. 96.
8. Nehru's reflections on the need to find a "middle way," which he described as keeping the ideal in view, while moving slowly in that direction without ignoring the facts of the existing situation, can be found in his remarks to Parliament

during the debate on the First Amendment Bill. See India, "Proceedings Other than Questions and Answers," pt. 2, *The Parliamentary Debates: Official Report* (16 May 1951):8821-22 (18 May 1951):9084-85 (29 May 1951):9615-18.

9. Gunnar Myrdal, *Asian Drama: An Inquiry into the Poverty of Nations* (New York, 1968), vol. 1, p. 115.

10. Jayaprakash Narayan, "Why Total Revolution?" *Everyman's Weekly* (22 December 1974).

11. India, Planning Commission, *Draft Sixth Five Year Plan, 1978-83, Revised* (New Delhi, 1979), p. 415.

12. India, *Economic Survey, 1979-80* (New Delhi, 1980), p. 7.

13. Ibid., p. 77.

14. Ibid., p. 122.

15. India, Planning Commission, *Draft Five Year Plan, 1978-83* (New Delhi, 1978), p. 2.

16. The World Bank, *World Development Report, 1979* (August 1979): 162.

17. *Draft Sixth Five Year Plan, 1978-83, Revised,* pp. 341-43; see also studies of size and growth of big business groups cited in Charan Singh, *India's Economic Policy: The Gandhian Blueprint* (New Delhi, 1978), pp. 73-74.

18. *Draft Sixth Five Year Plan, 1978-83, Revised,* p. 342.

19. *Economic Survey, 1979-80,* p. 76.

20. *Draft Sixth Five Year Plan, 1978-83, Revised,* p. 5.

21. *Draft Five Year Plan, 1978-83,* p. 2.

22. India, Planning Commission, *Fifth Five Year Plan, 1974-79* (New Delhi, 1976), pp. 6-7.

23. *Draft Sixth Five Year Plan, 1978-83, Revised,* p. 78.

24. The definition of "cultivators" and "agricultural laborers" was different in the 1961 and 1971 censuses. In 1961, some persons who were primarily agricultural laborers but cultivated a tiny plot of land for some part of the work day were classified as "cultivators" under a criterion that stated: "The basis of work will be satisfied in the case of seasonal work like cultivation, if the person has had some regular work of more than one hour a day throughout the greater part of the working season." In 1971 the criterion of work was changed to mean "the main activity of the person," i.e., "how he engages himself mostly." India, Registrar General and Census Commissioner, *Census of India, 1971: Provisional Population Totals,* paper 1, 1971, supplement (New Delhi, 1971), pp. 27-28. This definitional change may have been responsible for part of the jump in agricultural laborers as a percentage of the total work force from 16.7 percent in 1961 to 25.7 percent in 1971. Ibid., pp. 30-33.

25. See India, Ministry of Labour, Labour Bureau, *Rural Labour Inquiry, 1974-75,* Summary Report (Chandigarh).

26. India, Ministry of Agriculture and Irrigation, Department of Agriculture, *All India Report on Agricultural Census, 1970-71* (New Delhi, 1975), p. 26.

27. Narayan Datt Tiwari, "Growth with Social Justice and Self-Reliance," based on address delivered by the deputy chairman, Planning Commission, at the meeting of the National Development Council (New Delhi, 13 February 1981), *Indian and Foreign Review* (1-14 March 1981):12.

28. *Draft Sixth Five Year Plan, 1978-83, Revised,* p. 3.

29. "FICCI's Charter of Demands," *Economic and Political Weekly* (New Delhi, 8-15 November 1980):1919.

30. In January 1981, when the central government announced its scheme to issue

interest-bearing "special bearer bonds" of Rs. 10,000 each, with immunity to all purchasers from disclosure of the source of money invested, the Finance Ministry estimated the amount of black money in the economy at Rs. 25,000 crores (against an estimated GNP in 1978-79 of Rs. 85,655 crores). *Indian Express* (23 January 1981).

31. During the Fifth Five-Year Plan, the index of industrial production showed the following percentage changes in each of the five years between 1974-75 and 1978-79: +1.8; +5.4; +12.2; +3.4; +6.9. *Economic Survey* (1979-80):92-93.

32. Charan Singh, *India's Economic Policy*, p. 90.

33. See "Planning: Building on Sand," *Economic and Political Weekly* (6 September 1980):1502-3.

34. *Economic Survey, 1979-80*, p. 7.

35. John Mellor, "The Indian Economy: Objectives, Performance, and Prospects." In John W. Mellor (ed.), *India: A Rising Middle Power* (Boulder, Colo., 1979), p. 106.

36. Annual growth rates for the GNP in each of the five years of the Fourth Plan Period, 1974-75 to 1978-79, were: 1.0 percent; 9.7 percent; 1.5 percent; 8.1 percent; 4.2 percent. *Economic Survey, 1979-80*, p. 75.

37. Ibid., p. 7.

38. India, Planning Commission, Programme Evaluation Organization, *A Quick Evaluation Study of Food for Work Programme* (August-October, 1979), An Interim Report (New Delhi, December 1979), ch. 4.

39. Kumudini Dandekar and Manju Sathe, "Employment Guarantee Scheme and Food for Work Programme," *Economic and Political Weekly* (12 April 1980): 711-12.

40. S. Guhan, "Rural Poverty: Policy and Play Acting," *Economic and Political Weekly* (22 November 1980): 1975-82.

41. In 1952, the Planning Commission wrote that "for the purposes of our calculations regarding possible rates of development in India in the next few decades," population would continue to grow at the rate of 1.25 percent per annum—the rate during the previous ten years. India, Planning Commission, *The First Five Year Plan* (New Delhi, 1952), pp. 20, 23. By contrast, the annual growth rate rose to over 2 percent by 1961 and stabilized at almost 2.5 percent during 1971-81. The population reached 548 million in 1971 compared to planners' estimate of 500 million in 1977, and rose to more than 683 million in 1981. *Indian Express* (19 March 1981).

42. Jawaharlal Nehru, *Fortnightly Letters to the Chief Ministers, 1948-63* (5 August 1964), unpublished.

43. India, Planning Commission, *Fourth Five Year Plan, 1969-74* (New Delhi, July 1970), p. 117.

44. Charan Singh, *India's Economic Policy*, p. 3.

45. Data cited in Sheila Bhalla, "Islands of Growth: A Note on Haryana Experience and Some Possible Implications," *Economic and Political Weekly* (6 June 1981):1023.

46. Ibid., p. 1029.

47. P.S. Appu, "Kosi Area Development: The Pivotal Role of Institutional Reform" (New Delhi, April 1973), mimeo.

48. S.R. Bose and P.O. Ghosh, *Agro Economic Survey of Bihar* (Patna, 1976), chs. 3, 4.

49. It has been estimated that at least 10 percent of the cultivated land in Bihar

has passed into the hands of the middle peasantry from both these sources over the past three decades. See Pradhan H. Prasad, "Caste and Class in Bihar," *Economic and Political Weekly,* Annual Number (February 1979):481-84.

50. See Harry W. Blair, "Rising Kulaks and Backward Classes in Bihar," *Economic and Political Weekly* (12 January 1980): 64-74.
51. D.B. Miller, *From Hierarchy to Stratification: Changing Patterns of Social Inequality in a North Indian Village* (Delhi, 1975), p. 169.
52. Marcus Franda, "An Indian Farm Lobby: The Kisan Sammelanl" (American Universities Field Staff, 1980), p. 2.
53. Ibid., p. 3.
54. The canal systems were initially designed with traditional cultivation techniques in mind to spread water as thinly and widely as possible, and provide protection in time of drought, rather than to supply the higher water levels per acre required by high-yielding varieties. In addition, the canals have no cross regulators to allow for controlled rotation of watering, or channel systems that reach directly into the farmer's field. Available irrigation water is usually sufficient only for one wet-rice crop during the main growing season. However, the growth cycle of high-yielding varieties is unsuited to the monsoon patterns of much of the rice-growing area. The new varieties are best cultivated as a second crop during the sunny, dry season. In practice, the efficient adoption of modern techniques requires the installation of minor irrigation works to tap underground water as an assured source of supply year round. See B. Sivaraman, "Scientific Agriculture Is Neutral to Scale: The Fallacy and the Remedy," Dr. Rajendra Prasad Memorial Lecture, 27 December 1972, Indian Society of Agricultural Statistics, 26th Annual Conference, Kalyani.
55. Charan Singh, *India's Economic Policy,* p. 11.
56. James P. Grant, "Development: The End of Trickle Down?" *Foreign Policy* (Fall 1973):43-65.
57. The following paragraphs are based on Francine Frankel, "The Politics of the Green Revolution: Shifting Patterns of Peasant Participation in India and Pakistan." In Thomas T. Poleman and Donald K. Freebairn (eds.), *Food, Population, and Employment: The Impact of the Green Revolution* (New York: Praeger, 1974), pp. 127-38.
58. Miller, p. 94.
59. For an interesting analysis of growing politicization among the Indian masses, see D.L. Sheth, "Structure of Indian Radicalism," *Economic and Political Weekly,* Annual Number (February 1975):319-34.
60. S. Guhan, "Rural Poverty: Policy and Play Acting," p. 1980.
61. M.A. Oommen, *Kerala Economy since Independence* (New Delhi, 1979), pp. 20, 25.
62. Ratan Khasnabis, "Operation Barga: Limits to Social Democratic Reformism," *Economic and Political Weekly* (June 1981):A-45.
63. E.M.S. Namboodiripad, "Castes, Classes, and Parties in Modern Political Development," *Social Scientist* (New Delhi, November 1977):25.

Part Two

IRAN

Introductory Essay

The ancient land of Iran was thrust sharply into the American conscious-ness in the late 1970s. The overthrow of Shah Mohammed Reza Pahlavi, the reemergence of Ayatollah Khomeini, the revolutionary turmoil, the seizure of American hostages, the slogans that were simultaneously reli-gious and anti-American—all these events which caught by surprise even many experts on Iran, posed both elementary and profound questions. Why had these sudden events taken place? What were the forces that overthrew a pro-Western monarch who had been so long supported by the United States? What part did religion play in the revolution? How significant was the relatively new oil wealth? What did all this portend for the future? Was the revolution particular to Iran or could it be expected to spread to other Islamic countries? How deep—or superficial—was the declared opposition to America, Western values, modernization?

Some readily available but important information is a necessary prelimi-nary to assess not only the response to these questions, but the questions themselves. Of the people who live in the Persian Gulf region, more than 98 percent profess allegiance to the religion of Islam. Although most Mos-lems in the world profess Sunni Islam, the Moslems in the Gulf region are mainly Shi'is, and this is true of Iran. But if the religion of Islam is pervasive in the Persian Gulf region, is it equally influential? How deeply does it penetrate and permeate the culture?

On one level this is easy to state. The body of Islamic religious law (the *Shari'a*) was intended to apply to all areas of behavior, and one cannot discuss the historical development of Iranian culture without reference to that law. But in the nineteenth and twentieth centuries Western influences in cultural, economic, and political realms produced social changes at a rate that made it difficult to apply the traditional *Shari'a*. In various social areas decisions were made outside of Islamic law. This was an ongoing process which has been at least temporarily disrupted, and variously labeled as secularization, Westernization, modernization. But even at its most extensive, it did not displace Islam as a vital force. As one contemporary scholar has written of Islam: "Its significance in the belief and behavioral patterns of the great majority of the people cannot be too greatly emphasized." It is in the name of Islam that attacks have been launched on materialism and immorality, the alleged consequences of modernization. It is in the name of Islam that criticism is directed against pornography, various relations between the sexes, interest, insurance, aspects of technology and science, foreign investments and multinationals. One must take Islam into account to answer our questions about the present and future course of Iran.

In his examination of the patterns of religion and development in Iran, William Beeman—after asserting the identity of Iran as an Islamic state—points out the discrepancy between the intensity of religious fervor that marked the revolution and the more relaxed religious practice and set of beliefs that preceded it. He seeks to locate and describe what he terms "base elements" or "core symbols" expressed through religious doctrine and on which Iranian social and ideological life rests. Focusing on two sets of cultural principles—one which contrasts the internal life to the external, the other which contrasts hierarchical relations to those of equality—he shows how they operated in different sections of Iranian society in recent decades and how they are used today to justify the revolution.

The present regime of the Islamic Republic, according to the revolutionists, embodies and defends the core values of Iran. Those who oppose it, attack those core values. Islam is the medium through which these values are articulated. Those who wish to conceive and implement plans for modernization (technological, scientific, economic, and cultural development) must cope with that religion, with those values.

As a political scientist, R.K. Ramazani poses and responds to a different set of questions. Acknowledging the importance of religious leadership in the revolution in Iran, he points out that the religious leadership was never monolithic and that the revolution depended not only on the religious leaders but the entire society. Almost all sectors of Iranian society were united in their opposition to the Shah. They opposed him because of the discernible bad effects his policies had on a range of issues—economic, political, cultural, and religious. Ramazani views skeptically the easy characterization of the revolution as a "revolt against modernity." That description, he finds, obscures more than it clarifies, as do a number of other common descriptions.

Ramazani challenges a number of current concepts about contemporary Iran. Just as a past overemphasis on modernization (equated with economic growth) overlooked the complexities of Iranian society, present overemphasis on traditional Islam could do the same. There are lessons to be drawn from recent events in Iran, that will throw light on what we can realistically expect in Iran and other Gulf societies. Ramazani offers generalizations that will serve as a guide if we are to learn those lessons. Although the lessons are available to every nation, Ramazani concludes by showing the particular implications they have for U.S. policies.

J.F.

3

Patterns of Religion and Economic Development in Iran from the Qajar Era to the Islamic Revolution of 1978-79

William O. Beeman

Development and Its Religious Substratum

Many commentators on the revolutionary events of 1978-79 in Iran have interpreted them as indicating a strong upswing in Shi'a Islamic orthodoxy. Although Iran's identity as an Islamic state is not in question, both Iranian and foreign observers over the years have regularly reported the Iranian population to be somewhat lax in both knowledge of doctrine and adherence to strict Islamic practice. The religious fervor which characterized the revolution seems to constitute a significant change in the basic religious orientation of the Iranian people. The leaders of the postrevolutionary Islamic Republic were committed to effecting such a change in the population. They viewed the prerevolutionary period as one of corruption, led by a corrupt shah—thus accounting for previous laxity in religious observance.

In the discussion which follows the apparent shift in religious orientation in Iran is seen neither as a question of corruption and purity nor as one of decline and revival. Iranian religious behavior and belief is viewed as oriented by a set of symbolic principles which underlie not only religious practice, but also many other aspects of Iranian social, economic, and political life. This symbolic substratum, rather than orthodox Shi'a doctrine, provided the inspiration and strength underlying the fervor of the original revolution.

The religion of Iran, textbooks announce, is Ithna 'Ashari (Twelver) Shi-'ism, so called because it espouses twelve Imams—descendants of the prophet Mohammed. But the true religion of Iran lies far beneath the surface doctrines of Shi'ism. Moreover, even those Iranians who are lax in their observance of strict formal adherence to the laws and advisories of strict orthodoxy will nevertheless claim to be fully religious persons.

Iranian Shi'ism has been built up over the centuries on a base of native pre-Islamic belief and flavored with particularly Iranian aesthetic and philosophic doctrines. These particularly Iranian elements have given religious life in Iran a very different character from that of any other Islamic state. To understand this belief system, it is necessary to delve below the surface forms of religious practice and doctrine and gain an understanding of the base elements, the core symbols of society, upon which formal religion is built.

Religious doctrine often serves as a concretization of these core symbols, both making statements about the truth of the conceptual world in which society exists, and prescribing the behavior of society's members. Religion also serves as a formal statement of symbolic categorization in cultural life. It helps people regulate their lives by placing certain aspects of all the ideological attitudes available in their cultural system at the center of their personal value and action system, relegating other aspects to the periphery. Religious systems are not merely static arrangements of idealizations. They are dynamic, and occasionally make their dynamic nature explicit. Clifford Geertz's classic study of another Islamic society—that of Java—demonstrated the enormous distance that can separate the practice of religion from the demands of doctrine.[1] Such is the case in Iran.

Basic Dimensions of the Iranian Religious-Cultural Orientation

Underlying all Iranian social and ideological life are several major cultural principles. These serve as leitmotifs for public and private conduct. They are incorporated into both religious and secular philosophies of human interaction and are thus extremely important for an understanding of difficult social processes such as development.

These cultural principles are arranged in two large arenas of contrast. The first contrast is between the *internal* and *external* as culturally defined. The second is a contrast between *hierarchy* and *equality*. Within the dimension of hierarchy, two polar positions emerge: superior and inferior.

Although these principles exist in contrast to each other, they are seen most frequently in a state of dynamic tension, in a kind of cosmic equilibrium. Each principle implies a state of affairs within society in which it is in balance with its opposing principle. When affairs create a disequilibrium, widespread social disturbance is the result—such as the 1978-79 revolution.

Internal versus External

The internal/external contrast is found in many societies.[2] In Iranian ideology the contrast between the internal and external is especially strong. Because they are in a state of tension, the two dimensions continually threaten to destroy each other. Of the two, the internal is by far the more positively valued, and in many ways the principal human spiritual struggle is seen to be the striving of the pure internal core to conquer the corrupt external periphery.

This contrast is explored in depth in a recent study by M.C. Bateson et al.[3] The authors discuss the differences between the exemplary traits of *safa-ye baten*, "inner purity," and the bad traits of the external world which lead one to become *bad-bin*, "suspicious, cynical, pessimistic." The bad external traits, epitomized in adjectives such as *zerang*, "shrewd," *forsat-talab*, "opportunistic," *motazaher* or *do-ru*, "hypocritical," *hesabgar*, "calculating," and *charbzaban*, "obsequious, insincere," are qualities which many Iranians feel they must combat in themselves as well as in the external world.

The internal is the locus of the purest aspects of human spirituality, but it is also the principal focus for proper religious practice. A common popular religious saying in Iran is: "Knowledge of self is knowledge of God." The internal is reflected in architecture in the *anderun*, the area of the household where the family convenes to the exclusion of outsiders. Iranians believe that they have an especially rich inner life, and concomitantly, that no one can really fully understand their inner core.

The external is the abode of the material world and all that it implies. Although man must live in the world, Iranians view the external world as a potential danger for man's spiritual nature. Corruption comes from the external world as tangible attacks against man and his culture, and as a seduction of man away from the core values of society and the proper relations with men and higher spirituality. Desire for the external world and all in it is given a name in philosophical and popular usage. It is one of the central concerns in the doctrine and practice of Sufism, where the killing of one's "passions" *(nafs)* is one of the prerequisites to achieving mystic enlightenment. Iranian concern with this problem is reflected extensively in expressive culture. One of the principal themes of Iranian literature, films, and popular drama involves characters caught between the drive toward inner morality and the external pull of the corrupting world.

The distinction is not entirely absent from formal religious doctrine. One of the hallmarks of Shi'ism is the distinction between exoteric *(zaher)* and esoteric *(baten)* knowledge.[4] Allamah Tabataba'i, one of the great modern scholars of Shi'ism, makes it clear that the ability to understand the inner core of religious truth has a great deal to do with an individual's personal qualities: "[The Qur'an possesses] deeper and wider levels of meaning which only the spiritual elite who possess pure hearts can comprehend."

Keddie, likewise, shows how this doctrine was used to create a religious elite structure in the community of believers:

> There early arose the idea that in addition to the obvious, literal meaning of the scriptures, there was a more profound, inner meaning open only to the initiate. Among the Shi'i sects the idea became common that this meaning had been handed over secretly by the Prophet to Ali, and by him to his descendants, in whatever line the particular sect happened to believe. . . . And the philosophers' approach to *zaher* and *baten* was also attuned to their intellectual and political position. According to them, the Qur'an contained crude religious notions for the masses, and at the same time had deliberate obscurities and ambiguities which would lead the philosophically minded to contemplate and to achieve a true rational understanding of religion.[5]

The internal/external distinction exists in the political and historical consciousness of Iranians as well. The struggle between the pure core of Iranian civilization and the external forces that threaten to destroy it is one of the principal popular idealizations of Iranian history.

For ordinary Iranians the conquest of Iranian territory by the Greeks, Arabs, and Mongol hordes might well have happened yesterday. Foreign domination of the Iranian economy in the nineteenth century culminating with the Anglo-Russian partition of the country into spheres of influence in 1907 was a continuation of this pattern of conquest, as was Allied occupation of the country during World War II, and Soviet interference in Azerbaijan and Kurdistan following the war. Foreign domination was always viewed as the greatest of insults to the Iranian nation, but popular wisdom has it that Iran has always risen from the ashes of domination and conquest to reestablish itself as a great civilization. The basic ability of the internal to conquer the external is verified in this Iranian popular view of world events.

In extreme situations of personal suffering or national need, the resources of this symbolic core can be marshalled for political action. Religious life in Iran idealizes sacrifice and martyrdom for the sake of core principles.[6] Chief representative of those willing to be martyred rather than submit to external coercion was Imam Hosein—grandson of the prophet Mohammed—martyred on the plains of Kerbala near present-day Baghdad, rather than acquiesce to the demands of the caliph of Damascus, Yazid, that Hosein acknowledge his right to leadership of the faithful.

The image of Imam Hosein continues to play a central role in popular religious life in mourning ceremonies held throughout the year, in which Iranians are encouraged not only to take him as an example of correct pious behavior but to analogize his sufferings with their own. Thus a pattern developed in Iran which tends to view force and coercion from external sources negatively, to tend to blame external forces for any difficulties facing individuals or the nation as a whole, and to be willing to resist that which seems to emanate from a source external to Iranian core culture.

Hierarchy and Equality

Although hierarchical differentiation is a nearly universal feature of social life, few societies take the obligations of hierarchical position as seriously as Iranian society. Persons placed in a position of superiority should ideally rise to that position and retain it by fulfilling obligations to inferiors which ensure their support and respect. Inferiors in turn retain their ties to specific individuals in superior positions by reciprocal observance of obligations of their own. In contrast to hierarchical orientation in Iranian society are ties of intimacy and equality between individuals. These involve mutual obligations of a severe and absolute nature which often prove impossible or nearly impossible to fulfill.

Obligations incumbent upon a superior in a hierarchical relationship prescribe that although demands may be made of inferiors, rewards and favors must also be granted. In general, the superior individual is bound to those in an inferior role by a concern for their welfare and a desire to provide them with opportunities for advancement, comfort, and benefits. The tribal khan, the rural landlord, the religious sheik, the teacher, and the shah are all models of superior individuals who have the right to make almost unlimited demands on those bound to them in inferior roles, but who must also be unstinting in their concern for the welfare of those of whom they have charge. Any hint of exploitation on their part automatically voids the relationship.

Inferiors express their own demands through making petitions for things they need or desire, providing tribute and service to superiors as the balance of the bargain. The inferior person is in fact in an advantageous position with regard to the superior. If he is unable or unwilling to fulfill his obligations in the relationship, he has resort to his own inferiority as an excuse. In situations where power relationships are not defined, individuals will often jockey for the inferior position rather than the superior one as a means of "getting the lower hand" in the relationship.[7]

Hierarchical relationships are accepted as the norm in life—no one is exempt—even a minister is inferior compared to a national or spiritual leader; even a street sweeper is superior to younger street sweepers. Status in this regard is relative, changing according to situation and circumstance. There is no necessary stigma attached to being in an inferior position to another, unless it is undeserved or imposed against one's will. For this reason, both parties in the relationship respect each other. Lack of mutual respect is enough to bring about a breach in the relationship. Contempt on the part of the superior or insubordination on the part of the inferior will cause a rupture.

Relations of intimacy and equality are very demanding and difficult to maintain in Iran. Reciprocity in such relationships should ideally be absolute. The parties involved should be willing to do anything at all for each other's benefit, and share material and spiritual substance completely. The relationship is therefore often never fully realized to the satisfaction of the parties involved. Many avoid even beginning a relationship which promises this sort of intimacy for fear that they will be bitterly disappointed with its ultimate inadequacy. The most ideal form of this relationship is embodied in the Sufi notion of "Unity with the Absolute," also a theoretical goal, impossible except through long and arduous spiritual guidance.

Thus, in Iranian life relations tend toward hierarchy, where roles and obligations between individuals are clearly set. Breach or rupture occurs when individuals fail to fulfill their obligations to each other. When obligations are carefully observed, harmony generally prevails.

Historical Sectors of Iranian Society

Iranian cultural principles are brought into play in small ways in everyday social interaction, but they have found more lasting expression in shaping conflicts which pit the major sectors of society against central authority and against each other. For each of the major sectors—the religious establishment, tribes, village society (including landlords), and the bazaar—the obligation to define and defend core values from the corruption of the periphery, and the drive to establish rights and obligations of authority and subservience have constituted major themes both in their history and in the history of Iran.

Mullahs, Monarchs, and Maldars

The contrast between the internal and external, between hierarchy and equality, is epitomized in the centuries-old Iranian question of the proper relationship of religious to secular authority. The Safavids (1501-1722), who were responsible for the institutionalization of Twelver Shi'ism as the Iranian state religion, began as a Sufi mystical sect. Later they claimed direct descent from the prophet Mohammed through Musa al-Kasem, son of the sixth Shi'a Imam, Ja'far al-Sadeq. Shi'ism assumed a highly sectarian cast during this period, and persecution of Sunnis, Sufis, and non-Moslems seems to have been common. Indeed, continual harassment of Sunni Afghans may have been one factor leading to their destructive attacks in 1722 marking the effective end of the dynasty.[8]

During the Safavid Era, the Shi'a clergy became concentrated in Iran. Many were invited to settle there from the Levant and Mesopotamia. They were incorporated into the state government and given important administrative and legal posts. As Safavid rule began to decline in the years following Shah Abbas (1588-1629), many of the religious leaders who had acquired considerable power during this era began to urge the population to follow their guidance instead of that of the shahs, some of whom were weak and impious.[9]

Shi'ite doctrine during the Safavid period continued earlier practice of emphasizing the person of the twelfth Imam—the Mahdi, who would come on the Day of Judgment to "full the earth with justice and equity as it is now filled with injustice and oppression."[10] Religious leaders stressed that the only true "inner" religious truth was possessed by the Imams. Man needed to follow the Mahdi, as the only legitimate representative of God's law, or failing his presence on earth, that of the best representative of the Mahdi one could find.[11] This was generally the wisest and most pious individual available, usually a mullah or *mujtahid.* The most popular mullahs accumulated enormous power as their following grew and they posed a considerable challenge to the state.

Additionally, many of the ulema had acquired enormous wealth. They were charged with the administration of religious bequests *(waqf),* much of which was in the form of property to build virtual empires of their own.[12] Keddie comments that the ulema leaders "often had what amounted to private armies, made up particularly of religious students, who could cause disturbances and terrorize the government, particularly when they were joined by popular crowds."[13]

In the late eighteenth and early nineteenth centuries because of political unrest within Iran, the principal *mujtahids* had moved to the shrine cities of present day Iraq: Kerbala, Kufa, Najaf, and Samarra, where the principal Shi'ite martyrs had been buried. These cities were located in the Ottoman Empire. Thus religious authorities were physically removed from the secular authority of the rulers of Iran, especially during the rule of the nineteenth-century Qajars (1779-1924).

Troublesome Tribes

The question of hierarchy in political life was not exclusively limited to dealings with religious authority. Other sectors of society claimed full authority to govern their own affairs outside of the sphere of the central

government. Chief among these were the Iranian tribes. The pastoral nomadic tribal population of Iran was estimated to constitute as much as half
of the total population of the country during the first half of the nineteenth
century. It was proportionately less by the end of the century due in part
to a large general population increase during this period.

Tribes have always proved troublesome for Iran's rulers. Tribal leaders
generally insisted on maintaining a rough local autonomy for their own
people. They had a system of self-governance and a sense of their own ethnic
identity that precluded absorption into a central state system. One of the
more disturbing aspects of their independence was tacit acceptance of rob-
bery as an honorable profession in the tribes—so long as it was not committed within the tribe itself. Many villagers and even city dwellers came to fear
tribal raids, especially during hard times.

Tribal subsistence often involved utilization of ecological riches unavail-
able for exploitation in any other way. Tribesmen needed to be free to
migrate along prescribed routes to support a highly efficient meat, wool,
and dairy industry. When left to pursue their own course, the tribes would
migrate from summer to winter pasture in such a way that they would leave
the lowlands before the grass was dried out by the heat of summer, and
arrive in the highlands once the snows had melted. The process was re-
versed in the fall. Because the time difference between the availability of
grass at either end of the migration route left a gap of up to two months,
the flocks had to be carefully herded up and down the mountain slopes so
that they would never outrun their food supply.

Protecting this complicated ecological adaptive pattern required skillful
leadership. Although the simultaneous movement of several thousand families and several hundred thousand animals required a good deal of internal
autonomy for tribal subgroups, preserving the entire system from outside
encroachment necessitated a strong central figure. The tribal khans and
sheiks were formidable opponents when angered. Normally they were on
good terms with the government, as long as they were left alone. Some
eventually became coopted into government service and left tribal life altogether for the life of the city. Nevertheless, tribal leaders rarely abandoned
their power bases entirely, standing ready to challenge the government at
any time they felt the encroachment of the throne.

Landlords and Peasants

A third, formidable section of the Iranian population consisted of peasant farmers, very few of whom owned the lands they farmed. Landlords,
few of whom lived in the village(s) they owned, fostered a sharecropping
system with their tenants. The system was theoretically based on a division
of crops with the tenants on the basis of proportions of the five basic

elements of agricultural production: land, water, human labor, animal labor, and seed. Under one of a number of formulas found throughout the country, for example, if the landlord provided three of these elements he would take three-fifths of the crop.

Some farmers had no land to farm and were employed for cash wages by other farmers or by the landlord himself. These landless farmers were called *khwushnishin* ("he who sits well or comfortably"), a term also applied to nonfarmers engaged in services such as shopkeeping, artisanry, barbering, ritual practice, or building. In the nineteenth century and down to land reform in 1963 the life of these landless peasants did not differ drastically from sharecropping farmers, nor as a class were they much worse off.[14] Agricultural life was very delicately balanced. Water was scarce in most areas of the country except for the north and the northwest. Farmers developed some of the most ingenious mechanical devices and social institutions for maximizing water and cooperating in its distribution.

The *ganat* system was one of the most original methods for obtaining water ever invented by man. A long tunnel was made from a source of water near the base of a mountain or hill, dug through a series of vertical shafts spaced at frequent intervals. The slope of the land was calculated so that the water would emerge in a gentle flow from the source to the village where it was to be used. These *ganat* were often in excess of twenty-five miles long, and required considerable engineering skills to keep them maintained. Villagers contributed expensive cooperative labor or cash to hired laborers to maintain the *ganat*. At times, the landlord would own the *ganat* and be responsible for its maintenance.

Once water was obtained for the village, it had to be equitably allocated. Throughout Iran a remarkable system of cooperative labor, operating under various names, provided for the distribution of water to all agriculturalists, preserving the differentiated nature of each farmer's landholdings. This system, designated here by one of its more common names, the *bonih* system, consisted of the division of the village into cooperative labor groups or *bonihs*. Although the *bonih* system is seen in Iran in areas not dependent on irrigation, it generally served as the organizational base for water allocation where irrigation was essential. Each group was allocated a specific number of hours, as a proportion of the total irrigation cycle. Thus if the village needed to water its crops (e.g. wheat) on a ten-day cycle, there might be twenty *bonihs,* each with twelve hours of irrigation time. Each *bonih* would then be subdivided into shares in proportion to the land each man owned. In this way, land measures and water rights became inseparable. Men often measured their land according to the amount of water it took to irrigate it instead of using surface measures. The *bonih* often turned into a cooperative labor group. Members of the same *bonih* would plow, sow, and reap together as well as irrigate. The system was efficient, tightly integrated, and superbly adapted to rural agriculture in Iranian villages.[15]

The landlord was a formidable figure in village life for the peasants. He could be cruel and greedy. Often he treated villagers as chattel, either through his personal conduct or through his representative in the village. Nevertheless, he had certain obligations vis-à-vis villagers which he was required to fulfill. He was charged with correct crop distribution at the end of the season, and had to provide for the welfare of his villagers in lean times. He would often provide clothing for peasants at the Iranian New Year, and he could be approached for special aid: medical treatment, a loan, support for building religious structures, schooling for a bright youngster, and other such needs.

The landlord was the principal link between villagers and the external world of the urban centers. He was responsible for the marketing of crops, including any surplus that villagers might have.[16] In the nineteenth century landlords became more independent, and consolidated their control over the affairs of the rural countryside. Landowning became fashionable, and large landowners became formidable rivals of the throne. Especially in the waning years of the century, many landowners controlled land and wealth which rivalled that of the royal family. Keddie notes that the taxation system under the Qajar shahs was also favorable to landlords.[17]

Landowning was in some ways the universal destiny of the wealthy. The clergy developed extensive holdings, tribal leaders would settle out on huge parcels of land, sometimes adjoining summer or winter pastures, and urban merchants would look to rural agricultural land not only as a fine investment, but also as a pleasant retreat from city life. Even civil servants often came by land in less honorable ways; the government could encroach on private lands and confiscate them for "state purposes."

The Bazaar

Perhaps the most independent sector of Iranian society was the bazaar. Bazaar merchants were used to tolerating the central government as long as it did not interfere too severely with their business dealings. The bazaar was operated on a guild system with rigid codes of financial and personal behavior. Financial dealings within the bazaar were largely based on personal connections and good faith. A man's business reputation depended on his personal conduct in dealing with others. All this contributed to making the bazaar an extremely closed and close-knit sector of society. The tight inner organization of the merchant class also led to resistance against the government whenever the prerogatives of the commercial sector were compromised.

The bazaar was and is still today the heart of the Iranian commercial world. It has its own banking practices, provisions for the transfer of goods and money, and an almost organic system of raising and lowering prices. It has resisted government control in every possible way. In the nineteenth century the bazaar insisted on conducting business with foreign coins (the Maria Theresa Thaler being favored) to avoid coming under the unwelcome yoke of the throne's monetary system. Lest one think that the bazaar may have overestimated its strength at times, it is sobering to remember that even up to the last months of the Pahlavi regime, Iran's second most important export, after oil, was carpets—exported through the bazaar.

The bazaar has never shaken one aspect of its mentality that has been the bane of the Iranian central government for over a century. This is the fear of long-term, high-risk investment. Although many twentieth-century industrialists who made long-term investments came from the bazaar, the predominant desire in the bazaar is for an investment which provides a 100 percent return in a matter of days. In this atmosphere, innovation and change have a difficult time making any headway.

Checks and Balances

The nineteenth-century court in Iran maintained an extraordinarily tenuous hold on authority. The religious establishment was wealthy and powerful and disapproved of the throne. Tribal leaders were not openly hostile, but would offer a severe challenge if provoked. Landlords were growing wealthier and more protective of their own prerogatives year by year, and the bazaar was independent and isolated from government operations. All these traditional sectors were relatively financially independent and had their own private forces to counteract the government if need be.

It is in this context that the dynamics of development must be considered. If development is to be carried out in a systematic way, some means must be established to reach out into all sectors of society. The government of the Qajar dynasty was incapable of doing this, and the troubles of that century and the present one can be laid partly to that inability.

The History of Modern Development in Iran

Modern economic development was more difficult to bring about in Iran than in any other Asian nation. Iran never lost its integrity as a nation during this period, yet it became almost entirely dependent on Western countries for the impetus for modernization. Internal control of the country was very weak, which also limited the power of the central government to act, or even to protect its own policy decisions when they met with resistance from the public at large. In the twentieth century the two world wars combined with internal political strife to cripple the Iranian government at crucial junctures, making the nation even more dependent on outside resources for development.

The reign of Mohammed Reza Pahlavi brought enormous but short-lived prosperity to the nation. This prosperity could not be effectively translated into the infrastructural changes needed to transform Iran into the great world power desired by the throne. The pressures of wealth began to erode the fabric of Iranian social structure. To the chagrin of the more traditional sectors of the population, influence of outside nations became essential to the continued survival of development programs and the throne began to exhibit the twin signs of megalomania and paranoia that should have warned the world that serious upheavals were likely. Unfortunately, the nation was in the throes of revolution before these signs could be heeded.

The Qajar Period: Establishing the Pattern

The shahs of the Qajar era were faced with increasing economic difficulties throughout the nineteenth century. As Iran came into greater contact with the Western world, the development of a transportation and communication infrastructure for the nation became imperative. A series of humiliating military defeats resulting in loss of territory to Russia and failure to establish sovereignty over Western Afghanistan under Fath Ali Shah (1797-1834) demonstrated the need for the state to provide better military resources. A new bureaucracy began to emerge—demanding cash wages rather than whatever they could extort from the public in the exercise of their jobs.

Iran began to feel pressure on its traditional manufacturing sectors from European industrial powers. Charles Issawi quotes British consul K.E. Abbot writing in the 1840s:

> [In 1844] a memorial was presented to His Majesty the Shah [then Mohammed Shah] by the traders and manufacturers of Cashan [*sic*] praying for protection to their commerce which they represented as suffering in consequence of the introduction of European merchandize into their country.

> [In 1849] . . . the manufacturers have, however, rapidly declined for some time past in consequence of the trade with Europe which has gradually extended into every part of the kingdom to the detriment or ruin of many branches of native industry.[18]

Loss of income to the private sector through foreign competition was a serious matter for the throne as well, since the Qajar rulers had little source of income during the first half of the century other than taxation. But they taxed with a vengeance. Despite their rapaciousness, they still fell short of the income they needed to maintain the state. An important source of income lay in the sale of government posts, but this, too, proved inadequate to support the throne.

Foreign manufacture proved to be a double threat to Iran. If it eroded local industry, it also provided fatal attractions for the country's upper classes. A few members of the aristocracy began to travel to Europe, viewing how the upper classes lived. The Qajar shahs took the lead in importing expensive toys and luxury goods. They took a superficial attitude toward the notion of modernization, feeling that mere importation of advanced technology and foreign goods would suffice to bring the nation up to European standards.

More seriously, they did not have the income to pay for this consumer-oriented modernization program. The shortfalls in revenue became crucial during the reign of Naser od-Din Shah (1848-96), who set a pattern for his successors by indulging in three ruinously expensive journeys to Europe. His first journey was planned by one of the most remarkable of Naser od-Din's ministers, Hajji Mirza Hosein Sipah Salar, a man who had had extensive experience living abroad and did all within his power to persuade the Shah to transform his government into something resembling European rule. The journey to Europe was planned as a sort of royal "eye-opener," to provide the Shah with direct experience of the modern world.

Naser od-Din took well to modern ideas in at least one realm: the pursuit of new sources of income. Peter Avery describes well the establishment of the pattern that was to persist for the rest of the century in dealing with foreign financial interests:

> [Naser od-Din] conceived a new plan for raising money and, incidentally, making himself more independent of his fickle subjects. He decided that if he could not take the offensive against foreigners (as in the disastrous attack on Herat), it might be possible to induce them to pay for his quiescence. But loans from foreign governments have strings attached to them, and it was not long before another scheme, that of selling concessions to foreign individuals, commended itself to him. Individuals were less powerful than governments. They paid readily for concessions the granting of which was both lucrative and gave the impression that the shah and his friends were anxious to see their country efficiently exploited. This indeed was a modern approach and showed how easily some of the more dubious ethics of the West had been absorbed.[19]

Naser od-Din learned his lesson well indeed, and proceeded to sell numerous concessions to foreigners. The British, Russians, Belgians, French, and many others obtained concessions for the development of mineral rights, the right to develop telegraphic communications (thus introducing the first extensive cadre of foreign technicians to the country), road building, railroads, even the administration of Iranian customs. Much of the funds thus obtained were squandered by the throne. During the Shah's celebrated first European journey, the first significant religious opposition to the modernization schemes of the Shah and the Sipah Salar began to be felt. The clergy began to accuse the government of trying to make Iran like Europe, emulating Christendom. Their pressure was so great that the Shah was compelled to issue an order prohibiting the Sipah Salar's reentry into Tehran.

One of the principal bones of contention had to do with the largest concession ever offered anyone. In 1873 the Sipah Salar, faced with a problem of meeting enormous state financial obligations, offered a general concession of equally enormous scope to the English baron Julius de Reuter. This concession included the right to construct railways, work mines, and found a national bank. The nobility of Iran had learned that such concessions often meant enrichment for themselves as well, so many were in favor. The clergy looked askance, but the "deal" would have probably gone through had the Russians not expressed their displeasure with the deal and had the Shah not found the London financial community also unenthusiastic. The bank scheme was eventually salvaged from the general concession, but the rest of the plan was cancelled on the Shah's return to Tehran.[20]

The Reuter concession affair in many ways epitomizes the development pattern which was to be repeated again and again down to the present. The nation was to be developed through concessions of one sort or another to foreign interests. The upper classes, including the throne itself, were to be partners in the plans and reap great economic benefits, while the people were left to receive passively the schemes thrust upon them. Religious leaders continued to play an important role in opposing these schemes. Their opposition was twofold: on the one hand, they opposed the gradual erosion of Iranian religion, customs, and ideals at the hands of foreigners; on the other they resisted the massive growth in wealth and power that the secular ruling classes gained at their expense. This opposition was a recurrent theme in Iranian political life throughout the latter part of the nineteenth century and the whole of the twentieth. This period saw a general pan-Islamic movement opposed to the West growing throughout the Moslem world under the charismatic reformer Jamal al-Din al-Afghani.

The tobacco rebellion of 1890-92 was perhaps the first important conflict in modern times involving all the elements that characterized Iranian protest throughout the twentieth century. A British subject was granted the concession of a monopoly over all purchase, production, and sale of Iranian-grown tobacco. This was too much for the public to take, and the ulema took the lead in stimulating public outcry. Nikki Keddie, acknowledged expert on the history of the Tobacco Rebellion, describes the events thus:

When foreigners arrived to buy up the tobacco crop in 1891, ulema-led protests developed in the major cities. The ulema had family and other ties to the merchants and guilds, and were largely dependent on popularity for their status. They were less vulnerable than others to government reprisal, and were seen as natural leaders. When a Shiraz mujtahid was expelled in 1891 for acts against the company, he went to Ottoman Iraq, where he first saw the Iranian born pan-Islamic and anti-Colonial activist, Jamal ad-Din al-Afghani, who had himself been expelled from Iran for propaganda against concessions to Westerners. The Shiraz mujtahid also saw in Iraq the leader of all the Shi'i ulema, Hajj Mirza Hasan Shirazi, and Afghani wrote a famous letter to Shirazi urging him to act. Major movements broke out in several cities; and in Tabriz the concession had to be suspended. Late in 1891 Shirazi issued a decree saying that the use of tobacco was against the will of the Twelfth Imam, and there followed a universal boycott of tobacco. Naser od-Din was forced to cancel first the internal concession and then after new disturbances, the export concession. The ulema, united partly by telegraphic communication, saw the extent of their political power.[21]

The outlines of this rebellion point out that the public was beginning to feel that the country's leaders were selling off national resources for personal profit. Disturbances continued until the constitutional revolution of 1905-11, which featured a similar unification of clergy and parts of the populace against the throne. These disturbances did not prevent the granting of what proved in the twentieth century to be the most important concession of all—the right to develop all of Iran's oil resources, a concession granted to the British subject D'Arcy in 1901. The resulting Anglo-Iranian oil company provided the capital for much of the subsequent industrialization in the country.

With the early concessions came foreign control, and the British and Russians were in the forefront of those nations anxious to control events in Iran to their own benefit. It is said that the country's government was controlled from the British and Russian embassies. The British-Russian partition of the country into two spheres of influence, even in the throes of the constitutional revolution of 1907, constituted a grave insult to the Iranian people.[22] Even as late as 1921, A.C. Millspaugh, appointed administrator general of the finances of Persia, reported: "It was intimated to me that Persian administrations were filled with Russian and British spies and that many if not most of the leading Persian officials put the interests of a foreign government ahead of the interests of their own country.[23]

The Reza Shah Period: Continuing the Pattern

The ascension of Reza Shah to the throne following World War II has been hailed by many as the beginning of a new era in Iranian history. Many important structural changes took place in Iran's central government, but

Reza Shah changed very little basic structure of the traditional social sectors. If Reza Shah had any policy at all with regard to these sectors, it was to destroy them when they resisted his schemes.

At least two new social forces appeared on the scene during the reign of Reza Shah. The army became strong, and took on an extremely powerful social profile. The bureacracy increased to an enormous degree and began to look for all the world like a European government with all its faults and inefficiency. The outer trappings of modern government could not entirely hide the basic Iranian patterns of social life, and despite many attempts to make the bureacracy function like a modern efficient state system—personalism, favoritism, and individual connections remained dominant in daily government functioning. Other new groups on the scene included cadres of professional men: doctors, lawyers, engineers. Writers and artists also began to emerge but in very small numbers. These new professionals constituted the core of an emergent bourgeoisie destined to first coopt and then replace the upper classes of the Qajar era.

Reza Shah had as his major goal the modernization of Iran. Like his Qajar predecessors, he faced enormous difficulties in penetrating traditional sectors of society. Tribal khans continued to resist acknowledgement of central authority. Reza Shah countered their opposition by arresting the most defiant tribal leaders and forceably settling as many of the tribes as he could. Landlords continued to dominate the rural landscape. Because many were wealthy urban elites on whom he depended for power, Reza Shah was unable to penetrate their bastions of privilege in the countryside. He himself seized large tracts of land and many villages and became a considerable landlord in his own right. The bazaar benefited greatly from increased trade during this period, but foreign competition increased as well, and the merchants tended to remain suspicious of the Shah.

Of all the traditional sectors, the clergy were probably the most disgruntled. One major objection concerned those considerable reforms instituted by Reza Shah which affected the status of women. Public education for women was begun, and women began to hold professional occupations for the first time. The most severe opposition to the Shah's policies from the clergy arose from his outlawing the veil and the head-to-foot chador. Civil servants were required to appear for their paychecks with unveiled wives, and gendarmes went through the streets tearing the illegal garments off unsuspecting women. Clerics could perhaps have lived with some women not wearing the chador in public as a matter of choice, but to make it illegal seemed close to blasphemy. A riot in Mashhad against the new dress code, which also demanded Western dress for men, was cruelly put down by armed troops, who actually violated the sacred shrine of Imam Reza. The religious establishment suffered other losses during Reza Shah's reign, almost all of their former legal and educational functions being taken away from them. New schools and a new civil court system replaced the traditional religious courts and *madressehs.*

Economic development projects during this period consisted largely of massive infrastructural construction projects. The most important of these was the trans-Iranian railway. The bazaar resisted investment in industrial manufacture—the start-up time was too long and expensive. Returns were unacceptably slow and too low to satisfy the merchants who were used to quick returns and high profits. Most industrial development during this period was undertaken by the government itself, bypassing traditional economic institutions.

The principal theme of the Reza Shah period was centralization. Tehran became the center of all decision making, and former power bases in the provinces were unable to maintain themselves with any strength. With the judicial and educational systems centered in the secular government, the ulema were left with only limited power over the people. Tribal groups were forceably contained, and on occasion made to settle.

During the Reza Shah period the government attempted to modernize the country not by transforming the existing infrastructure but rather through bypassing traditional economic institutions. The new industrial sector was an overlay of the traditional economy and was held almost entirely in government hands. Agriculture and animal husbandry remained almost unchanged, while new and much more powerful decision-making institutions arose in Tehran as the nation pushed forward toward increased centralization of power.

Like his predecessors, Reza Shah had a limited range of financial sources. Chief among these was heavy taxation. Consumer spending was also heavily controlled through restrictions on the import of consumer goods. Inflation was kept down through wage controls. Nevertheless, he was able to innovate on an old pattern, changing the old Qajar system of concessions into something new—industrialization with the state as partner. Although revenues from oil and other industries were small in the beginning and were used primarily for purchase of military equipment, this was the principal source that would be used by his son as the linchpin in his own modernization program.

Mohammed Reza Shah: Driving the Pattern to Its Conclusion

Mohammed Reza Shah came to the throne at the forced abdication of his father (again at the hands of foreign powers) as a very young man. American officials viewed him as somewhat weak and irresolute at the time, but were willing to grant him the opportunity to prove himself. World War

II was disruptive, but it also provided an opportunity for reform-minded national leaders to make a new beginning as they were out from under the heavy autocratic hand of Reza Shah, reportedly so terrifying that his own ministers would tremble in his presence.

Prewar economic and development planning was extremely limited in scope. In 1946 a commission was appointed to prepare a development plan for the country, and again in consultation with many foreign elements, the First Plan was launched in 1949, along with a new organization for its administration—the Sazeman-e Barnaneh or Plan Organization. Political turmoil characterized this period in Iranian history as the newly powerful secular nationalists, the Communist Party, and the throne all continued to struggle for power. The prime ministry of Mohammed Mossadeq fell during this period, and conflicts with the British led to cutting off oil revenues. The coup that toppled him from power and reinstated the Shah as government strong man caused enormous disruption. The end result was failure of the First Plan, which eventually expended only 16 percent of the 21 billion rials ($656 million) planned.[24]

The Second Plan extended from 1955 to 1962 and was very loosely defined. It had the quality of a manifesto rather than a planning document, and provided no guidelines or priorities for planners to follow.[25] The government's priority was to launch an investment program, rather than plan how to integrate its projects. The eventual money investment thus tended toward grandiose infrastructural schemes, many of which later proved to be cost-ineffective or useless. Although 26 percent of the money in the Second Plan was designated for agriculture, most was spent on dam construction or irrigation projects that benefited relatively few of the small farmers who dominated the agricultural sector.

Transportation received the largest share of funds, and road building thus undertaken was perhaps the area of the plan with the greatest impact on the economy in the long run. "Social affairs" also received a large share of the funds (26 percent), but this turned out to be a residual category for spending, with little accounting of how the money was spent. The entire program (which in the end exceeded its original budget by almost 14 billion rials—$100 million), ended up providing few tangible benefits for the population as a whole.

The Third Plan was the first comprehensive development plan. The Economic Bureau of the Plan Organization, which benefited from well-trained young Iranian economists, determined that the earlier plans had suffered from (1) lack of coordination between the activities of various government agencies and (2) lack of a comprehensive view regarding the availability and use of economic resources.[26] The goal of the Third Plan was ostensibly to raise real GNP in the country by an annual rate of 6 percent per year, for a total growth of 35 to 40 percent for the entire duration of the plan (1962-67). This goal reflected a simple-minded reading of economic growth theories fashionable at the time which promised economic takeoff if only the GNP could be steadily increased over a long period.

The plan took place concomitantly with the launching of the Shah's "White Revolution," and its provisions meshed with the new economic conditions brought about by the principal reform initiated in that movement—land reform. As landlords were divested of their property, they needed a new source for investment. The Third Plan provided considerable funds for loans and technical assistance to private industry during this period. The private sector responded enthusiastically and considerably exceeded the investment expected of it during the period.

Once again, however, most projects conceived during this period were large, new projects that were not coordinated with existing economic sectors. The aim was to increase national employment and, due to an increase in industrial activity, this did occur. However, rather than increasing employment within traditional sectors, new sectors were created which tended to siphon off quality labor from existing pools—primarily the agricultural sector, creating the beginnings of the chain of urban migration that eventually led to the decline of agricultural production in the nation.

Land reform had been designed as an enlightened program which would return land titles to the farmers. It had been forced on the Shah as the price for good relations with the Kennedy administration, which was promoting such reforms throughout the world as a defense against Communist penetration in Third World countries with repressive regimes. Whatever his motives, the Shah embraced the ideals of land reform with a vengeance. The entire program had many admirable goals, but it also had many flaws in its execution. Much has already been written about the difficulties of land reform.[27] In brief, the principal reasons for the ultimate failure of land reform to stimulate agricultural production stemmed from the following difficulties:

1. The government failed to differentiate between sharecropping farmers and landless agricultural workers who received no land. Once the landlords had been removed, these peasants had no source of cash wages. They therefore left the villages as soon as new employment opportunities arose. This left the landed peasants short of labor during times of year when labor-intensive activities were undertaken—plowing, harvesting, winnowing.

2. Not all peasants were poor, especially those with outside funds—as from smuggling opium and other goods. When land became available, these representatives of the village bourgeoisie bought up all the land they

could, and in cases where several absentee landlords had been previously involved, they sometimes ended up with greater holdings than the original owners.[28]

3. Landlord support for maintenance of important water resources, canals, *ganats,* etc., was removed, and reestablishing a system for cooperative payment for these functions was difficult.

4. The entire marketing system for agricultural crops was eliminated with the landlord and nothing replaced it, leaving peasant farmers at the mercy of produce brokers from the cities. These merchants would often buy a whole crop in advance of the growing season for much less than its value. The peasants, strapped for cash, would have no choice but to agree. Under these circumstances, they had no real incentive to work at producing better crops or higher yields.

5. Young village men had for years adopted a pattern of leaving the village for a short period of their life before marriage to seek casual labor elsewhere. They would usually return, marry, and carry on agricultural production. New industry and construction, largely government-financed during this period, gave them incentives never to return. Thus after a period, villages consisted of nothing but old men, women, and young children.

6. Government price supports for wheat and other staples never kept pace with the increased cost of production. As agricultural labor was drawn away from the village, higher wages had to be paid to retain the few laborers that existed. This increased total cost of production. By the mid-1970s it cost farmers about 14 rials (20 cents) to produce a kilogram of wheat. The government paid only 10 rials to purchase that same wheat. The results are obvious.

7. From the Third Plan onward, although great lip service was paid to designing agricultural development plans that would aid small farmers, massive irrigation projects and dams continued to dominate the construction side of planning. Farm cooperation and agribusiness schemes were then set up to better utilize new irrigation resources. Rather than improve existing farming conditions for agriculturists, farmers were often coerced into participating in these schemes, sometimes being forced to exchange title for their land for "shares" in a corporation. The farmers quite correctly wondered what kind of land reform it was that first gave them title to land and then took it away from them.

The Fourth Plan (1968-72) was designed to increase real GNP by 9 percent per year. In the end it exceeded this by 2 percent, largely due to increased oil production. The plan organization had learned a great deal from previous plans, and this one was executed more efficiently. Nevertheless, the principal gains in the economy were made in the private and public industrial sectors. Although 1.2 million new jobs were created during this period, nearly 250,000 agricultural jobs were abandoned. As industrialists took over, the bazaar began to lose its centrality in the Iranian economy.

Industrialization took on a particularly interesting turn during this period as foreign capital became available to an unusual degree. Joint venture companies were established during this period involving Iranians and foreigners in turnkey operations. The foreign investor would come in and deliver a construction plant, lock, stock, and barrel on a shared cost basis. Government officials and the royal family were prime partners in these ventures because they provided the clout needed to avoid bureaucratic red tape. As these ventures began to achieve success, the nation began to experience a boom. The eventual source of all capital, however, was oil. Iran was unsuccessful in achieving a significant increase in nonoil exports. Most of the new industries manufactured consumer goods for internal consumption. Thus both the capital to *make* goods and the capital to *buy* them came from oil.

There is no question that Iran achieved some real growth during the period of the Fourth Plan—the world began to take notice to an increasing degree. Nevertheless, the growth was top-heavy. It was taking place among new classes of urban elites that had not existed twenty-five years before. Traditional sectors of the economy were experiencing a decline. The country was again awash in foreigners, most of whom seemed to be prospering at the expense of Iran and Iranians. These individuals, to add insult to injury, seemed not to care much about Iran, nor to respect Iranians. They were protected by the government to an extraordinary degree, allowed special privileges, and paid enormous wages in proportion to their Iranian counterparts.

The Shah continued his father's policy of centralization. Land reform was one important measure for breaking the back of the powerful landlords, some of whom had maintained private armies. Forceable settlement of the tribes continued with some extraordinarily bloody confrontations between army and tribesmen. The bazaar found itself saddled with new financial and banking regulations, as well as demands for stricter accounting procedures for purposes of taxation. Finally, the clerics had their last bastions of wealth and power removed during land reform, as personal holdings and religious bequests of land, which had been in their keep, were placed under a government office in charge of a minister appointed by the throne.

The clergy had already suffered considerably from industrialization. Enrollments in religious schools had reached an all-time low. Few young men now aspired to religious life. Even if they completed a term of study at a traditional *madresseh,* they would often abandon their robes for a car repair shop or factory. The government moved to fill the gap in support provided by the *waqf* lands and other sources of income eliminated in this period by providing a regular subsidy to the clergy, but this was a stopgap effort at best. By 1974, many felt that the back of the religious leadership had effectively been broken, and that they no longer constituted a political challenge to the throne.

Life in Iran was becoming increasingly frenetic and uncomfortable. The nouveau riche industrialists and professional classes with their international values and ways were viewed with deep suspicion by the population. In many ways these people did not seem to be Iranian at all. Their values fell into the realm of the external and denied the basic spiritual qualities so central to Iranian culture. When they professed an acquaintance with poetry or mystical philosophy, it seemed faddish and hypocritical. The great writer Jalal al-e Almad was one of the principal critics of this growing class of individuals. His writings, including the powerful essay *Gharbzadegi* ("Westoxication"), often bitterly called into question the erosion of the Iranian spirit during the modernization process. He spent much time in the country's villages and wrote about rural people with much care and affection. Other writers, Gholam Hossein Sa'edi and Samad Behrangi among them, wrote in a similar manner of the core values of Iranian life and severely criticized the government for selling out to superficialities while harming the core of the Iranian population. Modern poets took up the theme of alienation and longing for some form of redemption. The price of modernization was a spiritual one, and it was very dear indeed. The government's response was to harass and arrest these writers and suppress their writings. Many of the more vocal died in mysterious ways.

The Coup de Grâce: OPEC and After

Following the oil price increase of 1973, Iran began to reel out of control. Real growth continued unabated, but it continued to be spread only among the top echelons of society—people who had no real place within the nation's traditional structure. The Shah finally achieved the elusive goal that had been pursued since the days of Naser od-Din Shah—financial independence from the population as a whole. In 1959 oil revenues contributed only 9.7 percent of Iran's total GNP. By 1974 the contribution had risen to 47 percent.[29] By some estimates the government was receiving fully 80 percent of its revenues from oil. Since those in power were not elected, this gave them almost unlimited license in the exercise of power.

For both the Shah and his largely technocratic ministries, such power was very dangerous. It was almost as if Iran had turned into a private economic laboratory with mad scientists in charge. In Iran the most prestigious occupation after medicine was engineering. The engineer even received a social title, *mohandes* (geometrizer). Urban, rural, and planning engineering took their place in the land as technical specialties. At Pahlavi

University in Shiraz, sociology students petitioned to have their degree designated as social engineering.

Life in rural and urban areas became even more uncomfortable as the population was poked and prodded in interminable experiments to decrease inflation, increase productivity, and improve social indicators. It seemed at times that statistics mattered far more than people. The streets of Tehran, clogged with new cars assembled in Iran since 1968, were made one-way one week, and then turned around the other way the next. Parking regulations changed daily. The government legislated mandatory opening and closing hours for small businesses, then would change the hours in the next month. Birth control schemes were introduced without proper medical follow-up, causing many rural women to become sick without any idea of what to do. Farmers were offered credit, then threatened for nonpayment of their debts when the credit schemes were suddenly withdrawn. This was clearly not progressive change, as has often been claimed in assessing the Pahlavi regime, but rather irresponsible and reckless experimentation.

By 1975 the increase in GNP topped 70 percent in real market prices but inflation was exceeding 60 percent. In the next year the inflation rate topped the growth rate, causing negative real growth of about 2 percent. Agricultural production, lagging nearly 1 percent behind the birth rate (2.3 percent vs. 3.2 percent) now went into real decline. The folly of tribal settlement came home to roost as millions of pounds of meat had to be imported from abroad to make up for the destruction of this traditional sector. Ordinary Iranians, particularly those on fixed incomes or on rigidly limited government salaries, were beginning to suffer mightily. Housing costs were rising at yearly increments exceeding 100 percent. Domestic food production, in severe decline, necessitated importing food. For the first time in recent history, Iranians were buying wheat abroad.

The Shah moved to control the situation by appointing Jamshid Amouzegar, his former oil minister, as prime minister. Under former prime minister Amir Abbas Hoveyda, a series of controls in the form of a "campaign against profiteering" was instituted in 1975-76. This consisted of establishing draconian price controls for foodstuffs, along with strict penalties for violators, including the jailing of neighborhood grocers who overcharged or undercut government price standards. Amouzegar, a genuine technocrat, continued these stiff measures. Eventually 10,000 inspectors were sent to examine store accounts. Guild courts imprisoned 8,000 merchants, exiled 23,000 from their home towns, and fined 200,000 more.[30]

It soon became clear that Amouzegar was going to control inflation by cracking down on those few sectors of the economy where the neglected bazaar had found a foothold: real estate and the aforementioned lucrative market in specialized produce: fruits, vegetables, nuts, eggs, and such.

Punitive limitations were placed on the transfer of land and credit lending was virtually stopped. Effects in the bazaar were immediate—merchants stopped paying back bank loans *en masse* and antigovernment propaganda began to surface.

This gave the religious establishment an opening and the revolutionary exhortations of Ayatollah Ruhollah Khomeini, who had opposed government plans for development since 1963, began to take hold throughout the population. When the government moved to discredit Khomeini through a planted article in the daily paper *Ettela'at,* street riots began in the holy shrine city, Qom. The government confronted rioters as it had in the past, with violence, but this time counterprotests broke out throughout the nation. The clergy saw their opening, and once again, as in the past century, spearheaded the opposition.

Many middle- and upper-class Iranians wondered whether they should oppose the throne. They were disturbed by developments in recent years, but had maintained hope that much of the difficulty would eventually pass as Iran became more prosperous. For these individuals, most of whom observed the tenets of Islam in the loosest possible manner, the turning point was seeing unarmed young men and veiled women being gunned down by government troups on the streets of Tehran and other cities. For Iranian citizens, even wealthy ones, this was the ultimate outrage—the sign that the throne had ceased having any respect for the population. The fragile bond that had obtained between the Shah and the people was finally severed and general rioting began. At this point, the Shah ceased to have any legitimacy as a leader for the population as a whole. It was only a matter of time before he was expelled.

The Shah's Crimes

Looking back on the Shah's regime, we find that his difficulties were of two sorts. He faced a number of practical difficulties partly inherited from earlier generations. These might have been dealt with had he not chosen a course of national development that violated the basic values of the Iranian religious-cultural system. The Shah, like his father and the Qajar rulers before them, had to deal with a diverse, unruly, and highly independent population. The desire to rule without the need to curry public support had somehow been built-in as a feature of kingship. When the Shah finally achieved this elusive goal, he quickly discovered that even an absolute ruler needs to be in favor with the public at some level.

The Shah had in the end failed to adhere to the duties of one in a superior position. He had, in the eyes of the public, shamelessly used the Iranian nation in a mounting game of aggrandizement. When the people protested, he stood by while they were murdered. This was enough to disqualify him from a relationship which would guarantee the people's loyalty. Moreover, the Shah seemed to be carrying out his plans for the nation in a way which violated all Iranian ideological tenets concerning the proper relations between the inner and outer worlds of spiritual value. Development of Iran was to take place with the collusion of foreign elements. This made the actions, insofar as they affected Iranians adversely, further proof that the source of all corruption was from "outside," making the people's judgment on the Pahlavi dynasty—the "source" of the imported influence—all the more severe. The fact that the principal influence of foreigners seemed to drive the population away from spiritual values and toward material desire only put the seal on this set of beliefs.

Traditional sectors of the economy may not have benefited from the reign of Reza Shah, but at least, with the exception of the ulema and those tribes that defied the throne, their basic structure was left relatively unchanged. Land reform, industrialization, economic tinkering, and direct military force all were used by Mohammed Reza Shah as tools not just to modernize but to destroy the infrastructure of existing institutions. The institutions that came to replace these older sectors—the professional classes and technocrats—seemed bizarre to the mass of the population: ultimately creatures of the corrupting external world and totally unsupportable.

The Shah may well have fallen prey to the kind of "Westoxication" described by Jalal al-e Ahmad in a particularly pernicious way. The goals of modernization were in the end used by him to justify the use of extreme measures in an old struggle—that between the Iranian monarchy and the rest of the population, with whom, in terms of Iranian basic cultural orientation, it had always enjoyed the most delicate of relationships.

Epilogue: Clerical Development

It is not too difficult, even after three years, to predict what will take place under the current regime in Iran. The clerical leaders in power at this writing (Spring 1982) suffer from the opposite disease that afflicted the technocrats during the Pahlavi era. They know a great deal about personal morality and traditional Iran and its values but very little about the modern world.

One cannot turn back the clock. Whether they were put there for the wrong reasons or not, the automobiles, televisions, chemical plants, cargo ships, oil rigs, and mines now exist in Iran. Their owners have largely fled the country but the facilities remain. Some of these facilities are likely never to be reactivated. Left to rust and decay, much machinery is nonrepairable and lacking adequate manpower. The nation will likely have to start over on many projects.

Traditional sectors of society, like a coiled spring, have reasserted themselves in the absence of the tight enforced centralization of the Pahlavis. Tribes control vast sections of the land once more. The bazaar has shown that it will resist any measures to nationalize trade, and some of this resistance has been channeled directly against the clerical leaders that merchants supported during the revolution. The agricultural sector is the area where the most hope lies. Iran was once an agricultural nation and a noticeable drive and energy are being seen throughout its village regions. Left to their own devices and allowed to charge fair market prices for their goods, farmers have boosted Iran's agricultural output every year since the revolution. Volunteers throughout the land continue to work on village redevelopment projects. Some of the work is technically simple, but there is great enthusiasm which did not exist during the Pahlavi era.

The drive toward decentralization threatens once again to bring basic Iranian cultural orientations into conflict with authority, however. The Islamic court system established after the revolution presumes the infallibility of Islamic Law and of its administration by qualified judges. Thus there is no right of appeal. Consequently, thousands of individuals have been summarily executed since the inception of the new regime; some are very young, and some have committed crimes no greater than passing out leaflets criticizing the clerical regime. The official position is that opponents of the regime are committing a variety of blasphemy in their opposition. Those who plant bombs or commit murder, even in the name of justice, are executed with barely any hearing at all. Others who aid and abet such activities, even in small ways, are accused of "warring against God" or "spreading corruption on earth."

Such accusations rely on acceptance of the proposition that the regime of the Islamic Republic is the embodiment and defender of Iranian core values. Those who oppose it are therefore the embodiment of the external, the corrupt. Official identification of the internal opposition as affiliated with the United States, or occasionally with "godless" world Communism reinforces this image. Thus far the population as a whole has not reacted to these strong repressive tactics. This would indicate that for the time being, the clerical leaders' definition of affairs (coupled with a great deal of muscle from the tough but largely untrained Revolutionary Guard) is plausible enough to prevent the kind of mass movement that would be necessary to bring about yet another revolution.

The nation's present leaders are at a loss for a development policy at this time. Their principal activities have lain in the area of politics and morality. They wish to avoid the kind of Western-based growth-oriented capitalist development that characterized the Shah's regime and the traditional Islamic doctrine that defending the sanctity of private property seems to preclude Marxist-style planned economic schemes. The new regime will be looking for a third way to development. This is nothing new. Even under the banner of Islam, Iran is Iran, and Iranians will behave like Iranians. The founders of Islam themselves could not change that basic fact—those who inhabited the Iranian plateau eventually became Persianized. If there is an Islamic path to development in Iran, the world can be sure that that path will first be Iranian and then Islamic.

Notes

1. Clifford Geertz, *The Religion of Java* (New York: Free Press, 1960).
2. Ibid.; id., *The Interpretation of Cultures* (New York: Basic Books, 1973).
3. M.C. Bateson, J.W. Clinton, J.B.M. Kassarjian, H. Safavi, and M. Soraya, "Safa-yi Batin: A Study of the Interrelations of a Set of Iranian Ideal Character Types." In L. Carl Brown and Norman Itzkowitz (eds.), *Psychological Dimensions of Near Eastern Studies* (Princeton, N.J.: Darwin Press, 1977).
4. Seyyed Hossein Nasr, *Ideals and Realities of Islam* (New York: Praeger, 1967); and M.S.G. Bâtinîya Hodgson, *Encyclopedia of Islam,* 2nd ed., 1960, vol. 1.
5. Nikki R. Keddie, "Symbol and Sincerity in Islam," *Studia Islamica* 19 (1963).
6. Sharough Akhavi, *Religion and Politics in Contemporary Iran* (Albany: SUNY Press, 1980); William O. Beeman, "Martyrdom vs. Intervention: The Cultural Logic behind Iranian Resistance to American Military Intervention," *Leviathan* (Fall 1980): 2-8; id., "Images of the Great Satan: Symbolic Representations of the U.S. in the Iranian Revolution." In Nikki Keddie (ed.), *Religion and Politics in Iran* (New Haven: Yale University Press, 1983); Michael M.J. Fischer, *Iran: From Religious Dispute to Revolution* (Cambridge, Mass.: Harvard University Press, 1980); Nikki Keddie, "Religion, Society, and Revolution in Modern Iran." In Michael Bonine and Nikki Keddie (eds.), *Modern Iran: The Dialectics of Continuity and Change* (Albany: SUNY Press, 1981).
7. For a demonstration of the ways in which status jockeying in Iran is expressed in verbal behavior, see William O. Beeman, "Status, Style, and Strategy in Iranian Interaction," *Anthropological Linguistics* 18 (7, 1976): 305-22.
8. Fischer.
9. Nikki R. Keddie, *Iran: Religion, Politics, and Society* (London: Frank Cass, 1980), pp. 91-92; id., "Religion, Society, and Revolution in Modern Iran," pp. 22-23.
10. Keddie, *Iran: Religion, Politics, and Society,* p. 86.
11. Keddie describes the doctrinal struggle that led to this formulation: "The second half of the eighteenth century . . . saw developments of socio-political significance within Shi'ism. There was a doctrinal struggle between the Akhbaris, who thought that the Koran and Shi'i traditions sufficed to guide believers, and the Mujtahidis or Usulis, who said that each believer must choose a living mujtahid whose dicta he was bound to follow. The Mujtahids finally won and this reinforced the power of the mujtahids, giving them a force unequalled in Sunni lands, where the ulama had no such power to interpret basic doctrine." *Iran: Religion, Politics, and Society,* pp. 92-93.
12. Even today most of the city of Mashhad is built on *waqf* land consecrated to

the shrine of Imam Reza, the eighth Imam of Twelver Shi'ites who is buried there.
13. Keddie, *Iran: Religion, Politics, and Society,* p.144.
14. Eric Hooglund, "The Khwushnishin Population of Iran," *Iranian Studies* 6 (4, 1973).
15. Javad Safi-Nezhad, *Taleb-Abad: Nemuneh-ye Jame'i az Barrasi-ye Yek Deh* (Taleb-Abad: an example of community through the investigation of a village) (Tehran: Institute for Social Studies and Research, 1967); id., *Bonih: Nezam-ha-ye Towlid-e Zera'i-ye Jam'i Qabl az Eslahat-e Arzi* (the bonih: the structure of collective agricultural production before land reform), 2nd ed. (Tehran: Tus Publications, 1974); Ann K. Lambton, "Land Reform and Rural Cooperative Societies in Persia," pt. 1, *Royal Central Asian Journal* 56 (June 1969)pp:142-55; Eric Hooglund, *The Effects of the Land Reform Program on Rural Iran* (Ph.D. dissertation, Johns Hopkins University, 1975); Ismai'l Ajami, *Shishdan-gi* (Shiraz: Pahlavi University Press, 1348/1969); William O. Beeman, review of Ismai'l Ajami, *Shishdangi, International Journal of Middle Eastern Studies* 8 (1977):285-88.
16. Ann K. Lambton, *Landlord and Peasant in Persia: A Study of Land Revenue Administration* (London: Oxford University Press, 1953); id., "Land Reform and Rural Cooperation Societies in Persia"; Nikki R. Keddie, "The Iranian Village Before and After Land Reform," *Journal of Contemporary History* 3(3, 1968):69-91.
17. Keddie, *Iran: Religion, Politics, and Society,* p. 146.
18. Charles Issawi, *The Economic History of Iran* (Chicago: University of Chicago Press, 1971), pp. 258-59.
19. Peter Avery, *Modern Iran* (New York: Praeger, 1965), p. 83.
20. Ibid., pp. 88–90.
21. Keddie, *Iran: Religion, Politics, and Society,* p.96.
22. Mohammed Djawad Sheikh-ol-Islami, *Iran's First Experience of Military Coup d'Etat in the Era of Her Constitutional Government* (Ph.D. dissertation, Ru-precht-Karl University, Heidelberg, Germany, 1965).
23. A.C. Millspaugh, *The American Task in Persia* (New York: Century, 1925), p.34.
24. Farhad Daftary, "Development Planning in Iran: A Historical Survey," *Iranian Studies* 6 (4, 1973):180.
25. Ibid., p.183.
26. Ibid., p.189.
27. Hooglund, "Khwushnishin Population of Iran"; id., "Effects of the Land Reform Program on Rural Iran"; id., "Rural Participation in the Revolution." In *MERIP Reports* no.87, *Iran's Revolution: The Rural Dimension* (May 1980):3-6; Lambton, "Land Reform and Rural Cooperative Societies in Persia"; id., *The Persian Land Reform, 1962-1966* (London: Oxford University Press, 1969).
28. Mary Hooglund, "One Village in the Revolution." In *MERIP Reports* no. 87, pp. 7-13.
29. Firouz Vakil, "Iran's Basic Macro-Economic Problems: A Twenty Year Horizon," *Economic Development and Cultural Change* 25 (4, 1977):716.
30. Jonathan Kandell, "The Tehran Bazaar," *New York Times* (29 June 1979).

Selected Readings

Abrahamian, Ervand. "Structural Causes of the Iranian Revolution." In *MERIP Reports* no.87, *Iran's Revolution: The Rural Dimension* (May 1980):21-29.

Allaway, Tony. "Shah's Efforts to End Unrest and Win Over the Religious Community." "New Premier Charged with Preparing Iran Poll." *Times of London* (28 August 1978).

Banani, Amin. *The Modernization of Iran, 1921-1941* (Palo Alto: Stanford University Press, 1961).

Beck, Lois. "Revolutionary Iran and Its Tribal People." In *MERIP Reports* no.87, *Iran's Revolution: The Rural Dimension* (May 1980):14-20.

Beeman, William O. "Status, Style, and Strategy in Iranian Interaction." *Anthropological Linguistics* 18(7, 1976):305-22.

———. "What Is Iranian National Character? A Sociolinguistic Approach." *Iranian Studies* 9(1, 1976):22-48.

———. "The How's and Why's of Persian Style: A Pragmatic Approach." In Ralph W. Fasold and Roger W. Shuy (eds.), *Studies in Language Variation* (Washington, D.C.: Georgetown University Press, 1977), pp. 269-82.

———. *Iranian Interaction Styles* (Chicago: University of Chicago Press, forthcoming).

Bill, James. "Iran and the Crisis of '78." *Foreign Policy* 57(2, 1978-79):325-40.

Browne, Edward G. *The Persian Revolution of 1905-09* (Cambridge: Cambridge University Press, 1910).

Business Week. "Iran Rethinks Its Grandiose Goals" (17 November 1975):58-63.

———. "Iran: The Shah Cools His Overheated Economy" (26 December 1977):46-47.

Corina, Maurice. "Iran Imposes Barter Rules for Imports in Face of Declining Revenue from Oil." *Times of London* (17 January 1977).

Cumming-Bruce, Nicholas. "Harsh Action Brings Results." *Times of London* (26 September 1977).

Crittenden, Ann. "Businessmen Tell Troubles to Diplomats." *New York Times* (30 May 1977).

Daftary, Farhad. "Development Planning in Iran: A Historical Survey." *Iranian Studies* 6(4, 1973):176-228.

Esposito, John L. (ed.). *Islam and Development: Religion and Sociopolitical Change* (Syracuse: Syracuse University Press, 1980).

Ehlers, Eckhart, and Grace Goodell. *Traditionelle und moderne Formen der Landwirtschaft in Iran* (Marburg: Marburger Geographische Schriften, vol. 64, 1975).

Gage, Nicholas. "Iranian Opposition's Quandary: Coalition or Military Rule." *New York Times* (8 November 1978).

Good, Mary Jo DelVecchio. *Social Hierarchy and Social Change in a Provincial Iranian Town* (Ph.D. dissertation, Department of Sociology, Harvard University, 1977).

Goodell, Grace. *The Elementary Structures of Political Life* (Ph.D. dissertation, Department of Anthropology, Columbia University, 1977).

Graham, Robert. *Iran: The Illusion of Power* (London: Croom Helm, 1978).

Halliday, Fred. *Iran: Dictatorship and Development* (Harmondsworth, Middlesex, England: Penguin, 1979).

Hoffmann, Paul. "However Slight, an Opposition Does Exist in Iran." *New York Times* (2 April 1978).

Howe, Marvin. "Iranian Women Return to Veil in a Resurgence of Spirituality." *New York Times* (30 July 1977).

Ibrahim, Youssef M. "Strife Cripples Iran's Economy." *New York Times* (28 October 1978).

Johnson, Gail Cook. *High-Level Manpower in Iran: From Hidden Conflict to Crisis* (New York: Praeger, 1980).

Kandell, Jonathan. "Iran Arrests Head of Secret Police, Other Officials, and Businessmen." *New York Times* (8 November 1978).

―――. "Iran's Affluent, Indebted to Shah, Give Him Little Support in Crisis." *New York Times* (18 November 1978).

Keddie, Nikki R. "Iran: Change in Islam: Islam and Change." *International Journal of Middle East Studies* 11(4, 1980):527-42.

Looney, Robert E. *The Economic Development of Iran: A Recent Survey with Projections to 1981* (New York: Praeger, 1973).

Millspaugh, A.C. *The American Task in Persia* (New York: Century, 1925).

Morris, Joe Alex, Jr. "New Broom Stirs Lots of Dust in Iran." *Los Angeles Times* (7 October 1977).

Mottahedeh, Roy Parviz. "Iran's Foreign Devils." *Foreign Policy* 38 (Spring 1980):19-34.

Nasr, Seyyed Hossein. "Cosmographie en l'Iran pre-islamique et islamique: le problème de la continuité dans la civilisation iranienne." In George Makdisi (ed.), *Arabic and Islamic Studies in Honor of Hamilton A.R. Gibb* (Leiden: E.J.Brill, 1965), pp. 507-24.

Pullapilly, Cyriac K. (ed.). *Islam in the Contemporary World* (Notre Dame, Ind.: Cross Roads, 1980).

Ramazani, Ruhollah K. *Iran's Foreign Policy, 1941-1973* (Charlottesville: University of Virginia Press, 1975).

Ross, Jay. "Iran Switches Economic Priorities, Plans Slower Industrial Development." *Washington Post* (20 August 1978).

Rubin, Barry. *Paved with Good Intentions: The American Experience and Iran* (New York: Oxford University Press, 1980).

Schultz, Ann T. "Iran's New Industrial State." *Current History* 72(423, 1977):15-18.

Singh, K.R. *Iran: Quest for Security* (New Delhi: Vikas, 1980).

Sparhawk, Frank. "Iran's Modernization Failure and the Muslim Background." *Humanist* 40(2, 1980):8-12.

―――. "The Opposition in Iran." *Wall Street Journal* (3 August 1978).

Watts, David. "Is the Shah Unifying Those Who Are Against Him?" *Times of London* (26 May 1978).

Weinbaum, Marvin G. "Agricultural Policy and Development Politics in Iran." *Middle East Journal* 31(4, 1977):434-50.

Zabih, Sepehr. *Iran's Revolutionary Upheaval: An Interpretive Essay* (San Francisco: Alchemy, 1979).

Zonis, Marvin. *The Political Elite of Iran* (Princeton: Princeton University Press, 1971).

4

Iran, Islam, and the United States

R.K. Ramazani

The Iranian Revolution was at inception a "revolution of rising alienation." I shall flesh out the basic elements of that concept before relating it to the larger area of the Middle East and Southwestern Asia, and then indicate its main implications for the American approach to the region.

First, the Iranian Revolution involved the society at large. It is necessary to emphasize this, partly because of the excessive focus on the role of the ulema or religious leaders. I do not mean to belittle the overriding importance of religious leadership in the Iranian Revolution. As early as January 1964—after the Shah's bloody suppression of the uprisings in Qom and elsewhere in Iran in June 1963, and before the exile of the Ayatollah Ruhollah Khomeini—I pointed out the historical continuity of the conflict between the ulema and the monarch, and warned that the Shah's suppression of the religious leaders would not resolve that basic conflict. Nearly fifteen years later, that conflict constituted a major aspect of the Iranian Revolution which led to the overthrow of the monarchy.

Neither historically nor in the recent revolution, however, have the ulema represented a monolithic bloc of religious leaders against the ruling monarch. In the Constitutional Revolution of 1905-11, there were religious leaders such as Sayyed Muhammed Tabataba'i and Sayyed 'Abdullah Behbehani who supported the revolution, and there were others such as Shaikh Fazlullah Nuri who opposed it in the name of Islam and in support of the then notorious monarch Muhammed 'Ali Shah. In the nationalist movement of 1951-53, even the same religious leader, Sayyed Abulqasem Kashani, who first supported the Musaddeq government against the Shah, subsequently threw in his lot with the monarch. Even the Ayatollah

Khomeini himself had not always opposed the Shah's regime, the Pahlavi dynasty, or the Iranian Constitution of 1906-07, as evidenced by his *Secrets Exposed (Kashf-e Assrar)*, written in 1943. All he demanded at that time was the implementation of the constitutional provisions for the religious review of all man-made laws in accordance with Islamic Law.

Despite disunity among religious and secular leaders and their followers, the common bond of emotional opposition to the Shah's regime kept all of them more or less together in the course of the revolution. The revolution included not only bazaar merchants, intellectuals, and other groups similar to those in the two major previous uprisings of this century, but also the masses of the rural and urban lower classes. It was their participation in the massive demonstrations and crippling strikes of 1978-1979 that broke the back of the Shah's regime. Religious leadership, particularly that of the Ayatollah Khomeini, was important in mobilizing the masses by invoking Shi'i Islamic symbols. The Ayatolla's ability to universalize his own personal grudge against the Shah and turn the historical tension between the ulema and the monarchy into an irreconcilable conflict between good and evil was no doubt important. That should not detract from the fact that he would not have succeeded unless the masses were psychologically prepared to respond to his appeal.

Second, the factors that contributed to the alienation of the society at large were multifaceted and complex. They stemmed from the adverse effects of the late Shah's policies and attitudes on a whole range of social, economic, political, cultural, and religious issues. Excessive emphasis on any single aspect of the regime's policies would fail to explain the phenomenon of massive popular alienation. The Shah's grandiose and ruinous economic programs, his political repression, his massive arms purchases, his insensitivity to religious tradition, his perceived role as the lackey of the United States, and other factors, contributed to growing opposition against his regime.

This is why the characterization of the Iranian Revolution as antimodernist, antireligious, bourgeois, and the like, leaves much to be desired. For example, when one says that the Iranian Revolution was a "revolt against modernity" it does not help explication, unless one clarifies what one means by modernity. The same is true of characterizing it as a religious uprising. What does it mean? Does it mean the revolution's leadership consisted mainly of religious leaders, does it suggest that the followers were religiously inspired, does it propose that religious symbols were utilized, or does it mean that all or some of these considerations were decisive? It is also true that members of the professional middle class participated significantly in the revolution, but does that make it a bourgeois revolution? I think not.

Third, the revolution was both a product and a process. It was a product in the sense that it represented a popular reaction against the adverse effects of a whole range of the late Shah's policies. It was a process in the sense that it reflected at a given time an ongoing tension between demands for change *and* continuity. I say "ongoing" because the Iranian Revolution has not resolved or managed that tension. Nor did its historical antecedents in the twentieth century succeed in doing so. The establishment of an Islamic Republic in keeping with the Ayatollah Khomeini's vision of the "government of God" in Iran has been plagued, from inception, by the challenge of other visions. These range all the way from other kinds of ideas of an Islamic political and economic order, such as the one advocated by former president Bani-Sadr or the Ayatollah Sharia'tmadari, to those of the Mujaheddin-e Khalq (Islamic Marxist), the Fadayeen-e Khalq (Marxist-Leninist), the Tudeh Party (communist), the National Front (centrists), and others. The end is not yet in sight, and the underlying ideological and power conflict will probably continue, regardless of the longevity of the present revolutionary regime.

Fourth, the Iranian Revolution reflected not only a popular reaction against the adverse effects of the Shah's policies, but also against those of the United States. The reason for this is partly the close identification of the United States with the Shah's regime, not only because of the covert American intervention in Iran in favor of his return to power in 1953—as is so often asserted within and outside Iran—but also because of the mounting American economic, military, and diplomatic presence in Iran over a quarter of a century subsequently. The public at large resented the American "special relationship" with the Shah.

Anti-American sentiments in the Iranian Revolution resembled antiforeign feelings in their historical antecedents. In the Constitutional Revolution, tsarist Russia was the main target of the hostility of the revolutionaries partly because of Russian domination of Iran, and in the nationalist movement Britain was the principal target because of perceived British dominance of Iran through the Anglo-Iranian Oil Company. It is not always easy to draw the line between antiforeign expressions as an escape from the harsh realities of the society and as a genuine reaction to perceived sufferings at the hands of foreign powers. But one thing is clear. Many Iranians show a pathological obsession with conspiracy theories. They tend to see the hand of foreign powers in everything. The late Shah himself is a classic example. For nearly thirty-seven years he courted and cultivated American influence in Iran toward the consolidation of his power against perceived domestic and foreign foes. At the end, he squarely blamed the United States for his downfall. Today the Ayatollah Khomeini is not the only leader who characterizes the United States as the "principal enemy" (*doshman-e assli*). Almost every major sociopolitical force in Iran, regardless of ideological predisposition and social composition, tends to blame the Iranian predicaments largely on foreign powers, particularly the United States.

Fifth, the Iranian Revolution reflected more than a "revolution of rising alienation" from the Shah's regime and the United States in the purely psychological sense of the term. Popular alienation had also a profound ethical dimension. I say ethical rather than religious to avoid the impression that it was simply a matter of reasserting Shi'i Islamic ethics. To be sure, for the Ayatolla Khomeini and his supporters the standards and norms of conduct he envisaged for the new political order were based on Islamic precepts as he interpreted them. In mobilizing the masses against the Shah during the revolution of 1978-79, he never tired of invoking the concept of legitimate government. He regarded all previous governments as illegitimate, as the usurpers of the rightful rule, which he believed belonged to religious leaders. The fact that in the tradition of Shi'i Islam the Twelfth Imam is considered to have been in occultation since 873 A.D. and the Messiah, Mahdi, or *Shib al-Zaman* (Master of the Age) is yet to appear made no difference to Khomeini. As a charismatic revolutionary leader, he believed that Iranians could not and should not await the coming of the Mahdi. It was incumbent on them to launch a political revolution against the Shah's illegitimate regime and establish an Islamic Republic in its place. This is what he has tried to do.

It would be wrong to equate the general search for a new moral foundation for Iranian society merely with the particular Khomeini formulation of Shi'i Islamic ethics. This is why as long as Khomeini talked in general terms, the disparate forces of opposition to the Shah responded overwhelmingly to his religiously based symbols against oppression (*zulm*), oppressors (*mustakbarin*), and for justice (*adalat*) and the oppressed (*mustaza'feen*). But once he and his supporters began to spell out what they meant by "legitimate government," it was immediately apparent that there was no real consensus on the core ethical standards, principles, and criteria by which public policy—political, economic, social, and others—could be judged.

This general ethical-psychological alienation of the population that largely characterized the Iranian Revolution reflected a profound and continuous contradiction between ideal and reality in Iranian society. Because of the primacy of religious leadership in the Iranian Revolution, much attention has been paid to Shi'i tradition as the key to understanding the revolution. Doctrinal differences between the Shi'i and Sunni schools of thought and the historical conflict between the Sunni and Shi'i communities have been highlighted. This emphasis per se cannot reveal the deeper and broader problem of an ancient contradiction between ethical ideal and social reality in Iran. Shi'ism itself was a reflection of that basic tension.

Long before the coming of Islam to Iran, that ideal was expressed in the ancient motto of "good thoughts, good words, and good deeds" (*pendar-e nik, goftar-e nik, va kerdar-e nik*). This ideal was not classbound, and applied to individual, interpersonal, intergroup, and international relations. At the domestic political level, for example, it has always been expressed in the expectation of society at large to have "truthful" and "just" rulers, whether in pre-Islamic or Islamic Iran. That expectation was stated in the ancient inscription: "By Ahuramazda's will," said King Darius, "I am of such nature that I am a friend to the just; I am no friend to the unjust. What is right, that is my desire. I am not a friend to the man that followeth falsehood." Adda B. Bozeman tells us that as early as the sixth century B.C., Iranians "for the first time in historical known terms" were concerned about moral principles in international relations, and even applied them in their own practice for two centuries when the "tyranny of empires plagued the fabric of community everywhere." Arnold Toynbee was so enamored by the ancient Iranian example of tolerant universalism that he wished to see it applied as a model for unifying mankind in the present world community.

Yet Iranians, as well as others, have been deeply aware that in practice throughout the millennia they have fallen far short of their ideals, domestically and internationally. Domestically, they have witnessed falsehood and injustice not only in individual, interpersonal, and intergroup relationships, but also in the character of rule. Authoritarianism, despotism, dictatorship, and similar forms of domination have often characterized Iran's political leadership. The Shah, for example, aspired to the model of Cyrus the Great, but like many of his predecessors, practiced a capricious rule. The Ayatollah Khomeini's regime presumably aspired to the model of the good government of 'Ali ibn Abu Talib, the first Shi'i Moslem leader, but in practice his regime has come to be viewed increasingly by various segments of the population as a betrayal of that ideal. Internationally, also, Iranians have often witnessed the gap between the ideal of tolerant universalism and the reality of xenophobia.

The ethical-psychological alienation of the Iranian people from the Shah's regime that characterized the Iranian Revolution reflected at base a tradition of dissatisfaction with the continuation of that ancient and tenacious gap between a vague ideal and the reality of good society and government. Different individuals or groups espoused different ideals. Khomeini and those who supported his line judged the Shah's policies by the ethical norms and standards of Shi'i Islam as they interpreted them. Some modern-educated elements of the middle class judged them by democratic-liberal standards, while others applied those standards that underpin "Islamic Marxism" or Marxism-Leninism. Despite the diversity of ethical and moral perspectives, all major groups seemed to agree that the Shah's policies were not what they should have been. The Iranian Revolution reflected both normative and psychological concerns, or both ideal and material interests of the population at large despite diversity in the perceptions of both the ideal and reality.

Assuming that the Iranian Revolution could be characterized as I suggested above—what does it tell us about the rest of the Middle East and Southwest Asia? What are the prospects for the occurrence of similar revolutions in the region? I am not concerned here with the "export of the Iranian Revolution." First, since the outbreak of the war between Iran and Iraq (September 1981), the Khomeini regime has not had the capacity to propagate the "Islamic Revolution" in the region in the way that it did soon after the seizure of power by revolutionary forces. The war, together with mounting domestic economic and political problems, has dampened revolutionary zeal.

Second, during my visit to the area after the war, I was struck by pessimism about the Iranian Revolution as a model for imitation. Even the Shi'i populations of such countries as Bahrain and Kuwait—which had initially sympathized with the Khomeini regime—are now wary about the wisdom of any such experimentation in their own countries. Discussion of the export of the Iranian Revolution as a threat to other societies of the region is misplaced. The real threat lies in the human conditions of those societies themselves. If their conditions, as those of prerevolutionary Iran, are conducive to rising popular alienation from their regimes, that is what should concern us.

Speculation about the repetition of the Iranian Revolution elsewhere in the Middle East and Southwestern Asia vary widely. They may be categorized in terms of the response of optimists and pessimists. Optimists discount the prospect of recurrence of such a revolution elsewhere in the region, for two reasons. First, they point to differences between the positions of the Sunni and Shi'i ulema in the political processes of the other regional states and Iran before the revolution. They contend that the Sunni ulema have been relatively well integrated in the power structure of the Sunni states, are largely dependent on the political elite, and are not so close to the masses; in contrast, the Shi'i ulema in Iran enjoyed relative independence from the power elite and maintained a close relationship with the masses. Second, they emphasize doctrinal differences between Sunni and Shi'i religious leaders, particularly their different concepts of the legitimacy of political leadership. Mistakenly, they contend that in Shi'i Islam no temporal authority is considered legitimate in the interval between the occultation of the Twelfth Imam (873 A.D.) and the expected reappearance of the Mahdi, whereas in Sunni Islam temporal rulers are considered legitimate. Yet Khomeini himself did not refute temporal rule categorically until the 1970s.

The pessimists fall into two broad categories. First, there are those who consider it inevitable that all remaining monarchies in the region will eventually fall. Some arrive at such a conclusion from observing the course of events since the fall of the monarchy in Egypt in 1952, while others simply believe that the fall of monarchies worldwide is the wave of the future. From either perspective, the result is the same: it is only a matter of time before the ruling families in all the Gulf states will be overtaken by a different form of political order.

The word *different* here is of key importance because, until the Iranian Revolution, most pessimists would use *new* in the sense of the inevitable passing of traditional societies and the emergence of modern ones to take their place. It was widely believed that modernization in the form of increasing industrialization, spreading education, improving communication and transportation, growing urbanization, etc. would transform traditional, parochial, multiple mosaic, or heterogeneous societies such as Iran into integrated national communities; would turn subjects into citizens, communalism and tribalism into nationalism; would change primordial loyalties, values, attitudes, ethnic and linguistic particularities, and other such "anachronistic" features of the old societies of the Third World into all the ingredients necessary for the creation of a civic society.

The Iranian power elite during the Shah's regime never tired of equating the rate of economic growth with development, modernity, progress, and other related concepts. I remember from an interview with the late prime minister Amir Abbas Hoveyda how seriously he and his ministers believed in the overriding importance of the GNP or per capita GNP. That kind of thinking about economic and social development was not always discouraged by Iran's American friends. The Johnson administration discontinued American economic aid to Iran in 1967 in recognition of its economic progress defined primarily in terms of economic growth. Some American observers believed that Iran was perhaps approaching the takeoff point.

Since the Iranian Revolution, interest in the study of continuity and tradition in developing societies has intensified (witness the sudden rise of so many experts on Iran and Islam). The Iranian Revolution is regarded as a rejection of the theory of social mobilization and of the inevitability of change from traditional to modern societies. Moslem societies are believed to be experiencing the resurgence of Islam with all its implications for the revival of Islamic values, concepts, institutions, etc. All kinds of societies in the Moslem world, stretching from Mauritania to Malaysia, are viewed as being gripped by some form of Islamic stirrings. Theories emphasizing primordial values, loyalties, and institutions are now finding new evidence for the view that modernization, or economic development, or secularization, etc., may well lead to national disintegration rather than integration. Khomeini discounted national boundaries as early as World War II when he said that territorial states were the "creatures of limited ideas." Now he says Iran must grow in power until it has "vouchsafed Islam to the entire world."

Just as yesterday's overemphasis on modernization defined as economic growth hindered understanding of the complexities of Iranian society, today's excessive stress on traditional Islam may do the same. Those who found proof of continuity instead of change in the Iranian Revolution may soon have to revise their views. The Islamic Republic has proved incapable of coping with the multifaceted problems of Iranian society, and there are few observers who do not believe that the fall of the regime is imminent. That fall would be superficially interpreted as the resurgence of modernity. If so, there would be further proof for the optimists that the Iranian Revolution will not be repeated in other countries of the region.

Faulty comparisons between prerevolutionary Iran and other societies in the Middle East and Southwest Asia can find no better illustration than comparisons made between Iran and Saudi Arabia. Regarding Islam, optimists assert that the resurgence of Islam poses no threat to the stability of the present regime in Saudi Arabia because the country is the cradle of Islam itself; because the modern state of Saudi Arabia was founded partly on the fundamentalist tenets of Wahhabism; and because the ulema are involved in the political process in a way that was unknown in the history of the relationship between the ulema and royalty in prerevolutionary Iran. Pessimists point to the attack on the Grand Mosque in Mecca (November 20, 1979) by a disparate group of Moslem fundamentalists led by Juhayman al-Utaiba as proof of popular dissatisfaction with the modernization policies of the royal family and with the religious establishment that supports it.

Regarding political participation, optimists assert that the Saudi traditional political process is democratic in contrast with Iranian despotism because Saudi subjects have easy access to their rulers through the ancient tribal institution of the *Majlis*. Pessimists assert that this anachronistic institution is used by the royal family to avoid democratizing its rule despite its promise to do so after the uprising in Mecca.

Regarding socioeconomic welfare, optimists assert that popular alienation for economic reasons is avoidable in Saudi Arabia, as contrasted with prerevolutionary Iran, because Saudi Arabia has a much smaller population (about five million) as compared with Iran (about thirty-five million) and much greater wealth by which it can satisfy societal needs. Pessimists assert that the uprising of the Shi'i Moslem population at al-Qatif, in the Eastern Province in 1979, reflected the age-old Saudi discrimination against the country's Shi'i minority. To the Saudi officials who claim that this problem is being resolved now, the pessimists point out that no resolution of the problem can possibly be expected from the present regime as long as there is no chance for meaningful input by the Shi'i populations into the Saudi Arabian decision-making process.

The inconclusiveness of such comparisons makes it all the more necessary to ask whether the policies pursued by various regimes are conducive to a process of popular alienation similar to that which occurred in prerevolutionary Iran. There is no easy answer to this question, as the controversy between pessimists and optimists illustrates. One is not necessarily better off in addressing such a question by enumerating the objective conditions of the Gulf societies such as, for example, their heterogeneous populations, limited indigenous manpower, vast oil reserves, general poverty in other natural resources, tribal structure, etc. Many of these conditions become problems relative to certain goals and strategies adopted by the ruling elites. For example, if it were not for the Saudi Arabian new Five-Year Plan (1980-85) —which calls for spending hundreds of billions of dollars on economic development—the paucity of indigenous manpower would not have posed as serious a problem as it does. The aspiration of the ruling elite to freeze the import of foreign manpower for reasons of internal security makes the problem all the more manageable.

Granted both the empirical and judgmental difficulties in comparing the Gulf societies and prerevolutionary Iran—are there any lessons of the Iranian experience that might be relevant in terms of other societies in the region? The search for an answer might be aided by returning to the principal elements of the Iranian Revolution set out at the beginning of this discussion. On the basis of those major factors, the following generalizations are offered as a guide for research on potential domestic convulsions similar to the Iranian Revolution in other societies of the region:

1. All or at least major segments of the population of a society must feel adversely affected by the policies pursued by the ruling regime.
2. There must be a strong charismatic leader, religious or otherwise, capable of leading the entire society in opposition to the ruling elite.
3. Popular alienation must spring from a perception of suffering not only at the hands of domestic rulers, but also of a foreign power popularly perceived to sustain a despised regime in power as a means of dominating the whole society.

4. There must be a tradition of cumulative popular dissatisfaction with government in society.
5. The alienation of the public at large must stem not only from a perception of the harm done by government policies to the material interests (power, wealth, etc.) of the people, but also from a feeling that those policies have violated the moral or ethical standards of the society at large.

Since this formula is constructed on the basis of empirical evidence, it is free from the biases usually read into the Iranian experience presumably as a guide to understanding the potential fragility of the other regional societies. Since it does not characterize the Iranian Revolution as a purely Islamic revolution, it rejects the view that wherever there are signs of agitation by Moslem fundamentalists—such as in Kuwait, Egypt, Syria— an Iranian-type revolution is necessarily around the corner. Since it does not simplistically characterize the Iranian Revolution as a bourgeois uprising, it rejects the notion that wherever there are signs of rising middle classes, a similar revolt will be inevitable. Since it does not regard the Iranian Revolution as a purely nationalist reaction against the perceived domination of the United States, it rejects the notion that such a perception alone will necessarily lead to a similar revolution elsewhere. The list could be easily extended; the main point is that it would be better not to formulate generalizations for anticipated trouble in other societies of the region on the basis on an inadequate study of the Iranian experience. Much research remains to be done on problems of continuity and change in Iran and the other societies of the Middle East, especially the Gulf region.

To caution against oversimplification is not to invite complacency. On the basis of my own research on both Iran and the Gulf—although I do not see an impending domestic convulsion in the next couple of years in the Gulf region—I believe the ingredients of potential alienation are discernible in most Gulf societies in varying degrees of intensity and scope. This is no place to discuss in detail any one of these societies, but I shall summarize two major tendencies that cut across various national boundaries as the primary sources of potential alienation in the next five years.

First, the reluctance of all Gulf governments to address the problem of the rising demand for economic and political participation is a potential source of popular alienation. The Iranian Revolution destroyed the traditional passivity of the public in all Gulf societies vis-à-vis their governments. With it the effectiveness of traditional methods and techniques of the ruling elites for developing various forms of balancing acts has been seriously eroded, if not destroyed. The Iraqis and the Kuwaitis have revived legislative assemblies, and the Saudis have promised the establishment of a consultative council, for example; but few, if any, of the politically aware groups are fooled. Shrewdness and skillful manipulation of the public by the ruling elites have reached their limits. The Shah's proverbial "genius" in playing the balancing act worked for decades, but that was before the Iranian Revolution. The same basic game is played in other oil-rich Gulf societies today on a much larger scale than in prerevolutionary Iran because of greater financial capacities relative to the size and number of groups being economically coopted. The game is working at the moment, but the opportunity to address the people's basic demands for a better distribution of wealth and power is slipping away daily.

With respect to the Gulf states' plans for economic development, I sense the same superficiality I observed in Iran's plans some twenty years ago. I wrote in March 1962 in the *American Behavioral Scientist* as follows:

> It is reasonable to assume that even if more numerous and more competent social scientists become available, modernization efforts will continue to be only in part relevant to the society's needs at the deepest level, unless the elite in power somehow becomes more broadly based. In other words, a ruling elite can hardly be expected to display deep social concern unless it strikes deep roots in the society. For this reason, it is safe to assume that until a more homogeneous and representative elite does emerge and is entrusted with the task of making and executing public policy, modernization will continue to be hampered by numerous deficiencies, including the slow recognition of social research for planned socioeconomic transformation.

The point is not that the economic planning deficiencies in the other Gulf states today are identical to those of prerevolutionary Iran. The main suggestion is that governmental reluctance to broaden and deepen participation in Gulf societies is bound to affect the economic development planning adversely no matter how solicitous of societal needs the ruling elites may be. The prevalent but unarticulated notion that with vast oil resources whole societies can be massively subsidized and hence satisfied, partly derives from the theory that satisfaction of social and economic needs will stem the tide of the rising demand for political participation. Even Henry Kissinger admitted after the Iranian Revolution that this theory—and its supporters, including himself and the Shah—had been proven wrong by the experience of Iran. The only alternative to sharing economic and political power with the old and new groups in society is losing it altogether.

Second, the other major source of potential alienation of society at large in the Gulf societies is the massive arms purchase by the richer Gulf states. All societies need to defend themselves against perceived external enemies, but no amount of military hardware can buy domestic political legitimacy and authority for ruling elites. The Iranian Revolution proved that point conclusively, but no lesson seems to have been learned. For example, between 1950 and 1980 the Shah's regime purchased and received over $9 billion worth of military equipment from the United States, but with a population one-seventh of Iran's, Saudi Arabia's purchases amounted to $11 billion during the same period. Arms purchases, even when they are so massive, do not necessarily cause revolutions, but they can contribute to popular alienation in two major ways: they can create domestic, social, and economic dislocations, as they did in Iran, and they can produce popular resentment against the arms-supplying foreign state and its nationals, as they also did in Iran. In twenty-five years of close relationship between the United States and the Shah's Iran, no single aspect of their multifaceted ties contributed as much to public dissatisfaction with both the Shah's regime and the United States as their security cooperation. From extensive interviews during two field trips since the Iranian Revolution, I have come away with the clear and strong impression that similar popular dissatisfaction is simmering among various societal strata in the Gulf region.

I now turn briefly to the third and last concern of this discussion: the implications for the American approach to the Middle East and Southwest Asia. The American approach to Iran emphasized strategic considerations for a quarter of a century. Neither President Kennedy's brief insistence on social and economic change in the early 1960s, nor President Carter's apparent demand for political liberalization in the late 1970s made a major difference in the overall American strategic approach to Iran. The thrust of American policy from the Eisenhower to the Carter administration was strategic. Iran was considered by every American president a "strategic prize." The primary value of the Shah's regime to the United States was strategic, first as a leading regional ally in the cold war, and then as an American surrogate in the Persian Gulf and adjacent regions. All other considerations, including the basic need to encourage the construction of viable social, economic, and political institutions with deeper roots in Iranian society, took a back seat in the American approach to the Shah's Iran. For this important reason, the United States refrained over the decades from pressing the Shah too hard to accord highest priority to the satisfaction of the material and moral interests of Iranian society.

At the inception of the close Tehran-Washington relationship, when it was strongest, the United States refused to use its leverage to obtain from the Shah's regime assurances that it would respect Iran's Constitution. The CIA intervened covertly in Iran to return the Shah to power (1953), presumably to prevent a communist coup d'état, but when the Shah volunteered that he therefore owed his throne to American intervention, he was assured by the American agent involved that he had no obligation toward the United States whatever. President Kennedy pressed the Shah to make social and economic reforms before granting further American military aid, but the ink on the Shah's land reform decree was hardly dry before he prematurely congratulated the Shah for his gallant efforts; and President Johnson resumed the supply of arms to him with great zest. President Carter first demanded political liberalization, but then soft-pedaled it for fear of undermining the "island of stability" in the region; he continued to sell arms to the Shah months after the start of the Iranian Revolution.

The same is happening today in the American approach to the entire area, especially toward Saudi Arabia. Once again, no lesson has been learned from the Iranian experience. The watchword today is "strategic consensus." That is the overriding American thrust toward the area both publicly and privately. The Reagan administration has picked up the Carter administration's commitment to the defense of the region with added zeal to ensure the uninterrupted flow of Middle Eastern oil. The Carter Doctrine was prompted not so much by the Soviet invasion of Afghanistan, but by the Iranian Revolution.

Whatever the United States needs to do to protect Western access to the region's oil supplies should be less cause for concern than what it might fail to do, because of oil, to encourage or press the ruling elites within the region to put most of their money and efforts where they really belong—in the material and moral reconstruction of their own societies. The ruling elites are tempted to cultivate close security ties with the United States to bolster their regimes, whereas the people of the area are increasingly demanding their share of power and wealth from the regimes. Too close an identification of the United States with such regimes will invite popular alienation from America. Our current emphasis on strategic considerations will pay off only in the very short run as it dwarfs long-term and deeper American interests in these societies. Those interests include the peaceful satisfaction of the rising expectations of the peoples of the region before mounting dissatisfactions turn into violent revolutions of rising alienation in other Gulf societies as well.

Part Three

MEXICO

Introductory Essay

As both of the following essays make clear, Mexico is a land of rich and varied cultural strains, religious beliefs and practices, political ideologies, and traditions. It is a land of paradoxes. In the rich tapestry of Mexico's modern history, one can discern several prominent threads—political, ideological, economic, and religious. It would be impossible to give an adequate sense of Mexico's modern development without referring to each of these. And it would be unrealistic to project the general direction Mexico, with its recently enhanced strength and prestige, is likely to follow without noting the part each of these has played in the past and is likely to play in the future.

Many of Mexico's resources, constraints, and formidable problems are evident in the paradoxical statements that describe the country today. Born out of the violent Revolution of 1910 and continuing as the Institutional Revolutionary Party (PRI), the present regime is authoritarian. Although the state is heavily involved in the economic structure of the country in terms of both ownership and direction, it depends on private capitalism for economic growth. The authoritarian character of the regime is certified by the fact that Mexico City is where most important decisions are made, including many that are not so important. This power to make centralized decisions is not accompanied by the power to see that they are carried out. The latter is diffused within the bureaucracy and geographically across the country.

With a high degree of articulated social consciousness—another legacy of the revolution—Mexico has a population divided by extreme income inequalities that are more severe than in other Latin American countries with fewer resources. Since the Revolution of 1910, almost every president has boasted of how much land he has distributed, but there are now one million more adult landless peasants than in 1910. With a population generally judged to be religious—a judgment sustained by the crowds who cheered Pope John Paul—the revolutionary regime is officially secular. Severe restrictions are placed on public activities of the Catholic Church.

Another factor in Mexico's development that must be regarded as both a resource and at least a constraint is its proximity to the United States. Citizens of the United States are, at least initially, tempted to see that relation as raising problems for the United States and as having more benefits for Mexicans than for them. Here the most extreme view is that which sees poor Mexicans flowing north across the border while dollars flow in the opposite direction. Both current data and historical reflection modify that view considerably. The contribution to the United States economy made by, for example, seasonal farm workers who return to Mexico is difficult to calculate, but it is significant enough to upset the easy assumption that the benefits are all one-sided. Mexico's recently discovered petroleum reserves gives it a leverage it did not previously have with the United States and other countries. It also provides an opportunity to deal more equitably with many of its severe social problems.

These are only some of the statements that might describe present-day Mexico and its potential for development. The essays which follow offer more historical and detailed description and they drive toward a resolution of the issue with which we are concerned. With what sets of values will Mexico respond to its present social, economic, and political problems? How will it choose to develop long-standing and newly discovered resources? Will it be able to reduce the striking inequities that the revolution, now many decades old, proposed to attack? What role will the church play in the decision making? And what will be the influence of those religious values and rituals that have been transmuted into Mexico's social and political structure?

Douglas C. Bennett approaches some of these questions by examining three major traditions that are intertwined in modern Mexico: those that derive from Catholicism, those that accompanied the introduction of capitalism, and those that emerged in the revolution. He situates the Mexico formed by these values within the external constraints of a world capitalist system and Mexico's own resources, human and natural. He reveals the crucially important role the state plays and will play in attempting to resolve the profound and paradoxical problems Mexico faces. And it is in the character of that state, Bennett shows, that one must look for the religious and cultural values of Catholicism.

Complementing this description and analysis, Claude Pomerleau shows how religion has historically beguiled Mexico and how different regimes have attempted to cope with it. In bringing this up to date, he examines recent changes within the religious tradition of public morality and the areas in which that tradition interacts with official government ideology.

That interaction raises unique institutional issues, he asserts, but it also presents interesting challenges. And if any large-scale economic program for development is to succeed, it must tap the deep values of society. At this level it will encounter an entity, the church, whose support will be needed. If a constructive relation is not formed, the church, the state, and society will suffer.

J.F.

5

Catholicism, Capitalism, and the State in the Development of Mexico

Douglas C. Bennett

The Independence movement, the Reform movement and the Díaz dictatorship were distinct and contradictory phases of one continuing effort to break free. The nineteenth century was a complete break with form. At the same time, the liberal movement was an attempt to create a utopia, and thus provoked the vengeance of reality. Our independent history, from the time we were first aware of ourselves as individuals and of our geographical area as an individual nation, has been a break with tradition, with form, and a search for a new form that would contain all our native particulars and would also be open to the future. Catholicism was closed to the future; liberalism replaced the concrete Mexican with an inanimate abstraction; neither could express both our individual desires and our universal longings.

The Revolution began as a discovery of our own selves and a return to our origins; later it became a search and an abortive effort at synthesis; finally, since it was unable to assimilate our tradition and offer us a new and workable plan, it became a compromise.

—Octavio Paz, *The Labyrinth of Solitude*

Among the many paradoxes of contemporary Mexico are these three: (1) It is a very religious country, as the 1979 visit of Pope John Paul II served to indicate; yet it is officially anticlerical (under the Constitution, the church is forbidden to own land, the government regulates all forms of religious activity, and all primary education must be secular). (2) It has followed, particularly for the past fifty years, a capitalist path to economic development; yet the state plays a large, even entrepreneurial role in the economy. (3) It had a social revolution, and that tradition espousing democracy and social justice is still the source of legitimacy for all public policy; yet there are deep, enduring patterns of inequality and authoritarian rule.

I will address here the role of ideas and values in the emergence of these paradoxes. The focus will be on three strands of ideas and values that have gone into the making of modern Mexico: those deriving from the church and Catholicism, those that have accompanied the coming of capitalism, and those that emerged in the revolution. My argument can be briefly summarized. The conservative coalition of hacienda owners, commercial interests, and the church that dominated Mexican society from early colonial times through and beyond Independence, came to be challenged in the mid–nineteenth century by elites espousing different programs and values, ones that had accompanied the coming of capitalism in Europe. In the nineteenth century there were two distinct waves of this: first, liberalism, which helped dethrone the conservatives and force a separation of church and state, but which could offer no stability to Mexico; and second, positivism, which emphasized order and progress more than liberty, and which guided capitalist development during the last decades of the century, but along such unequal and exclusionary lines that a revolution was brought on in 1910. The revolution was a rejection of both pasts—Catholicism and liberalism/positivism. It brought forth a number of demands, such as for land reform, but no coherent program. Those who gained control of the Mexican state following the revolution drew their economic and social program once again from the ideas and values of capitalism. This time the source was the United States and not Europe, and the borrowing was more pragmatic. Catholicism and the church were forced into their own sphere. In recent years, a pattern of informal accommodation has been worked out between church and state. The values and traditions of Catholicism do play a role in the development of modern Mexico, but their influence is not to be sought in the shaping of the economy, narrowly conceived, but rather in the character of the state and in its relationship to economy and society.

Ideas and values are important in development because they guide critical choices, but recognition of this point needs to be supplemented by appreciation of several others concerning the approach or perspective to be employed here. First, there are structures which constrain and limit the range of human choice. "Men make their own history," Marx insists, "but they do not make it just as they please." Particularly for countries not at the center of the world capitalist system, these structural constraints are external to a significant degree. They concern the institutions and practices which govern international flows of trade, investment, and finance; they concern the character of industrialization elsewhere in the world; and the ability of core states to mobilize power (both military and diplomatic) to insist upon arrangements to their own liking. These structural constraints are not simply external; there are structural constraints which are internal, and it is important to attend to compatibilities and contradictions between the external and internal in identifying the range of alternatives open to a historical actor. This point concerning the delimitation of the field of choice by structural constraints is fundamental to the study of development, but because the ideas and values that guide choice will be at the center of our attention, and not the structural constraints, there is a danger of seeming to overstate the field of choice or the efficacy of ideas.

Second, structures are created by human action. They are not given or natural. They embody values even as they restrict and delimit choices; and until they are changed by action, structures continue to transmit their values to succeeding generations. Third, while ideas and values guide purposeful human action, such action may not have the consequences intended by the actor. We need to be sure to distinguish intentions from consequences. Finally, most of the ideas and values of interest to us here are imported, not home-grown. They arose in response to circumstances quite different from those in which they have been employed in Mexico. This is one reason why intentions and consequences can diverge, particularly because these foreign ideas can mask as well as illuminate reality. Octavio Paz is particularly insistent on this point. He says of liberal ideas in the nineteenth century that "they merely served as trappings for the survival of the colonial system," and that "far from expressing our concrete historical situation [they] disguised it, and the political lie established itself almost constitutionally. The moral danger [they have] caused is incalculable." He speaks of positivism as "a historical superimposition much more dangerous than those that preceded it," and he argues that "the positivist disguise" served "to hide the moral nakedness of the [Díaz] regime from its own leaders and beneficiaries."[1] Even Catholicism is a foreign import, but the danger here is not so much that we will lose sight of this as that we will forget how much it was transformed in being accepted by the Indian population, and how much Catholicism is an institution and a set of ideas and values that varies by region, class, and even sex in contemporary Mexico.

Catholicism, Anticlericalism, and the State

Hernán Cortés, the conquistador who subdued what is now Mexico, carried with him the swords of both secular and ecclesiastic authority. He planted the flag of his monarch and erected crosses atop the Aztec ceremonial shrines that he did not raze. The task of converting the Indians to the new faith was immeasurably assisted by the miraculous appearance of the Virgin to one Juan Diego, in December 1531, at a site which had been sacred to Tonantzín, the Aztec mother of gods. The Virgin of Guadalupe, revered even by those with only the palest of religious beliefs, remains the spiritual center of Mexican Catholicism; but she is also a reminder that Mexican Catholicism is not identical to its European ancestor, having been transformed in its contact with Indian rites and practices.[2]

Colonial New Spain was a theocracy, a church-state or a state-church, in which sacred and secular authority intermeshed in a thousand ways. Under a grant from the papacy, the Spanish monarchs had the right (the *patronato real*) to appoint all church officials. The state collected tithes (the *diezma*) for the church, and monastic vows were binding under both civil and canon law. Through direct land grants from the crown and through donations, the church quickly came to acquire significant landholdings in New Spain. Less than a century after the Conquest the crown felt compelled to proscribe further bequests. Nevertheless, it has been estimated that by 1700 the church held half the arable land. Because of the proceeds from its lands, because of the *diezma,* because its landholdings were untaxed, and because of other fiscal benefits and concessions, the church's holdings of more liquid assets were also substantial.[3] Both before and after Independence it could extend financing to promote projects, both public and private, that it favored; and it could scuttle others by refusing credit.

Mexico's independence struggle counts two priests, Miguel Hidalgo and José María Morelos, among its heroes; but the church hierarchy followed the lead of the pope in condemning it. After the successful separation from Spain in 1821, the church arrayed itself in the camp of the conservatives together with *hacendados* and much of the military to insist on more or less of a continuation of the colonial arrangements including those between church and state. The Constitution of 1824 (Mexico's first) provided for church control over censorship and education, the continuation of ecclesiastic and military *fueros* (special privileges that would be adjudicated under martial or canon law, not civil law), and a high degree of centralization of authority in Mexico City.

The conservatives' liberal antagonists drew inspiration and justification from the tradition of the Enlightenment. Their model was not the Spanish Empire but rather the bourgeois republicanism of France and England. Their program called for liberty (an end to *fueros* and other feudal privileges), laissez faire, and the separation of church and state. The constitution they enacted in 1857 proved moderate in relation to their ultimate goals—it did not even call for a clear separation of church and state, for example—but was vigorously opposed by the church nevertheless, particularly because it called on the church to surrender its landholdings.[4] Conflict between liberals and conservatives continued unabated for fifty years, adding to the endemic instability of the new country (there were more than fifty governments between 1821 and 1876, and three foreign interventions). The church called on the faithful to disregard the Constitution of 1857, and threatened to excommunicate any official who took the oath of office under its provisions. When the conservatives raised the banner of rebellion, liberal president Benito Juárez began to press a series of reform measures with vigor. Marriage was made a civil contract, monastic orders were outlawed, public celebrations were restricted, and the number of holidays was reduced. Under the Ley Lerdo of 1856 only individuals (and thus not the church) were permitted to own land. Beginning in 1859, Juárez seized church lands and sold them at public auction. Unfortunately, many Indian peasant lands were also held communally. The new restrictions on landholding allowed the Indians to be displaced from their land through debt, legal subterfuge, and outright coercion. Concentration of landholding increased rapidly in the next few decades. By the end of the century, perhaps as much as 90 percent of Mexico's rural families were landless, and many of these were bound to the large haciendas through debt peonage.

Unable to win a military victory of their own, in 1862 the conservatives rallied behind a French expeditionary force seeking to place the Hapsburg Archduke Maximilian on the throne of Mexico. When Maximilian was finally defeated in 1867 and Juárez once again president in Mexico City, the old conservative coalition of church, army, and *hacendados* was shattered for good. The liberals, however, proved unable to establish political authority or a basis for economic growth. Theirs was a vision suited to conditions that were not to be found in Mexico.

General Porfirio Díaz, a hero of the struggle against Maximilian, seized power in 1876 and quickly centralized authority in his own hands. The order he established, which would last until Mexico exploded in revolution in 1910, provided the basis for Mexico's first sustained burst of economic growth. Under Díaz the church was allowed freer rein. Neither the Constitution of 1857 nor the reform laws were repealed, but Díaz did not press enforcement of their anticlerical provisions.[5] In this climate the church, whose strength had been primarily in the cities and towns, turned its attention to proselytizing in rural areas where pagan survivals were still common.[6]

But if Díaz was more tolerant of the church, what programmatic vision there was to his regime drew from positivism, particularly through the energies of a group that came to be labeled the *científicos*.[7] The difficulty with liberalism, these positivists argued, was that it had stressed liberty before Mexico was ready. What Mexico needed, in their view, could better be obtained under the banner of "order and progress." These positivists drew their inspiration from a more contemporary generation of European apostles of the coming of capitalism: Comte, Spencer, and the other social Darwinists. The doctrines of positivism thus lent ideological legitimacy to the authoritarian measures of Porfirio Díaz and to the steps he took to promote rapid capital accumulation. One of the *científicos,* José Ives Limantour, became Díaz's minister of finance and chief economic advisor, and he quickly placed like-minded officials in key economic posts throughout the Díaz administration.

During the Porfiriato, agricultural and mining exports expanded rapidly and trade partners were diversified to include Britain, France, Spain, and the United States. An extensive program of railroad construction was undertaken: in 1877 Mexico had only 417 miles of track; by 1901 it had 9,600 miles. Foreign investment, actively encouraged by Díaz and the *científicos,* quickly came to play a large role in a number of key sectors, among them banking, mining, petroleum, commercial agriculture, railroads, and electric power. The economic growth of the Porfiriato created huge fortunes for some (including Limantour and many of the other *científicos*), but excluded the large majority of Mexicans from its fruits. Díaz permitted the exploitation of hacienda laborers, and he used his troops to quell any signs of unrest in the mining and petroleum enclaves. For many, the Díaz years brought an absolute worsening of their economic situation.

In the last years of the Díaz regime, the Mexican Catholic Social Action movement began to take shape encouraged by Pope Leo XIII's *Rerum Novarum* (1891) and by similar movements in Europe, but shortly after the revolution broke out the church hierarchy opted to support leaders who were perceived as more eager to restore the Porfiriato than to undertake serious social change. Anticlerical sentiment returned to the center of Mexican politics.[8] Under the Constitution of 1917, the church was forbidden to own or acquire property, all places of public worship became the property of the nation, the church was denied juridical personality, the clergy was made a profession subject to law and disenfranchised, and the church was forbidden to "establish or direct schools of primary instruction" (Article 3). The conflict came to a head in 1926 when the church closed its places of worship and suspended the celebration of mass to force President Calles to rescind a number of anticlerical edicts. For the next three years there was armed rebellion (the Cristero rebellion) in some of the more religious regions.[9] Finally, in the 1930s, a kind of accommodation was reached between church and state. By 1940, incoming president Manuel Ávila Camacho could publicly profess: "I am a believer." In the ensuing four decades, the church and state have worked out increasingly comfortable but strictly informal ways of working with each other.[10]

Capitalism and the State

The Mexican Revolution quickly turned into a civil war. Just a few months after Francisco Madero issued his Plan of San Luis Potosí, Díaz had gone into exile. It would be nearly a decade before the character of the new regime was decided. A number of social forces joined together to oust Díaz: agrarian radicals (such as Emiliano Zapata and Pancho Villa), syndicalist workers, and bourgeois constitutionalists, to name only the most important elements. Once Díaz was gone, they could find no inclusive and coherent program around which to unite. Nothing shows this so clearly as the Constitution of 1917 which is an amalgam of liberal, constitutional ideas and radical, social ones.

In the end, none of the contending forces could completely dominate the others. The various factions coalesced into what Bradenburg has labeled a "Revolutionary Family."[11] In 1929 this was given a measure of institutional form in the founding of (what is now) the Institutional Revolutionary Party (PRI), and in the 1930s PRI was reorganized along corporatist lines, separate party sectors being accorded to labor, to peasants, and to the middle class. However, "PRI is better conceptualized as an apparatus through which the Revolutionary Coalition controls Mexican politics than as a mechanism for representing and implementing the demands of its component interest groups."[12] Since its founding, the PRI candidate in each presidential election has won by an overwhelming margin, and PRI has prevailed in virtually all lesser elections of any consequence.

The revolution and ensuing civil war decimated the Mexican economy. In addition to the loss of human life, it destroyed the currency and the banking system, disrupted lines of communication and transportation, and wiped out productive assets in agriculture, mining, and manufacturing. The task of economic reconstruction would be a formidable one—but along what lines or program would it proceed? While there were radical elements in the Mexican Revolution, in the early 1920s there was no socialist model anywhere in the world to be followed. The Bolshevik Revolution had only just happened. The dominant voices in the Revolutionary Family were members of the nascent bourgeoisie, primarily from the north (especially Sonora): Carranza and Obregón from landowning families, and Calles, a small businessman. In reconstructing the economy, their model was primarily the United States with its vigorous private sector, large and growing middle class, commercial agriculture, and broad spectrum of manufacturing industries.[13] The United States was more of a model in terms of showing them the shape and extent of what could be achieved than in terms of showing them a precise road to be followed. They realized from the start that the state would have to play a more active and vigorous role than it had in the United States. On the one hand, the U.S. model stipulated that primary reliance be placed on the private sector for investment, but on the other hand Mexico lacked the domestic entrepreneurial class that could play this role. In consequence, the state would have to bring a national bourgeoisie into existence, and it would have to be prepared to do whatever this fledgling national bourgeoisie would not or could not do.[14]

The reconstruction of the banking sector in the 1920s and 1930s set the pattern for what was to follow elsewhere in the economy. Its resuscitation was necessary to generate domestic savings and investments and to attract foreign loans. Under the new regime, foreign banks (and foreign ownership of domestic banks) were forbidden, and domestic private sector banks would be closely regulated by the Bank of Mexico, created in 1925 to perform central bank functions. A complex scheme of reserve requirements became the mechanism by which private investment was to be channeled away from speculative uses and into high-priority sectors, and by which savings could be extracted for public sector investments.

Over the next several decades a vigorous private banking system emerged under the careful ministrations of the state. Particularly after 1954, there was a determined effort to keep inflation low; and in consequence rates of domestic savings have been enviably high for a developing country. In the absence of an effective bond or stock market, the national bourgeoisie that emerged in Mexico has largely crystallized around the private banking system. It has come to be characterized by a series of groups—a dozen or so major ones and many smaller ones—each having a bank or bank complex at its center, whose savings are utilized for investments in affiliated manufacturing, mining, and/or commercial enterprises.

From the beginning, the guiding assumption was that primary reliance would be placed on the private sector banks. But it was also understood that a strong private banking system willing and able to make the necessary investments could not be created overnight. A series of state development banks was established to finance those activities that the state managers deemed necessary but which the private sector banks would not or could not undertake. Specific public sector banks were set up to finance agricultural credit, foreign trade, infrastructure and basic industry, and small business ventures.[15]

What happened in the banking system is important because it set the pattern for what would happen in other sectors: primary reliance was placed on the private sector, but the state stood prepared to do what the private sector was unable or unwilling to do. But it is important as well because it established a foundation for what would happen elsewhere. Through the resuscitation of the banking system an entrepreneurial class was brought into existence. The public sector banks that were created have often been the instruments through which the state has intervened in the economy when it has felt called upon to do so. Finally, the complex of public sector institutions demarcated by the Finance Ministry, the Bank of Mexico, Nacional Financiera (the state industrial development bank), and lesser public sector banks has provided a site for the training and preparation of the middle- and high-level state managers (*técnicos*) of the Mexican economy. While there is considerable turnover of personnel within the Mexican state bureaucracy, particularly every six years when there is a change of presidential administration, there has been a high degree of continuity of outlook in the government institutions that oversee the conomy. As new governmental institutions have been created in this area—a Ministry of Industry and National Properties, a Ministry of Planning, etc.—they have been staffed by *técnicos* imbued with the common outlook that was institutionalized early in the complex of state bank institutions.

In agriculture a dualistic strategy has been pursued. Because of the insistence of the peasants led by Zapata and Villa, land reform was written into the Constitution of 1917. Subsequent presidents have varied widely in their willingness to carry through land reform, the biggest redistribution coming in the 1930s under Lázaro Cárdenas. Through this land reform there has been an attempt to recreate the traditional pattern of communal landholdings—*ejidos*. Plots are individually worked for the most part and may be inherited, but they cannot be sold. In addition to these small holdings engaged principally in subsistence agriculture, large-scale commercial agriculture has also been promoted. Large-scale investments have been made in irrigation works and in other key inputs and infrastructure (fertilizer, marketing facilities, etc.). In the 1940s when significant tracts of land were being brought under irrigation, agricultural output grew more than 8 percent a year, but by the 1970s the growth rate had slipped to 2.1 percent per year, failing even to keep pace with population growth.

While there was some manufacturing investment during the Porfiriato, significant manufacturing activity did not begin until Mexico was cut off from world trade by the Depression and World War II. Begun as a predicament, import-substituting industrialization was continued after the war as a deliberate policy. Import quotas and tariff barriers were erected, and tax concessions established for "new and necessary industries."[16] Since 1940, manufacturing has been the most dynamic sector of the economy, growing at an average rate of 8.1 percent in the 1940s, 7.3 percent in the 1950s, and 9.4 percent in the 1960s. Since the late 1960s there has been an increasing concern that import substitution has been pushed as far as is sensible, and a policy emphasis on the promotion of manufactured exports in industries already well established has emerged.

To a significant extent, entrepreneurship in the Mexican economy has been performed by the large bank-industrial groups that formed in recreating the country's private financial system. Of these the Monterrey Group (now split into several distinct groups) is perhaps the best known. But disproportionately, entrepreneurship has been performed by people outside or marginal to Mexican society and its traditional values.[17] The Monterrey Group had its origins in Sephardic Jewish immigrants to Mexico. Lebanese and Spanish republican immigrants also played strong entrepreneurial roles. More significant than these "outsiders," have been transnational corporations. After the revolution, foreign investment was barred from a number of sectors where its presence had been strong during the Porfiriato, including banking and agriculture (foreigners were forbidden to own land). In 1938, foreign oil holdings were expropriated after the firms refused to comply with a wage settlement that had been upheld by the Mexican Supreme Court. But in other sectors, foreign investment has not only been permitted but to some extent quietly encouraged. To protect established markets, a large number of transnational corporations established manufacturing subsidiaries in the 1950s and 1960s after import-substitution policies were implemented. Particularly in the 1960s and early 1970s the government insisted upon Mexicanization: that all new firms in Mexico be majority Mexican-owned. One consequence of this policy was the creation of a number of lucrative investment opportunities for the larger bank-centered groups as foreign corporations have had to locate domestic partners for their Mexican subsidiaries.[18]

Finally, significant entrepreneurship has been performed by the Mexican state. It has undertaken projects not only in infrastructure (roads, telecommunications, electric power, port facilities) but also in a host of basic industries such as steel and petrochemicals in which private sector investment was not forthcoming either because of high capital costs or high risk associated with the project. In a number of cases, the state has bailed out private sector firms on the brink of failure. Once acquired, these state-owned firms have sometimes moved aggressively into new ventures or product lines. But with these occasional exceptions, state entrepreneurship has not sought to preempt opportunities for private sector investment. On the contrary, the Mexican state has consistently looked to nurture conditions for private capital accumulation.

From 1940 until the late 1960s, Mexican GDP grew at an average annual rate in excess of 6 percent, which, in the words of one analyst, "as a sustained growth record must be almost unequalled in the post-war third world."[19] Frequent reference was made in the development literature to the "Mexican miracle." The fruits of this growth were very unequally distributed, however. As Roger Hansen concluded in 1971, "a large part of the bill for the past thirty years of rapid industrialization has been paid in terms of foregone increases in consumption by the large majority of Mexican society located toward the bottom of the income scale. Between 1940 and the early 1960s, the rich in Mexico became richer and the poor poorer, some in a relative sense and some absolutely."[20]

The Mexican economy slowed, then sputtered in the mid-1970s because of accumulated difficulties with its strategy of economic growth, changes in the world economy, and tensions between the government and the private sector it had successfully brought to life. The discovery of substantial petroleum reserves in the past few years has reignited growth in the Mexican economy, but it is far from clear whether the oil revenues will be put to uses that will bring about a more equitable pattern of development. One preeminent issue is the creation of sufficient employment opportunities for the country's rapidly growing population. At present the number of new jobs being created each year is only about half the number of new entrants to the labor force.

Religious Values in the Political Economy of Contemporary Mexico

Discussions of the political economy of contemporary Mexico, if they mention the church and religion at all, generally touch only on these three points: that in the nineteenth century the church was forced to divest its substantial landholdings and withdraw from any directly political role; that the Cristero rebellion of the 1920s had slowed the postrevolutionary consolidation of the Mexican state; and that the only political party of any consequence that has arisen to challenge PRI has ties to church circles and to currents of Catholic social thought.[21] This is an insufficient portrait of the role of the church and of traditional religious values in the political economy of contemporary Mexico.

The influence of religious values is not to be seen in the basic construction of the economy, narrowly conceived. Private sector initiative, the development of commercial agriculture, the character of industrialization, and the unequal and exclusionary pattern of economic growth that has taken place all owe far more to the structures, models, and values of capitalism both in an international context and as it has been received and implanted in Mexico. The influence of the religious and cultural values of Catholicism is rather to be seen in the character of the state and in the manner in which it relates to the economy and society. The Mexican economy has grown as rapidly as it has because public and private elites took advantage of opportunities within the context of the world capitalist system. Mexico was fortunate in this regard to have a sizable domestic market for manufactured goods, substantial natural resource endowments (especially hydrocarbons), and both beaches and a colorful past to support a tourist industry (a significant source of foreign exchange). Because of international constraints, the Mexican economy almost certainly could not have grown as rapidly as it has (though it could have grown more equitably) if it had not chosen to follow a capitalist model. But this growth would also have been impossible if the state had not been able to maintain support from and control over the lower classes, and direct the allocation and structuring of capital. For both these tasks concerning legitimacy and accumulation, the legacy of the revolution has been important, particularly because it accorded the state a remarkable degree of autonomy. Also important in understanding the manner in which the state institutionalized itself with regard to business, labor, and the peasantry is an appreciation of the religious and cultural values of Mexico's Catholic past. Three issues warrant consideration: (1) the tutelary role of the state, (2) the character of regime support, and (3) nationalism.

The first two of these require introduction of what Alfred Stepan has labeled the organic-statist tradition: a normative approach to politics distinct from either liberalism or Marxism, whose intellectual foundations are to be found in Aristotle, Roman law, medieval conceptions of natural law, and modern Catholic social thought. This tradition has been neglected in the standard treatments of Western political theory, and it is more commonly encountered in countries which have been significantly affected by the institutions and values of the Roman Catholic Church.[22]

In Mexico this organic-statist tradition has been kept alive both because of and despite the strong political and intellectual currents of anticlericalism. This tradition views the community and not the individual as its moral center; it sees society as an organic whole and accords legitimacy to its component parts (individuals, families, private interests or associations) only insofar as they play their proper role within the whole; and it sees the state's role as articulating the common good and directing the component parts of society to find their proper, harmonious place within the whole.

Tutelary Role of the State

There is nothing unusual about the extensiveness of state activities in the Mexican economy. As Gerschenkron argued, the state has commonly played a major industrializing role in countries that embarked in the process only well after the industrializers of the first and second waves (Great Britain, the United States, Germany, etc.).[23] What is unusual for a state in a capitalist economy, and what is to be laid at least partly to the organic-statist tradition, is the strong tutelary character of the Mexican state in orchestrating the process of economic development. In the organic-statist tradition, Stepan argues, "the state is conceived of as playing a relatively autonomous architectural role in the polity."[24] To a significant extent, that is the role the Mexican state has played since the revolution. "The Mexican state aims," Laurence Whitehead attests, "not merely to administer an established social order but to direct a long-term process of social transformations."[25] While this tutelary role is to be seen in a wide variety of tasks and accomplishments of the Mexican state, nowhere is it more clear than in the substantial work of bringing to life a domestic bourgeoisie to carry forward the development of agriculture, commerce, and industry. The successful accomplishment of this task has tended to limit the autonomy of the Mexican state to direct future change; in a variety of ways the now vigorous domestic entrepreneurial class can veto projects and policies not to its liking.

The Corporatist Organization of PRI and Regime Support

Despite the revolution and the continuing salience of revolutionary myths and themes, the fruits of economic growth in Mexico have been very unequally distributed, and the poorest 40 percent have tended to be excluded from the benefits altogether. Central to the explanation of this paradox must be consideration of the corporatist organization of the ruling party. PRI has successfully positioned itself as the only legitimate heir to and interpreter of the revolutionary tradition, and through its tripartite sectoral organization it has maintained control over and yet enjoyed support from labor and peasants—precisely those segments of the population that have benefited least from the "Mexican miracle."[26]

It would be a serious mistake to explain the persistence of this corporatist form of political organization simply by reference to an enduring cultural heritage such as the organic-statist tradition. Such an explanation (to mention only one of several difficulties) would fail to account for why corporatist arrangements arise at particular times after long periods of abeyance, and why some corporatist arrangements endure while others do not. Corporatist political arrangements are created—consciously engineered—generally in times of crisis to limit and control societal conflict. Nevertheless, the organic-statist tradition is important in the installation and maintenance of corporatist regimes because it serves as a rationale and guide for those who undertake to establish them.[27] PRI's corporatist forms could not have been created or maintained so easily (or perhaps not at all) in the absence of the enduring legacy of the organic-statist tradition.

There is a further general point to be made concerning the character of regime support in Mexico. While the legitimizing themes of the revolution are distinctly anticlerical in *content,* Coleman and Davis have argued that the *process* of legitimation involves a quasi-religious reification of the nation-state. Particularly among the lower classes, the state is an object of veneration; patterns of behavior are carried over from the religious to the political sphere: "The PRI does benefit, even if in unintended ways, from the persistence of conventional patterns of interaction within religious authority structures. The patron-clientelistic exchanges of religious life have a direct analogue in the evocation of symbolic visions of the future by Mexican political elites who seek to contain political behavior within 'proper' channels. It cannot hurt the political elites to have religious elites reinforce tendencies toward the acceptance of deferred gratification."[28]

Nationalism

Through the nineteenth century the church slowed the development of Mexican nationalism. In doctrine the church was universalistic and in practice it served to exclude the masses from effective participation in the national community. Conversely, anticlerical sentiment in the nineteenth and early twentieth centuries promoted the emergence of a vigorous Mexican nationalism. More recently, as Frederick Turner has argued, church and state have moved "from exclusive conceptions to a common formulation and acceptance of the meaning of Mexican nationalism."[29] Now that the church has withdrawn its claims to extensive secular influence and church and state have worked out an informal but comfortable accommodation, common professions of a single faith and common symbols such as the Virgin of Guadalupe serve to reinforce rather than undermine Mexican nationalism. Only in such a context could President José López Portillo, charged with responsibility of upholding the Constitution of 1917, not only permit the visit of Pope John Paul II to Mexico in January 1979, but serve as his official welcomer at the airport.

Conclusion

The possibilities for Mexican development have been constrained by Mexico's place within the world capitalist system. The discovery of substantial hydrocarbon reserves will alter and perhaps loosen these constraints, but it will certainly not remove them altogether. Within the bounds of these constraints, several different strands of ideas and values, many of them initially of foreign origin, have been championed by different social forces to guide the course of Mexican development. The revolution constituted a violent rejection of the visions that had dominated the nineteenth century: one derived from Catholicism, others—liberal and positivist—drawn from the progress of capitalism in Europe. The revolution provided a moment of openness, but no coherent guiding vision of its own. There could be no possibility of an explicit tapping of Catholic values, but the Cristero rebellion ensured that religion would remain something to be reckoned with. In ensuing decades, Mexico has emerged as a religious but anticlerical country.

Particularly because of the proximity and increasing hegemony of the United States in the Western Hemisphere, it is unlikely that anything but a capitalist model for economic development could have been adopted after the revolution. But for growth to occur on a capitalist route in a late-late industrializer such as Mexico, particularly after ten years of civil strife, the state had to play a leading role in dampening popular demands, in seeing to the rebirth of domestic entrepreneurship, and in undertaking critical investments of its own infrastructure and basic industry. Mexico presents the apparent paradox of a country committed to capitalism but with the state playing a major entrepreneurial role.

One critical factor in allowing the state to play the role that it has in the economic growth of the last half century has been the persistence of an organic-statist tradition, derived from Catholicism, which legitimizes the state's playing a much larger and more tutelary role than in liberal-capitalist society. Catholic-derived values provide a key underpinning of the contemporary Mexican regime, but its public pronouncements continue to pay homage to the radical proclamations of the revolution for democracy, land distribution, and the rights of labor. The final and sharpest paradox of contemporary Mexico is that it is a country which experienced and continues to celebrate a social revolution but which is characterized by deep, enduring patterns of inequality and authoritarian rule.

Notes

This chapter was written while I was a Fellow at the Woodrow Wilson International Center for Scholars, Washington, D.C., and draws upon ideas developed in collaborative research with Kenneth E. Sharpe. I would also like to thank the participants in the Council on Religion and International Affairs Study Group on Religion and Global Economics, and particularly Claude Pomerleau, for a number of helpful suggestions.

1. Octavio Paz, *The Labyrinth of Solitude: Life and Thought in Mexico* (New York: Grove, 1961), pp. 122, 132.
2. On the Virgin of Guadalupe see Eric Wolf, "The Virgin of Guadalupe: Mexican National Symbol," *Journal of American Folklore* 71 (1958): 34–39.
3. Jan Bazant, *Alienation of Church Wealth in Mexico: Social and Economic Aspects of the Liberal Revolution, 1856–1875* (Cambridge: Cambridge University Press, 1971).
4. See Charles Hale, *Mexican Liberalism in the Age of Mora, 1821–1853* (New Haven: Yale University Press, 1968).
5. Karl Schmitt, "Mexican Positivists and the Church-State Question, 1876–1911," *A Journal of Church and State* 8 (Spring 1966): 200–13.
6. Jean Meyer, *The Cristero Rebellion: The Mexican People between Church and State, 1926–1929* (Cambridge: Cambridge University Press, 1976), pp. 194–95.
7. Leopoldo Zea, *Positivism in Mexico* (Austin: University of Texas Press, 1968, 1974).

8.   Robert E. Quirk, *The Mexican Revolution and the Catholic Church, 1910–1929* (Bloomington: Indiana University Press, 1973).
9.   On this period see Meyer; James Wilkie, "The Meaning of the Cristero Religious War against the Mexican Revolution," *A Journal of Church and State* 8 (1966): 214–33.
10. See Susan Eckstein, "Politicos and Priests: The Iron Law of Oligarchy Interorganizational Relations," *Comparative Politics* 9 (July 1977): 463–81.
11. Frank Brandenburg, *The Making of Modern Mexico* (Englewood Cliffs: Prentice Hall, 1964).
12. Roger D. Hansen, *The Politics of Mexican Development* (Baltimore: Johns Hopkins University Press, 1971), p. 107.
13. Octavio Paz puts the point this way: "But the ideological insufficiency of the Revolution became plain almost at once, and the result was a compromise: The Constitution of 1917. It was impossible to return to the pre-Cortesian world; it was equally impossible to return to the colonial tradition. The Revolution had no other recourse than to take over the program of the liberals, though with certain modifications." *The Labyrinth of Solitude*, p. 145.
14. This and the next several paragraphs draw heavily from Douglas C. Bennett and Kenneth E. Sharpe, "The State as Banker and Entrepreneur: The Last Resort Character of the Mexican State's Economic Interventions, 1917–1976," *Comparative Politics* 12 (January 1980): 165–89.
15. See Charles W. Anderson, "Bankers as Revolutionaries: Politics and Development Banking in Mexico." In William P. Glade and Charles W. Anderson, *The Political Economy of Mexico* (Madison: University of Wisconsin Press, 1968), pp. 103–85.
16. On the development of manufacturing in Mexico see Sanford Mosk, *Industrial Revolution in Mexico* (Berkeley: University of California Press, 1954); Timothy King, *Mexico: Industrialization and Trade Policies since 1940* (London: Oxford University Press, 1970).
17. On entrepreneurship in Mexico see Flavia DeRossi, *The Mexican Entrepreneur* (Paris: Organization for Economic Cooperation and Development, 1972); Salvador Cordero and Rafael Santín, "Los grupos industriales: una nueva organización económica en México," *Cuadernos del CES* (Mexico City: El Colegio de México, 1977).
18. On this see Douglas C. Bennett and Kenneth E. Sharpe, "The Ill Logic of Mexicanization," *Foro Internacional* (forthcoming).
19. E.V.K. Fitzgerald, "The State and Capital Accumulation in Mexico," *Journal of Latin American Studies* 10 (November 1978): 264.
20. Hansen, p. 71.
21. One observer has written of the Party of National Action (PAN): "The PAN is the legally participating descendent of those who waged civil war on behalf of the Spanish heritage of power, privilege and racial dominance resting on the symbiotic relationship of clergy, military and the wealthy families of the great landholding and commercial classes." L. Vincent Padgett, *The Mexican Political System* (Boston: Houghton Mifflin, 1976), p. 99.
22. Alfred Stepan, *The State and Society: Peru in Comparative Perspective* (Princeton: Princeton University Press, 1978), pp. 3–113. Cf. Howard Wiarda, "Toward a Framework for the Study of Political Change in the Iberic-Latin Tradition: The Corporative Model," *World Politics* 25 (1973): 206–35; Richard

Morse, "The Heritage of Latin America." In Louis Hartz (ed.), *The Founding of New Societies* (New York: Harcourt, Brace, & World, 1964), pp. 123–77.

23. See Alexander Gershenkron, *Economic Backwardness in Historical Perspective* (Cambridge: Harvard University Press, 1966).

24. Stepan, p. 33.

25. Laurence Whitehead, "Why Mexico Is Ungovernable—Almost," mimeo, 1979.

26. Evelyn Stevens, "Mexico's PRI: The Institutionalization of Corporatism." In James Malloy (ed.), *Authoritarianism and Corporatism in Latin America* (Pittsburgh: University of Pittsburgh Press, 1977), pp. 227–58.

27. Stepan, p. 46ff.; cf. Philippe Schmitter, "Still the Century of Corporatism?" In Frederick Pike and Thomas Stritch (eds.), *The New Corporatism: Social-Political Structures in the Iberian World* (Notre Dame: University of Notre Dame Press, 1974), pp. 85–131.

28. Kenneth Coleman and Charles Davis, "Civil and Conventional Religion in Secular Authoritarian Regimes: The Case of Mexico," *Studies in Comparative International Development* 13 (1978): 70.

29. Frederick Turner, "The Compatibility of Church and State in Mexico," *Journal of Inter-American Studies* 9 (1967): 592.

6

Religion and Values in the Formation of Modern Mexico: Some Economic and Political Considerations

Claude Pomerleau

Until recently in Mexico official church documents would have been reserved in specifying issues of the economy and politics, would have carefully distinguished religious from public issues, and would have avoided discussion of the latter. Such discretion was deemed necessary because of the extreme sensitivity of government officials to any criticism.[1]

The workbook of the Conference of Mexican Bishops for 1980–82 makes a notable departure from this practice. It lists the following issues challenging church policy in Mexico: the disintegration of family life, the special problems of youth, the interrelated corruption of society and government, the alienation and exploitation of peasants and indigenous groups, hunger and undernourishment, the patently unjust structures of production and consumption, inflation, the external debt, the absence of democratic institutions, an irresponsible policymaking process, the monopoly and misuse of political power, and widespread apathy about public affairs. The bishops also mention numerous related issues in the areas of education, religion, and the church.

The significance of the Mexican bishops' notebook does not come from the explicit and comprehensive reference to social, political, and economic problems. Rather, it lies in the fact that such criticism is made at all. Mexican law defines religious activity in a very restrictive sense, basing its interpretation on the anticlerical traditions of the nineteenth century and on the 1971 Constitution and subsequent legislation. For the past forty years, the bishops have accepted this qualified interpretation of the anti-clerical laws in return for substantial concessions and discrete exceptions in the fields of education and public worship. But the tone and content of recent official church documents indicate that some new conditions and pressures have produced new responses. As pressures inside and outside the church increase, relationships between it and Mexican society and government are also likely to change. The values and traditions which define and restrict the major public relationships have been changing during most of this century. This is especially true for religious values in which radical changes were initiated by the Second Vatican Council (1962–65) and for Mexican values, noticeably affected by the events and protests of 1968.

Mexico has an extraordinary assortment of cultural traditions, ideologies, and group values that cause a wide range of tensions in the formulation of public policy. In the past, when governments operated out of a narrow dogmatic view of power and society, such as the administrations of Porfirio Díaz (1876–1910) and Plutarco Elías Calles (1924–28), resulting social conflicts disrupted government operations. Most administrations since that of Calles have been able to maintain a balance between competing moral and ideological forces influencing public policy and power.

Today public policy is shaped within the context of this compromise which balances major developmental ideologies. Such a compromise has antecedents that reach back to the Colonial period and even to the Triple Alliance before the Spanish Conquest. The contemporary blend and balance of strategies have evolved out of an improvised and perhaps precarious balance between the two major moral systems which shaped Mexican thought and determined its national character since Independence. For simplicity and convenience, I call these systems of public morality the liberal and religious traditions. These two traditions represent opposing poles of integration in terms of values, ideologies, and rituals that shape and accompany the making of public policies. Although there is some overlapping of the two traditions, they represent distinct historical currents that help define and determine the role of the state in the formulation of social and economic policies. We must understand them if we are to understand the dynamics within state entities and even between individuals and groups in society. Public policy today is affected by the *modus vivendi* reached between government and church officials during the late 1930s, after a long period of conflict between the advocates of opposing moral positions.

The present arrangement is not new for Mexico. The administration of Colonial Mexico operated out of an analogous compromise between the Spanish religious and political tradition and the meso-American cultures with their integrated views of religion and society. The fusion of the two world views, accomplished during the sixteenth century, remained relatively stable during the next two centuries. Under the influence of the Enlightenment, the religious tradition began to change during the second half of the eighteenth century. Independence arrived abruptly and unexpectedly in the nineteenth century, putting great strain on the social and economic institutions inherited from the Colonial era. Attempts were made to restore a theocratic state but failed for many reasons, including radical changes in the religious framework and in public morality. The first attempts to restore the traditional order after Independence failed and a liberal synthesis gradually emerged. At first, liberals tried to transform the religious tradition; then, to supplement it; finally, in their frustration over the resistance of organized religion, the radical liberals and revolutionaries of the twentieth century tried to destroy the religious tradition altogether. Although a civil concept of the state (combining elements from secular philosophies from France and the United States) eventually triumphed, it had to exist alongside the traditional religious concept, rooted as it was in popular rituals and practices. Today the religious tradition is undergoing profound changes, more profound than anything experienced since the initial impact of the Enlightenment on Colonial society and religious theory.

The pressures and tensions transforming the religious tradition are causing similar tensions in the ideology of the revolutionary regime. These pressures on the moral foundations of the present government have forced changes in the relationships between government and society and caused increased concern over the symbolic role of the revolution in the public sector. The two moral pillars of political stability are beginning to shift, but it remains to be seen whether they will shift in the same direction.

For the past forty years Mexico's government has been remarkably stable, even stagnant. The government consists of a controlled party system with a rigid political hierarchy dominated by a powerful president who is replaced every six years through a semisecret process.[2] This system has allowed an extraordinarily high rate of economic expansion since the 1930s. However, postrevolutionary governments have promised more than they could accomplish. Ambitious promises continue to be made on the basis of the expanded production and export of oil. But a growing number of experts believe that there is a critical need for the reformulation of the public covenant between people and government, or at least for changes in the informal arrangements within the ruling elites that exclude or postpone many groups from effective participation in the formulation of social and economic policy. Without these minimum changes, Mexico could be heading toward a resumption of destructive social conflicts and increased government repression.[3]

I propose to examine some recent changes within the religious tradition of public morality and the role of the Mexican Catholic Church; the opposing tradition that I have named "civil religion" and which provides the moral canopy for governments that have inherited the revolutionary tradition; and finally, the areas of interaction between new religious forces and the official government ideology. I will first take a short historical excursus into the religious problem that has beguiled Mexico for so long and the response of recent governments to that complicated issue.

The Religious Problem and the State

The controversy over religion today is focused on the continued exclusion of organized religion from the public arena, especially in the area of social and economic policy. Because of religious conflicts of the past, the church is still officially considered the major obstacle to development and the major cause of the social and political problems of the past. Religious values are rejected as inappropriate and unacceptable, directly or indirectly, for the country's social and economic development. The tone of anticlericalism sounds like that of nineteenth-century France. Specifically and formally, organized religion is excluded from the public arena through obsolete political instruments.

For example, universities are subject to exaggerated and unnecessary pressures against the study of religion. Even Catholic universities are Constitutionally prohibited to teach religion. A notable exception is the Jesuit-run Iberoamericana in Mexico City, where the first course in the sociology of religion was introduced in 1979. Emotions still run high over the potential dangers of this religious actor—an absent actor, considering that the church has been excluded from the cultural and intellectual world of Mexico for most of the century. In light of political achievements since the revolution, as well as the social and economic difficulties facing the country, the return of organized religion in a responsible and limited way would be of considerable significance.[4]

The anxiety attendant on the participation of organized religion in Mexican public life is based on the dominant role of the church in forming the national character during the long period beginning in the early sixteenth century and lasting until the beginning of the nineteenth.[5] Although many historians praise the church for creating a distinct Mexican identity out of meso-American and Spanish elements, there is considerable controversy over the significance of the church and the social and political doctrines it developed after Independence. The role of religion in contemporary Mexico is usually dismissed as inherently destructive or irrelevant to modern society. Yet the mixture of Catholicism and native religious rituals and practices constitutes a major cultural contribution to the modern world. Underlying this cultural phenomenon, called *mestizaje,* is the world of religious symbols and values with its fiestas, saints, and public rituals, its doctrine of human community, and a broad vision of the common good.

Despite political and economic dependence on the Spanish crown and the dogmatic and comprehensive presence of church institutions, New Spain developed a vigorous intellectual and scientific life. Intellectuals, religious and lay, introduced the ideas of the Enlightenment into the country, and scientic rationalism became a major force in the academic community, especially in Mexico City. Alexander von Humboldt wrote in 1903: "No City of the new continent, without excepting the United States, presents such great and solid scientific establishments as the capital of Mexico."[6]

The act of open political rebellion that initiated the movement toward Independence constituted a public religious ritual that is constitutive of the modern Mexican community. The rebellion of the curate of Dolores, Reverend Miguel Hidalgo, had comprehensive economic and social implications that challenged the political order of the period and continues to be an enigma of contemporary nationalism. The lasting effect of Hidalgo's rebellion shows to what extent public institutions were shaped by the interaction of religion on society. Although the Catholic Church of Colonial Mexico allowed a wide range of practices, from corrupt ritualism to violent mysticism,[7] it was also the integrity and decency of the majority of the monks and friars and diocesan clergy that captured and retained the loyalty and imagination of Mexicans in a way that the military and civilian bureaucrats could not.[8]

The debate over the role of the church during the nineteenth century continues to be unclear, controversial, and disruptive. The intertwining of religion and society stabilized the Colonial order but also created some intolerable obstacles for the fathers of modern Mexico. Independence was followed by social violence and economic disintegration which lasted until the 1930s. Although a religious truce characterized the long tenure of Porfirio Díaz, the official philosophy of his regime was openly hostile to the value system of Catholic doctrine. Throughout much of the nineteenth century and briefly during the twentieth, political and religious leaders competed for the loyalty of the citizens through mutually exclusive philosophies of the common good. Church leaders and political conservatives tried to reestablish an integrated order including the cooperative interaction of political, economic, and religious activities on all levels, an order that they thought had proved satisfactory in the past. Liberals and supporters of a secular state were opposed to the political veto exercised by the church through its extensive legal and economic power closely related to its social influence. As supporters of the theocratic state maneuvered to overpower or destroy the creators of the liberal state, latent conflicts surfaced.

The search for suitable political structures radicalized both liberals and conservatives. The former proposed an open society and an autonomous state; the latter sought to retain a form of the theocratic system with its organic approach to society and hierarchy. Public order was repeatedly disrupted until the late 1930s. The secular formula eventually triumphed and was reluctantly recognized by church leaders and followers. From one perspective, it seems that the modern state was created from the fractured ribs of the theocratic state—the new system reestablishing the same paternalism, elitism, and concentration of political power that had characterized the theocratic order. Even when the leaders of conflicting ideologies had much to gain by cooperating over specific issues, personalities and institutional interests prevented compromise. Solutions were repeatedly blocked by disagreements over the source of authority and the role of religion.[9]

The long conflict between advocates of conflicting ideologies reached open warfare in the Cristero rebellion of 1926–29. This final conflict fragmented the church and produced widespread and lasting social and economic damage. The rebellion appeared to be a genuine religious conflict; economic factors alone could not explain the intensity and extent of the fighting. Catholics in the Center-West believed that their deepest religious beliefs were being systematically destroyed by the government.[10] In looking back on the rebellion, one might conclude that the Catholics lost the battle but won the religious war—even though the cost was high. The hierarchy lost credibility and lost touch with the grass roots. However, government revolutionaries and reformers were also damaged by the rebellion they could have avoided. The path they chose was that of creating a new moral base for national development. The task proved to be more difficult than expected.

Revolutionaries like Álvaro Obregón and Calles and their colleagues inherited an ideological controversy that had lasted the entire previous century. The controversy had been magnified by the disruptions of the 1910 Revolution. To stabilize the system and stimulate development, they consolidated and centralized the administrative system. The formulation of a new moral base for the legitimacy of the government produced an inevitable opposition and raised serious problems. Loyalty to the new doctrine was limited at first to the immediate beneficiaries. The church officially opposed the new civil doctrine, especially for its social and educational implications. The revolutionaries needed to elaborate a new moral framework that would serve to motivate leaders and formulate strong loyalties among the citizens. A monopolistic political party was designed to maintain unity among elites and transform the loyalties of the masses. The reformers recognized that the church was able to transform religious loyalties of urban workers and peasants into national political organizations—perhaps as effectively and extensively as the government. A suitable replacement for the church was needed to transform the revolutionary faith into effective social and political structures. The missing ingredient was a system of secular symbols and values that could relate individual citizens to the process of development—without taking a chance on mass popular organizations.

President Obregón had initiated that process on the cultural level by appointing José Vasconcelos minister of education. Vasconcelos created a rural elementary school system based on the religious concept of the rural mission. President Calles, as Obregón's collaborator and successor, disliked the indigenous and protoreligious tendencies of Vasconcelos and encouraged the Mexican disciples of Dewey to establish the new civil values for a modern Mexico along the lines of U.S. educational philosophy. Meanwhile Calles proceeded to break up the old order. He was an impatient man, convinced that the major stumbling block to the immediate transformation of the traditional moral order consisted of the clergy and the church. He explicitly stated his intention to crush the church once and for all[11] and assumed that individualism, again on the American model, would spread throughout the country. He failed to grasp the complex interrelationship between popular religious values and elitist politics in Mexican history. The Catholic response was as traditional as the values: rebellion. By the end of the conflict, Calles had spent most of his political capital.

President Lázaro Cárdenas (1934–40) inherited the political legacy of Calles. But Cárdenas was more astute than his mentor. He came from the Center-West region where religious traditions are deeply rooted, the home of Hidalgo and Morelos and one of the major regions of intellectual ferment during the nineteenth century. Cárdenas renewed the campaign for a revolutionary faith based on secular education and material progress. He sought to establish a new system of values through the extension of the rural school. Again, collective religious opposition threatened to ruin the project. By 1936 he recognized that the strategy must be changed to avoid repeating Calles's mistake. When he abandoned the crusade, he effectively settled for a parallel ideological system and church leaders were now anxious for a compromise.[12]

The church emerged from this conflict disoriented and disorganized. The same church that first gave the country a sense of national identity and purpose retained little of its original self-confidence. Although the church made considerable material and organizational progress during the 1940s and 1950s, religious leaders of those decades had little in common with the confident and critical religious leaders of the Social Congresses (1903–10) and the National Catholic Labor Confederation, which had hundreds of member unions throughout the country in the 1920s. Yet the church's success in the social and labor fields in earlier decades had produced the subsequent conflicts with Calles and Cárdenas. The intensity of the ideological conflict may help explain why church organizations such as Catholic Action (1929) consisted of artificial and isolating social structures, isolating Catholics (especially youth) from society.[13] The government, too, engaged in selective but counterproductive violence, eliminating most of the surviving leadership of the rebellion in the hope of destroying any future political opposition.

Today, while most Mexicans continue to be loyal to their particular expressions of religion, the church has done little to relate the transforming forces of society to the religious values held by the majority of Mexicans. However, there are indications that religious transformations, still isolated and uneven, may eventually force an open and comprehensive debate over the issue of religious values and their role in Mexico's development. There are substantial changes in religious practices in individual parishes, some dioceses, and in most religious orders. Occasional collective documents on social justice by the bishops are beginning to have a cumulative impact on the tone and content of religious reforms. There is also a strong movement described as "liberation theology" that is rethinking the role of religion in social change. This intellectual movement is gaining strength as its relationship to traditional Catholic doctrine on corporatism or solidarism becomes more explicit. The official revolutionary doctrine may best be understood as a civil religion, a concept developed by sociologists in the United States.[14] Mexico is significant for its attempt to replace traditional religion with a narrow and exclusive civil religion.

Civil Religion and the State

The 1910 Revolution was as controversial as any event in Mexican history. It is often described as a symbolic turning point in Mexican history: the end of an exclusively technical and closed elite and the beginning of a comprehensive system that includes more intellectuals, professionals, and artists than any regime since Independence. Nevertheless, many have noted the striking continuities and similarities between postrevolutionary and prerevolutionary governments. At the very least, the revolution has become a symbol for profound changes, some initiated before it and others that have remained only rhetoric.

Revolutionary elites have systematically and enthusiastically projected the revolution onto history as the normative symbol for comprehensive development and as the foundation of a new civil identity. The revolution was intended to replace the Spanish Conquest as the epic event that transcends regimes and ideologies. It is described as a concentration of energy capable of transforming all social and economic activity for the common good. The revolution is the Big Bang Theory of the Mexican social universe, proclaiming as it does the formation of the first new nation in Latin America. It was said about the uniqueness of Mexican religion: to no other nation have such favors been granted (Psalm 147). The secular state now makes similar claims for itself. It was said: "Mexicans belong to the Virgin of Guadalupe." PRI now insists that it belongs to the revolution.

These comparisons with religion are not accidental. These two faiths, the traditional and the revolutionary, both absorbed transcendent goals, utopian schemes, and sobering and intractable reality. Both were shaped by periods of violence. Both faiths began by attacking the traditional order and then found it an indispensable source of stability and continuity. Just as Guadalupe became the protectress of indigenous cultures and popular religion, so the revolution willy-nilly exalts the *indigenismo* in Mexican history through pre-Christian symbols and events.

The First Audiencia of New Spain was as crooked and oppressive as any subsequent Colonial government. The 1910 Revolution was also plagued by cynicism and reaction. In Mariano Azuela's novel about the Revolution, *The Underdogs,* Valderrama the poet says: "I love the Revolution like a volcano in eruption. . . . What do I care about the stones left above or below after the cataclysm? What are they to me?"[15] To transcend the violence and pervasive cynicism produced by the revolution, the revolutionaries established a surprisingly traditional political framework sustained by elaborate rituals drawn from the past. As religious groups challenged the new order and its leadership, revolutionary doctrines and symbols were expanded to include the following: (1) a constitution legalizing the social and economic goals of the revolution; (2) elections as a periodic ritual of common support for the revolutionary regime; and (3) a political party to organize, sustain, and define the rules of membership and the constitutive rituals. The party that emerged was more than a pragmatic association of mutual interests and goals but also considerably less than the doctrinaire vanguard party associated with Marxism.

The political party of the revolution is the principal instrument of political control that emerged from the revolution. The revolutionary elites consolidated their power through a party process that was first called the National Revolutionary Party by Calles, then renamed the Mexican Revolutionary Party by Cárdenas, and finally named the Institutional Revolutionary Party (PRI) by Alemán (1946–52). Each title symbolized a progressive development of the party, from a loose association of political associates and regional caciques (Calles) gradually including a broad umbrella of peasants, workers, and civil servants (Cárdenas), to its present position as the electoral arm of the privileged political families that monopolize power and name the president.[16]

Although PRI's organizational transformation has great significance for power and policymaking, the continuity of its symbolic role is also important for Mexico's political stability. PRI provides periodic electoral rituals and accompanying celebrations that maintain the loyalties of the political families called *camarillas*. No one can hope to become part of a *camarilla* without belonging to PRI. But belonging to PRI requires no more ideological conviction than baptism does for most Mexicans. The electoral act is efficacious as ritual, but not necessarily as an act of political choice. The restricted efficacy of elections is supplemented by the Constitution, a social and economic manifesto rather than a legal document. .

The Constitution provides the documents that give legitimacy to the system in terms of its social and economic goals. It does not define the form or substance of political power. Instead of interpreting the Constitution to apply to changing political forces, PRI bypasses, ignores, or changes it to avoid controversy. Although some articles have been repeatedly changed, such as those on education, practical political arrangements are usually determined by presidential decree without reference to the Constitution. This does not mean that it is inoperative; only that the Constitutional texts are as operative as the Bible for most Mexicans. While anticlerical laws are ignored and repeatedly violated by the clergy, the threat of enforcement is an important political instrument. In spite of such disuse or abuse, the Constitution represents a significant symbol of the secularization of the political process. Thus, when the archbishop of Mexico declared in 1926 that the church would ignore the 1917 Constitution, he triggered the Cristero rebellion. Today the hierarchy openly and repeatedly recognizes the legitimacy of this document, while political leaders are obliged to ignore it to survive.

An electoral campaign is held every six years and this, too, can be considered a ritual of national political integration. Even though most Mexicans do not vote and elections are openly rigged, the electoral campaign allows for a public celebration of continuity between the revolution and the official party.[17] Since elections do not allow for the organization and expression of an alternative government or set of policies, their significance can be explained in the context of the revolutionary mystique. Even the frequent protest of opposition parties over the rigging of elections and (in 1981) the arbitrary disqualification of previously legalized political parties, help to reinforce the façade of legality. Finally, elections require that politicians renew their contacts with the public, visit villages, and inaugurate public projects. This is especially important for the president-designate, for his visits throughout the country are a way of reassuring local politicians of the competence and determination of the new *camarilla* to wield power and represent their interests.

The most powerful symbol of the revolutionary ideology is the president, the supreme political father. One of the recognized accomplishments of the revolution was breaking the chain of personal power *(continuismo)* and the rotation of the highest leader. Recent research has done much to explain how power is obtained and exercised in Mexico, the capricious nature of succession, and the role of ritual and symbols.[18] Octavio Paz shows that the power of the Mexican presidency is different from that in any other Latin American country: it is more subdued, impersonal, and concentrated. Its exercise continues to resemble some aspects of Aztec priesthood and the office of viceroy. Although the president is scrupulously legal in public, his real power lies in his ability to circumvent the law; his legitimacy comes from his ability to distinguish between the ritual expressions of power and the shifting relations between groups, especially within his own *camarilla*.

All these revolutionary symbols and their highest expression in the presidency constitute the civil religion that stabilizes the political order and determines its relationship to the private sector and the church. It gives solidity to the pyramid of political power—but only because it parallels or integrates religious symbols.

The Role of Ideologies in Economic Development

Ideologies play an important but not dominant role in the policy process. They define the limits of bargaining, especially in times of stress or change, but do not necessarily determine procedures or outcomes under normal conditions. Under Calles, the social doctrine of the church was formally excluded from the bargaining process. Since Cárdenas, the militant advocates of an exclusive civil religion have been restricted to the role of a pressure group among others within the bureaucracy. Although Mexico has been described as unique in its ability to include a wide range of diverse ideological positions within the formal political structure, the primary goal of the ruling elites—according to a recent study of the relationship between state and society—is the separation of the major ideological groups from their social bases.[19] The government uses its revolutionary goals, through the dominant party and the military, to sever political institutions from their popular roots, especially those of the opposition.

The major exception to this ideological cooptation is the church. Instead of isolating the church from its social base, the government excludes it from the formal bargaining process. Under such an arrangement, religious leaders are forced to look for more effective ways of relating religious values and loyalties to the society around them. This alone would have produced changes in the church. However, since the Second Vatican Council, theologians and pastors have given special priority to developing traditional religious values among the urban and rural poor. The new approach to ministry was defined as the determinative objective of social ministry at the Puebla Conference of Latin American Bishops in 1979 in the numerous passages emphasizing a "preferential option for the poor" and calling for solidarity with and commitment to the poor.[20]

Such doctrinal developments in the church are likely to encourage the government to continue excluding religious leaders from any formal bargaining. Political leaders will continue to insist on the right to discipline religious leaders who enter the public arena openly to influence the policy process. However, the ideological context for bargaining over public policy continues to be civil religion. This civil framework formally excludes bargaining with groups that are not a part of the official party and will continue to give priority to maintaining the existing alliance over any other goal. Tensions between traditional religious leaders will challenge the existing limits of public bargaining in the future. Clarifications and modifications of the bargaining process are necessary. Growing rural violence, especially in the South, and the political transformation of the Mexican church, will make such clarifications inevitable. One of the problems facing the effectiveness of civil religion is that the structures of government and society have reestablished the myth of government as an open arena for corrupt, self-serving politicians. They have also reinforced the widespread passivity and submissiveness that accompanies authoritarianism and paternalism.[21]

The renewal of the church's social doctrine is based on the classical doctrine of state and society that has distinguished Catholic documents since the Middle Ages. These doctrines and related social values are based on the solidarity of all citizens according to their functional association (religious, professional, economic), and adapted to the changing industrial and social conditions that began in the nineteenth century. The renewed social doctrine of the church is also related to the classical doctrine of dualism, considered essential for a humanistic and constructive relationship between individual and society.

Church doctrine considers the dualistic theory of the secular and the sacred, as formulated by Augustine, to be normative for any understanding of religion and society. Augustine's theory of dualism was subsequently refined by Aquinas by superimposing the concept of the active (or public) life onto the Augustinian vision of the City of Man and the contemplative (or private) life onto the City of God. Public life in Catholic countries was secularized and the chasm between the private and public sectors became almost unbridgeable. Specific activities such as religious ritual and family life were exclusively restricted to the private sector, and other activities such as business, defense, and governmental processes, limited to the public arena, were supposedly outside of religious attention. Ideally, religious activities in this system would have to be privatized and public life secularized. In an extreme example of this dualistic doctrine, the moral limits to any public policies would be very tenuous. Some consider Mexico to be such an example.

The moral basis of public life and the ethics of social and economic policies have been a constant preoccupation of reformers since the Colonial era. Aquinas and Suárez (who subsequently adapted the theories of Aquinas to Spain) are considered normative moralists for Catholic social doctrine and pioneers of the ethical tradition of the church. Both theologians considered the common good of society to be the highest moral obligation of the state and the individual.[22] The progressive social and economic experiments initiated by the early missionaries in Colonial Mexico, men like Bartolomé de las Casas and Vasco de Quiroga, and the progressive social and economic doctrines of Jesuit reformers in the eighteenth century (later dramatized by Hidalgo) are rooted in the same moral climate that was condemned as corrupt and contemptible by radicals of the nineteenth and twentieth centuries.[23]

Tensions in Mexican society between the religious tradition and secular ideologies spring from differing concepts of the equitable development of society and economy. Some religious reformers in Mexico believe the church can make a contribution to the moral debate over public policy. They challenge the popular interpretation of the distinction between public and private activity as it is now applied. They reject secular or religious philosophies that exclude religious values from public life or reduce public authority to an instrument of class conflict or to the domination of one class over the other. This same doctrine has also provided the rationale for the criticism of authoritarianism and false paternalism. Most of these efforts at renewing the social tradition of the church have been made in the name of liberation theology. This theology is based on the social teachings of the Second Vatican Council as elaborated within the Latin American context by the Latin American bishops at Medellín, Colombia in 1968 and Puebla, Mexico in 1979.[24]

Instead of the classical vocabulary of active life for the public sector and contemplative life for the private sector, one interpretation of liberation theology replaces the active and contemplative with their modern equivalents: solidarity and liberation.[25] These modern terms define the relationship between the individual and the commonweal as did the concepts of action and contemplation for preindustrial society. Solidarity replaces the concept of hierarchy as the principle of overall organization, with the highest order of solidarity reserved for the common good of all.

While some liberation theologians have limited their vocabulary to one school or other of Marxist analysis, the thrust of liberation theology comes from the more comprehensive and radical tradition within the church. Liberation, the complementary concept, directs all groups toward the development of society. Liberation is a specific application of the more traditional concept of action. Action, in a society of repressive economic structures, must be specified in terms of the overall transformation of society. Liberation ensures that solidarity not become another form of passivity, another justification for class or ideological repression. The new theologians insist that no attempt to renew the religious values at the core of the individual identity can succeed without a corresponding transformation of social structures, the state being the highest but not absolute expression of such transformation.

The projection of Catholic social doctrine through the doctrines of solidarity and liberation has affected the Mexican church on all levels. Some insist that the church must reform *itself* before trying to reform society. However, the most liberal tradition of church theology has always insisted that the church understands itself and makes its religious message intelligible only by projecting it into history, by reflecting it off the structures and institutions that determine human behavior.

Within this perspective, it has been suggested by economists Charles Wilber and Kenneth Jameson that organized religion is likely to play an increasingly important role in redefining the moral basis of economic development.[26] They suggest four areas of interaction between organized religion and development, which have special application to the Mexican case: (1) individual decision makers and their characters; (2) modification or replacement of the dominant theories of development; (3) legitimation of a positive process of development; (4) provision of resources and ideas favorable to development within the transnational church.

All four areas of interaction must be qualified for the Mexican case in light of its distinct religious history. The most promising category for the influence of religion on development in Mexico is that of the church as a renewed actor in support of development. In spite of a divided hierarchy and weak national organization, individual bishops and local church communities have organized to strengthen community organizations for self-help projects; to train leaders for various programs of human development; and relate traditional religious categories such as sacraments, fiestas, pilgrimages, and salvation to concrete categories of community organization. The most dramatic expression of this transformation of religious categories is found in several dioceses of the Southwest where the training of clergy and lay leaders requires an extended period of living with the villagers and sharing in their lives and community organizations.

The second area of interaction between religion and development comes from the internationalization of the Mexican church. The past isolation of

Mexican Catholicism has been transformed by changes in society and the economy. The strengthening of the transnational character of the Catholic Church has forced the Mexican church into the debates and reforms of the rest of the Third World. Population shifts within Mexico and from Mexico to the United States have forced the Mexican hierarchy into the arena of social, economic, and political issues as they affect church organization.

Within the area of individual decision makers, the Mexican church is limited by legal and organizational realities to a specific sector of the business world where it has private schools, and to its parish structures, where some limited resources exist for training community leaders. The Mexican church has not renewed its parish structures and school system except on a limited basis. The final area of possible interaction between the church and development is that of opposing or undermining the forces of modernization and change. This has been the path followed in the past with destructive consequences for both the church and society. Furthermore, any form of organized resistance that would distinguish the church as a pressure group or identify it with a political party would cause a renewal of political repression against church members. In the Mexican context, whenever religious leaders translate organized church loyalties into instruments of political pressure or opposition, it produces a high level of ideological polarization within society.

The controversy over the role of religion in the economic development of Mexico is historically more complex and precariously balanced than in other Catholic countries. The religious problem raises unique institutional issues but also presents interesting developmental challenges. Changes have been introduced into the church and in society that suggest a more positive developmental role for religion than at any time since Independence. Given the renewed vitality of organized religion, it is unlikely that any program of economic development will succeed unless it taps the moral base of Mexican identity. For the government to play such a constructive developmental role, it must establish a more comfortable relationship with its own secular values of social change and radical equality.

Notes

1. For an interesting discussion of official government reactions to progressive church documents see George Getschow, "Mexico's Old Rivalry of Church and State . . . ," *Wall Street Journal* (21 July 1981): 1, 16.
2. For an important interpretation of Mexico's "esoteric democracy" see K.F. Johnson, *Mexican Democracy: A Critical View* (New York, 1978).
3. A critical academic perspective can be found in J.A. Hellman, *Mexico in Crisis* (New York, 1978), pp. 177–80. For a popular interpretation emphasizing instability, see Gene Lyons, "Inside the Volcano," *Harper's* (June 1977). For a

pessimistic view of a member of the Catholic hierarchy, see the interview with Bishop Arturo Lona of Tehuantepec (State of Oaxaca) in *Proceso* (6 April 1981).

4. For useful analyses of the religious problem see Jesús García G., *Acción anticatólica en Méjico* (Mexico City, 1939); Martín Quirarte, *El problema religioso en México* (Mexico City, 1967).

5. See J. Lloyd Mecham, *Church and State in Latin America* (Chapel Hill: University of North Carolina Press, 1966), pp. 340–79; David Brading, *Los orígenes del nacionalismo mexicano* (Mexico City: ERA, 1980), pp. 97–138.

6. *Ensayo político sobre el reino de la Nueva España*, p. 22. Quoted in Thomas Sanders, "Education, Culture, and Values in Mexico: The Colonial Period," *American University's Field-Staff Reports* (April 1977): 15.

7. T.F. Fehrenbach, *Fire and Blood* (New York, 1973), p. 91.

8. Lesley Byrd Simpson, *Many Mexicos* (Berkeley, 1974, 4th ed. paper), p. 91.

9. Two examples of the seriousness and continuity of the ideological debate can be seen from the writings of Donoso Cortés, one of the earliest philosophers of the modern interpretation of "solidarism," and Vicente Rocafuerte who defended the reconciliation of Catholicism and liberalism. They both wrote in the first decades of the nineteenth century.

10. A consensus on the causes and effects of the Cristero rebellion can be found in Jean Meyer, *The Cristero Rebellion* (Cambridge: Cambridge University Press, 1976); David Bailey, *Viva Cristo Rey!* (Austin: University of Texas Press, 1974).

11. Meyer, p. 44.

12. Sister Maria Ann Kelly, C.S.J., "Mexican Catholics and Socialist Education of the 1930's. In Lyle C. Brown and W.F. Cooper (eds.), *Religion in Latin american Life and Literature* (Waco, Tex., 1980), pp. 135–88.

13. Ivan Vallier, *Catholicism, Social Control, and Modernization in Latin America* (Englewood Cliffs, N.J.: Prentice-Hall, 1970) 1970), p. 129.

14. Russell E. Richey and D.G. Jones, *American Civil Religion* (New York, 1974). The idea of applying the concept of civil religion to Mexico comes from K.M. Coleman and Charles L. Davis, "Civil and Conventional Religion in Secular Authoritarian Regimes: The Case of Mexico," *Studies in Comparative International Development* (Summer 1978): 57–76.

15. Mariano Azuela, *The Underdogs* (New York: New American Library/Signet Paperback, 1962), p. 136.

16. Johnson, p. 77.

17. Paul H. Lewis, *The Governments of Argentina, Brazil, and Mexico* (New York: Crowell, 1975), p. 162.

18. An excellent discussion of the Mexican presidency can be found in K.F. Johnson, "Mexico's Authoritarian Presidency." In T.V. DiBacco (ed.), *Presidential Power in Latin American Politics* (New York: Praeger, 1977).

19. S.D. Purcell and J.S.H. Purcell, "State and Society in Mexico: Must a Stable Polity Be Institutionalized?" *World Politics* (January 1980): 194–227.

20. John Eagleson and Philip Scharper (eds.), *Puebla and Beyond* (Maryknoll, N.Y.: Orbis, 1979), pp. 265–67.

21. For a comprehensive review of political culture and pathologies in Mexico see Ann Craig and Wayne Cornelius, "Political Culture in Mexico." In Almond and Verba (eds.), *The Civic Culture Revisited* (Boston: Little, Brown, 1980).

22. For a survey of classical Catholic doctrine on the state, see Henrich A. Rommen, *The State in Catholic Thought* (St. Louis: Herder, 1945).
23. For a revisionist perspective on the role of development in Mexican history see Enrique González Pedrero, *La riqueza de la pobreza* (México, 1979). González Pedrero is a former senator and secretary general of PRI who presents Vasco de Quiroga as a great civilizer of Mexico. See also Victor Turner, "Hidalgo: History as Social Drama." In *Dramas, Fields, and Metaphors* (Ithaca: Cornell University Press, 1974).
24. Dennis P. McCann, *Christian Realism and Liberation Theology* (Maryknoll, N.Y.: Orbis, 1981), pp. 131–55. See also Encuentro Latinoamericano de Teología, *Liberación y cautiverio* (Mexico City: n.p., 1975), pp. 17–234.
25. Jon Sobrino, "The Significance of Puebla for the Catholic Church in Latin America." In *Eagleson and Scharper.*
26. Charles K. Wilber and Kenneth P. Jameson, "Religious Values and Social Limits to Development," *World Development* (July-August 1980): 467–80.

Selected Readings

General Church History

Cuevas, M. *Historia de la iglesia en México,* 5 vols. (El Paso, Tex.: Revista Católica, 1928)

Mecham, J. Lloyd. *Church and State in Latin America* (Chapel Hill: University of North Carolina Press, 1966), chs. 15,16.

Murray, Paul V. *The Catholic Church in Mexico* (Mexico City: EPM, 1965).

Schlarman, J.H. *Mexico: A Land of Volcanoes* (Milwaukee: Bruce, 1950).

Specialized Topics

Bailey, David C. *Viva Cristo Rey! The Cristero Rebellion and the Church-State Conflict in Mexico* (Austin: University of Texas Press, 1974).

Bazant, Jan. *Alienation of Church Wealth in Mexico: Social and Economic Aspects of the Liberal Revolution, 1856–1875* (Cambridge: Cambridge University Press, 1971).

Costeloe, Michael P. *Church and State in Independent Mexico* (London: Royal Historical Society, 1978).

Lafaye, Jacques. *Quetzalcóatl and Guadalupe: The Formation of Mexican National Consciousness, 1531–1813* (Chicago: University of Chicago Press, 1976).

Meyer, Jean A. *The Cristero Rebellion: The Mexican People between Church and State, 1926–1929* (Cambridge: Cambridge University Press, 1976).

Ricard, Robert. *The Spiritual Conquest of Mexico* (Berkeley: University of California Press, 1966).

Schmitt, Karl M. "Catholic Adjustment to the Secular State: The Case of Mexico, 1867–1911." In *Catholic Historical Review* 48 (July 1962): 182–204.

———. "The Mexican Positivists and the Church-State Question, 1876–1911." In *Journal of Church and State* 7 (Spring 1966):200–13.

The Contemporary Mexican Church

González-Ramírez, Manuel R. *La iglesia mexicana en cifras* (Mexico City: CIAS, 1969).
Informes de Pro Mundi Vita. "La Iglesia en México," no. 15 (Brussels: Pro Mundi Vita, 1979).
Pomerleau, Claude. "The Changing Church in Mexico and Its Challenge to the State," *Review of Politics* 43 (October 1981).
Wayland-Smith, Giles. "The Catholic Church and Social Change: A Research Note and Some Preliminary Findings on the Archdiocese of Yucatan" (Institute of Latin American Studies of Northwestern Pennsylvania, 1977).

Part Four

JAPAN

Introductory Essay

Traditional suppositions about economic development have assumed that there is only one path to achievement in this area, one modeled on the industrial experience and sociocultural ethos of Western nations. Empirical support for this belief is rooted in the historic fact that economic modernization and industrial society have originated in and largely been confined to Western Europe and North America. Consequently, economic modernization has long been associated with the process loosely called "Westernization."

Japan challenges this notion. It is the only non-Western society to develop a major industrial economy and it has done so within a cultural framework markedly different from that of the pioneering industrial countries of the North Atlantic. In sustaining an extraordinary period of modernization and growth for over twenty-five years, Japan has consistently maintained low rates of unemployment and inflation, and a high level of social stability. It is unique in having been able to transform a rural-agricultural society into an urban-industrial one while lowering crime rates at the same time.

From ranking among the poorest and most devastated nations in the late 1940s, Japan is now about to replace the Soviet Union as the second largest economy in the world. Projections suggest that it may well overtake the United States as the global economic leader within the next decade. Japan's GNP as a percentage of U.S. GNP, estimated in current dollars, has grown from 4 percent in 1950, to 8 percent in 1960, to 20 percent in 1970, reaching 50 percent in 1980.

Behind this performance are two little-realized facts which are important in understanding modern Japan. First, Japanese modernization began around 1868 and has a longer history than is generally perceived. Second, the period to which most study has been given, the past three decades, represents the second wave of Japanese industrialization. By the 1930s, Japanese economic power had developed sufficiently to support a modern, technically oriented war for many years. After this came catastrophic destruction, but the basic skills and aptitudes for industrial growth had long been established and proven.

Whatever the historical experience, Japan's record has been and continues to be enacted in an inhospitable geographic environment—Japan's level area is approximately equal to that of California, it has very few natural resources, and a high population density. Any explanation for its achievements must be sought in its human resources and cultural environment. Recognizing this, a large volume of recent scholarship has focused on Japanese policymaking and policy, management systems, and the character of economic culture.

There has been less attention on the *evolution* of the economic culture, particularly the relationship between the heritage of religious tradition and contemporary economic expansion. In an effort to balance perspectives, two scholars of Japan examine this connection and interaction in the following chapters. Both Koichi Shinohara and Ron Napier begin with the premise that the modern industrial corporation, vigorously encouraged by government supports, has been the engine of Japanese economic development. Both believe that a critical element in Japan's aggregate success has been the way in which Japanese society has organized and managed inheritance —Napier highlights structural inheritance and Shinohara discusses religio-familial inheritance.

Napier warns that we should not confuse modern Japan with all of Japan. "Our" Japan is only a highly successful and visible part of a larger whole. Modern Japan employs 30 percent of the labor force and embraces a system combining lifetime employment and advancement through seniority with generous financial and social rewards. This sector, highly favored by public policy, is linked to and in many ways rests upon the "other" Japan—the more traditional and less favored sector of subcontractors, undercapitalized small industries, and poorly compensated workers. Napier shows how these cultures reinforce each other and often generate a group-oriented ethic in the three areas most important to the Japanese (family, education, and workplace).

The modern sector which has largely produced the dramatic performance of Japan is of recent origin and its special features (e.g. lifetime employment, consensus decision making, seniority, regular bonus payments) are not more than two or three generations old. As this part of the Japanese economy continues to outperform the industrial West, it is startling to realize that most of these special features which contribute to Japanese excellence are regarded as work disincentives in other societies. Whether this structural inheritance, now so closely fused into Japan's economic culture, is a byproduct of a special period of economic success or will endure in hard times is examined by Napier. The current global recession, he concludes, may leave permanent scars on the industrial face of Japan.

Shinohara presents a more vertical explanation for the economic order, efficiency, and adaptability of modern Japan. The traditional streams of Japanese religion—Shinto, Buddhist, Confucian—formed an eclectic and overlapping belief system which began to crystallize about two centuries ago into the concept of *ie*. This interlacing of consanguineous and economic lineage evolved a group consciousness, with each *ie* serving as a focal organism around which religious, social, and economic interests clustered. The *ie* evolved into a kind of religiously sanctioned unit, a surrogate "religion" with responsibilities to members of the group—a very Japanese form of extended family.

The organization of *ie* was legally acknowledged as a basic social organization in 1898. The privileges of the head of the *ie* family were given official status in the code of civil law and the practice of *ie* succession was legally defined. At the end of World War II, however, new laws did not recognize the institution of *ie*. While *ie* has lost its legal status and continues to decline as a social form, Shinohara sees its ideological inheritance infusing and energizing modern Japanese economic development.

It is no coincidence, Shinohara implies, that Japan's modernization and economic growth began when the beliefs and structure of *ie* became institutionalized about one hundred years ago. *Ie* may have faded recently, but its spirit endures in the Japanese corporation. This spirit creates a sense of diligence, discipline, group consultation, and support, which has blended well with modern industrial values. The *ie* system, although conservative in theme, also allowed for a certain flexibility. For example, the removal of leaders who were inadequate or irresponsible—they were displaced, but not disgraced. The *ie* group accommodated new members when it needed renewal and frequently spun off subsidiary *ie* units. A major wellspring of modern Japanese economic growth, claims Shinohara, lies in this concept which is so fundamentally different from any developed by other industrial societies. The lesson here is encouraging for non-Western nations. The Japanese experience validates the proposition that there are many paths to successful economic development, and suggests that local cultural and spiritual ideas may even enhance this process.

In time, it is possible that the popular American perception of Japan as an ally may turn into that of Japan as an adversary. Resentment at market penetration, at the consequent unemployment created, at lack of trade reciprocity, could make many Americans unhappy with Japanese economic action. Reading Napier and Shinohara reminds us of the potential for this discord as two nations with similar economic goals compete against each other. Understanding the content of Japanese economic culture and the shadings it gives to policy may be one way in which such friction could be anticipated and reduced.

J.F.

7

Religion and Economic Development in Japan: An Exploration Focusing on the Institution of *Ie*

Koichi Shinohara

The question of the relationship between religion and economic development in Japan has often been raised in terms of Max Weber's thesis concerning the origin of the "spirit" of capitalism in the West.[1] The discussion has been rather unproductive so far because we do not yet possess an analysis that clarifies this relationship systematically and provides us with helpful conceptual tools for further exploration. The difficulty may be partly due to certain basic characteristics of the Japanese religious tradition. Although it is customary to conceive of Japanese religion in terms of separate traditions such as Shinto, Buddhism, and Confucianism, it may be more appropriate to analyze it as one coherent whole that works according to one set of dynamic principles. This is not to deny the diversity and inner tensions in Japanese religion; rather, it would enable us to focus upon the underlying unity that defines the context within which the diversity and inner tensions take shape.

To take an approach that focuses on this unity means that one cannot discuss the relationship between religion and economic development in Japan simply by examining the explicit economic attitudes of Shinto, Japanese Buddhism, and Japanese Confucianism as separate developments. We must first articulate their common underlying principles and then proceed to explore their economic implications. Our first challenge is to secure a conceptual framework appropriate for carrying out an exploration of these principles and their various economic implications.

I propose to examine the uniquely Japanese institution of *ie* or family as a first step toward building such a conceptual framework. Following a brief sketch of the distinctive features and history of this institution I will proceed to examine the religious character of the institution; here the close interrelationship among the indigenous (Shinto), Buddhist, and Confucian elements in Japanese religion will be illustrated. I will also focus on the merchant *ie* within this context. I will then discuss the significance of the concept and institution of *ie* in the modernization of Japan. This sequence of analysis should provide a useful context for our further discussion of religion and economic development in Japan.

The Institution of *ie*

The Japanese word *ie* is usually translated as "family." However, there are several unusual characteristics qualifying this institution in Japan which sometimes make this translation misleading.[2] *Ie* is best understood as the basic unit of communal life and consists of all those who live under one roof and eat meals prepared in the same kitchen. In theory, then, *ie* constitutes the indivisible unit of economic life. All members participate in the productive activities of the *ie* and are supported by the one common, pooled income of the *ie*. This sharing of communal life appears to be more fundamental than the blood relationship among its members for the constitution of *ie*. For example, the common practice of adopting a son *(yōshi)* for the purpose of continuing the lineage of *ie* reflects this preference and so does the fact that a married woman becomes a member of the *ie* of her husband and loses her status in her family of birth almost completely. Nakane reports that if a husband of a Japanese woman dies when she is still young and their children are small, she is much more likely to raise the children by herself than to go back to the *ie* of birth and raise the children with its help. Women in other societies (e.g. India) are more likely to choose the latter course.[3]

The *ie* is an institution that continues over generations. A new lineage of the *ie* begins when a male member other than the one who is designated as the successor of the main *ie* (honke) is allowed to establish a branch *ie* *(bunke)*. The institution disappears when the head of the *ie* dies without a successor. Relative deemphasis on the biological relationship and emphasis on the lineage of the *ie* seems contradictory. Certain unusual characteristics of the institution of *ie* come to the fore in light of this particular tension:

All power in the *ie* is concentrated in the figure of the head of the *ie* *(kachō)* who controls the property that belongs to it. Again, his power is not based on his biological relationship to other members of the *ie*. When the head of the *ie* retires and passes the position on to his successor (usually his oldest son), his power and prestige in the *ie* decline dramatically.

The second important figure in the *ie* is the successor. There can be only one successor and the property of the *ie* is handed over virtually undivided. When there is more than one son to the head of the *ie*, only one of them is chosen as the successor. Others are either given away as an adopted son *(yōshi)* to other families or, when the *ie* is in good economic condition, are allowed to establish a new branch, or most frequently they continue to live in the main *ie* in a status not significantly different from that of its employees. When a son is allowed to branch out, he is given a small portion of the property of the main *ie*, but it is made certain that this will not deplete the property of the main *ie* in any serious way. The primary concern is to preserve the lineage of the main *ie*. When there is no son to the head of the *ie*, a male member of another *ie* is adopted as *yōshi* and becomes the successor.

The general history of the institution of *ie* is unclear in many ways. As an institution among common people *(shomin)*, it is difficult to trace back beyond the early Tokugawa period. Nakane observes that ancestral tablets *(ihai)* in ordinary, peasant *ie* do not go back beyond the Kyōhō period (early eighteenth century); she concludes from this that the clearly defined conception of *ie*, closely associated with ancestor worship, emerged during the mid-Tokugawa period among ordinary peasants.[4] Historians point out that *kenchi*, the registration of cultivated field and peasants,[5] and *shūmon aratamechō*, the registration of the *ie* and their members at Buddhist temples, contributed to the emergence of a clearer conception of the *ie*.[6] The latter practice was adopted during the early Tokugawa period as a measure designed to ensure the extermination of Christianity in Japan.

Nakane observes that the institution of *ie* reached the peak of its influence toward the end of the Tokugawa period (1912–25) and collapsed after World War II.[7] The demise of the *ie* was largely caused by economic changes. The strong status of the head of the *ie* is based on his control over its property and income that derives from it. When members of the *ie* began to draw income in the form of a salary from outside bodies, the power of the head of the *ie* was fundamentally undermined and the institution declined.[8]

Certain changes in the place of the *ie* in Japanese society since the Meiji Restoration of 1868 were reflected in legislation. Whereas the use of family name *(sei)* was originally regarded as a privilege and generally limited to the samurai class during the Tokugawa period, the new government made its use mandatory within five years after it came into power. The civil code put into practice in 1898 gave official legal status to the institution of *ie*. The privileges of the head of the *ie* were recognized and the practice of the succession of the *ie* was legally defined. This code remained in force until the end of World War II. The civil code introduced in 1956 does not recognize the legal status of the institution of *ie.* The only compromise was the insertion of a provision that guarantees the inheritance of the genealogical table, ritual instruments, and grave site by the person who takes charge of ancestral ceremonies.[9]

The *ie* and the Japanese Religious Tradition

The religious significance of the institution of *ie* is most clearly visible in the cultic practices involving worship of the ancestor. Japanese students of folklore *(minzokugaku),* who studied these practices extensively, worked under the hypothesis that the ancestral spirit *(kami)* of the *ie* is in fact identical with the agricultural spirit *(kami)* of the field *(ta no kami).*[10] Every year this agricultural spirit comes down from the mountain *(yama no kami)* in the spring to enter the field, and in the fall returns to the mountain. For example, ceremonial practices associated with the New Year and Bon festivals, both involving *ie* as the basic unit of celebration, are interpreted as the reception and returning of the ancestral/agricultural *kami.* The underlying idea is that the ancestral/agricultural *kami* protects the *ie* and secures prosperity for it.

More generally, the seasonal cycle identified in this analysis also constitutes the background of the cultic organization of traditional Japanese villages. Japanese festivals are associated with specific shrines and participation is limited to those who belong to clearly defined circles consisting of a number of *ie.* These circles are often identical with *dōzoku* groups. Thus a circle would include the *ie* of the main lineage *(honke)* and the branch lineages *(bunke).*

The cultic organization of a Japanese village is normally very complex, and it is difficult to reconstruct historically the development of different circles. It is appropriate nevertheless to note a few general implications. The *ie* is the basic unit of organization. Individuals participate in the festival as members of their *ie.* Often the *kami* for whom the ritual celebration is performed is not explicitly identified. Or, in many cases, the identification is late and secondary. But the definition of the circle of participants in terms of membership in *ie* strongly suggests that it is in fact the more ancient, ancestral spirit for whom the ritual is performed. The mythological world view based on the identity of the ancestral *kami* and the agricultural *kami* also lies behind these festivals.

The Bon festival, described above as a festival of sending the ancestral *kami* back to the mountain, is celebrated as a Buddhist festival. Folklore scholars interpret the Bon festival as an example of the process whereby an indigenous practice acquires the superficial appearance of Buddhism. The process may still be partially traced in the evolution of the ancestral altar into *Butsudan* (Buddhist altar).[11]

Funerals and services in memory of deceased ancestors were traditionally performed by Buddhist priests. This gave rise to the Buddhist cult of ancestor worship. The Tokugawa policy of *shūmon aratamechō* required the *ie* to be registered at and affiliated with a Buddhist temple. This meant that in addition to the organization of the *ie* into circles that participated in indigenous festivals at local shrines, a separate set of Buddhist circles of *ie* developed, consisting of those which supported each Buddhist temple. Here again we observe the basic priciple that individuals were linked to Buddhist temples as members of their *ie*.

The institution of *ie* also played an important role in the development of Japanese ethical teachings. Confucian teachings of filial piety *(hsiao* or *ko)* and loyalty *(chung* or *chu)* were appropriated in Japan largely within the institutional framework of *ie*. *Bushido,* the warrior ethic of the samurai class, may be characterized as an extreme form of the ethic of *ie*.[12]

Regarding economic implications, I will examine more closely the *ie* ethic of the merchant class. The *kakun* or family instructions left by heads of major merchant houses *(ie)* for future generations can be used as the main source for exploring the merchant ethic.[13]

Merchant houses of the Tokugawa period trained their employees in the following manner. First, young boys about ten years of age were hired as *decchi.* These boys were sometimes children of relatives or of other merchant families but more often they were recruited from rural areas. As *decchi,* they performed miscellaneous errands, and were also expected to learn reading, writing, and arithmetic as well as the elements of their business. After ten years in the status of *decchi,* these young employees were promoted to the status of *tedai* and worked for another ten years as full-fledged members of the store. Once the ten-year service as *tedai* was completed, the employees were recognized as fully qualified merchants and either became *bantō* at the main store or were given the necessary capital to open their own branch stores outside.

Reference to the *ie* is found extensively in the family instructions of merchant houses. The business is understood as a property of the *ie,* that is, something that must be continued through generations. Its foundation was laid by ancestors through extraordinary efforts, and it is a moral duty for later generations, especially for succeeding heads of the *ie,* to preserve and pass it on in good condition to future generations. One interesting text teaches that one should realize that the spirit of the ancestor is present at all times and advises that one should consider oneself as a *tedai* of the ancestor.[14] Confucian moral concepts such as filial piety[15] and loyalty[16] are introduced to describe the appropriate attitudes toward earlier generations and the head of the *ie*. All those who work for the business are instructed to work in harmony with each other.[17] This point is often made through metaphor. For example, it is pointed out that an isolated tree is easily broken (by a strong wind), while trees in a forest are not.[18] Similarly, one arrow is easy to break but several arrows bundled together are not.[19]

Emphasis on the preservation of the work of earlier generations resulted in a degree of traditionalism.[20] One also finds in these documents characteristics pointing to a significant level of economic rationalism, particularly because of the precarious nature of the economic foundation grounding merchant houses. While the samurai's *ie* can rely on a fixed income and the farmer's *ie* can rely on the harvest of the land, the merchant's *ie* depends on the small profit that arises in commercial exchange. This means that one must be shrewd and work diligently. Incompetence and luxury on the part of the head of the *ie* is bound to lead to ruinous consequences. So one finds the explicit instruction that if a successor to the head of the *ie* happens to be incompetent or undisciplined, he should be replaced regardless of his standing in terms of blood relationships.[21] Here ethical and economic considerations clearly supersede the traditionalistic considerations based on kinship ties.

In describing the "spirit" of capitalism, Max Weber distinguished the smaller capitalist enterprises of city dwellers from the large-scale, politically oriented state capitalism. He identified economic rationalism in the former. Despite the fact that successful Japanese merchants were regularly forced to provide loans to feudal powers, instructions and similar literature often warn against the dangers involved in large-scale transactions involving feudal powers *(daimyō)*.[22] The ideal is that of a merchant who works hard,[23] avoids luxury,[24] values honesty,[25] and acknowledges the importance of small customers.[26] A passage from a contemporary writer, Saikaki, summarizes this attitude in a humorous vein:

> Five portions of rising early in the morning, twenty portions of the business of the *ie*, eight portions of working late at night, seven portions of thrift, ten portions of good health—if one grinds these fifty portions into fine powder, carefully mixes them without making a mistake in measuring the amount, and takes it regularly both in the morning and in the evening, then one will surely become a man of great wealth. However, for this medicine to take effect, it is important that one avoid the following poisons: indulgence in good food, sexual licentiousness, wearing silk as everyday clothes; allowing one's wife to go around in vehicles and daughters to be addicted to *koto* harp and *karuta* game; allowing sons to become crazy about musical instruments; to be absorbed in [such aristocratic pastimes as] *kemari* game, *yōkyu* game, incense ceremony, *renku* poetry; renovation of the house, the love of tea ceremony, going out to enjoy cherry blossoms, boating, taking a bath in the middle of the day; going out in the evening to seek pleasure, gambling, *sugoroku* game;

for a merchant to learn swordsmanship; pilgrimage to shrines and temples, religious faith based on concerns over next life; mediating conflicts, becoming a guarantor [of loans]; campaigning for permission to open a new rice field, taking part in exploratory mining; drinking sake at meal time, addiction to tobacco, going to the capital city when there is no business to take care of there; becoming a sponsor for the sumo wrestling to raise funds for shrines and temples, becoming the organizer of a fund-raising campaign for a shrine or temple; manual work that is not related to the business of the *ie*, gold trimmings on the sword; associating with actors, becoming known at a geisha house; loans with interests higher than 9.6%.[27]

We find here both a considerable unwillingness to participate in new economic ventures and a distinctly "this-worldly" form of asceticism.

Ie and Modernization

The institution of *ie* influenced Japanese modernization in many fundamental ways. I want to point out a few important instances of this influence.[28] The property of *ie* was passed on virtually undivided from the present head to his successor. The development of the *ie*-based *zaibatsu* would have been impossible otherwise.[29] But only those merchant houses of the Tokugawa period which were willing and able to take major risks in adjusting to the new situation became major forces in Japanese industry.

The institution of *ie* provided workers for Japanese industry. Workers in early Japanese industry were recruited in rural areas. Most of them were women[30] and during the 1890s the majority of these female workers commuted to their factories.[31] Their wages constituted a supplementary income to the agriculturally based economy of the *ie* and this meant that the wages could be kept low. It was only at the beginning of the twentieth century that dormitories for female textile workers were built. The pattern of recruiting young women and second and third sons as the main source of labor for Japanese industry appears to have been established around the same time.[32] Even workers who left their *ie* in rural areas on a more permanent basis, kept their primary tie with the *ie*. This meant that the responsibility for supporting these workers in cases of misfortune such as serious sickness remained with the heads of their *ie*.[33] Again, this resulted in cheaper labor. Kamishima Jiro emphasized the importance of these "single" workers in Japanese industrialization and coined the term *tanshinsha shakai* (society of single people) to characterize urban life in modern Japan.[34]

The attempt to give an *ie*-like character to business corporations *(kazokushugi, kigyō ikka)* emerged as a secondary response to the development of *tanshinsha shakai*. There was an effort to meet the unfulfilled need for the communal life of *ie* on the part of employees by creating a new *ie*

-like community at the working place so that the company became a quasi *ie*. The modern institution of the emperor system *(tennōsei)*, first spelled out in the Meiji Constitution (1898) and the Imperial Rescript on Education (1890), was an attempt to define the new political reality of Japan as a modern state by using the model of *ie*. In a similar manner, the family ideology *(kazokushugi)* of Japanese companies attempted to meet the new situation created by Japanese industrialization by organizing the workers into *ie*-like communities.

Two practices are often referred to as typical expressions of the *ie*-like character of Japanese companies: the pattern of lifetime employment and wage distribution based on seniority. These became established in the late 1920s.[35] The tendency to enter into more private spheres of employees' lives, that properly belong to the concerns of the *ie*, is stronger in larger, more progressive and modernized corporations.[36] The *ie*-like character of Japanese companies should not be interpreted merely as a residual influence of the tradition. This character is a reappropriation and reactivation of certain important elements of the tradition in a new context.[37]

In summary, we can advance the thesis that while the *ie* as the basic institutional framework of Japanese family broke down, all other Japanese groups and organizations acquired certain *ie*-like characteristics. Nakane Chie perceptively and persuasively analyzed the fundamental characteristics of modern Japanese society using the concept of vertical society *(tate-shakai)*, and her analysis clearly illustrates how characteristics closely associated with the institution of *ie* may still be identified in all Japanese groups today.[38] A brief review of some themes in Nakane's analysis may be useful here:

Large-scale Japanese institutions (e.g. business corporations, civil service bureaucracies, and universities) are constituted by a large number of small groups. These groups, which may be either formal or informal, are characterized by intensive and extensive contacts among their members. Nakane uses the term *frame* (an attempt to translate the Japanese word *ba,* location) to describe the context which binds the individuals into such a group. The important point is that it is not a commonly shared personal attribute or set of such attributes but rather an accidental context of close and continuing interaction that constitutes these groups. Emotion plays an important role in the interaction among members and the sense of group unity *(ittai-kan)* is highly valued.

The relationship among group members is governed by the commonly accepted linear rank order rather than the principle of functional differentiation. Every group member is familiar with all aspects of the group's activities, and the members freely take each other's places when that becomes necessary. The ranking is determined not by ability but by neutral criteria such as seniority. The system is strongly egalitarian. Although the position of the head of the group is secure and free from competition, his leadership is open to relatively uninhibited criticism and pressure from other group members. This leaves little room for strong leadership, and in part explains why Japanese society does not produce powerful leaders. This also means that the society does not rely on strong leaders and perhaps explains why Japanese society works well even when, as is frequently the case, the leaders may be rather incompetent.

As units that provide for all basic needs of members, these groups are not functionally differentiated among themselves. They are similar to each other and compete with each other. Competition in Japanese society takes place more typically among groups rather than individuals. The emphasis on rank order is also seen in the larger context of the organization of the institution as a whole. The institution is constituted as a pyramidal hierarchy of small groups. It can work very efficiently under certain circumstances because communication along vertical lines travels quickly from the top to the bottom and consensus is easier to achieve. But the horizontal relationship among groups on the same level can be a source of difficulty. Factionalism between groups is rampant in Japanese society. Japanese society can be better understood in terms of the dynamics of the interaction among groups than in terms of universally applicable norms.

This analysis indicates that the patterns of behavior characterizing the traditional institution of *ie* continue to shape the behavior of Japanese people today. The *ie* as an institution has declined and dominant institutions in contemporary Japanese society are organized formally in terms of very different principles. It is still the case, though, that the manner in which Japanese people today relate to larger social contexts through their membership in smaller groups resembles their traditional *ie*-oriented behavior. Larger social units come to be organized not as bodies constituted by individuals with specific qualifications and rights but as a network of smaller groups.

Concluding Comments

Max Weber maintained that "ethical and ascetic Protestantism established the superior community of faith and a common ethical way of life in opposition to the community of blood, even to a large extent in opposition to the family."[39] He argued further that "from the economic point of view, it [the establishment of the community of faith] meant basing business confidence upon the ethical qualities of the individual proven in his impersonal vocational work."[40] A way of life based on the natural ties of blood relationship tends toward personalism and traditionalism. In contrast, a way of life based on the community committed to universalistic ethical norms tends toward impersonalism and rationalism. Economic rationalism may result from the latter but not from the former, according to Weber. The significance of our brief examination of the Japanese institution of *ie* can be evaluated and fruitfully summarized in the light of Weber's discussion.

The "fetters" of blood relationships were partially overcome in the *ie*. This gave the *ie* a somewhat abstract character insofar as it was governed by a number of principles, some of which were based on considerations of blood relationship while others were economically or religiously founded. Because of this abstract character, patterns are still primarily governed by considerations of interpersonal relationships rather than abstract ethical norms. They are largely compatible with the rationalism of modern economic behavior.

Let me return in conclusion to the general question posed at the outset: How should one understand the relationship between religion and Japanese economic behavior? The analysis above argues that one cannot fully explore this relationship in terms of the economic implications of universalistic ethical norms found in dominant religious traditions. This explains why a Weberian approach that normally focuses on such norms and implications does not lead to persuasive analysis of the Japanese situation. The significance of religion for economic behavior in the Japanese case is more clearly understood if one remembers that religion is the source of most fundamental ideas concerning the cosmic order and recognizes that a central institution such as the *ie* is supported by these ideas.[41]

Notes

1   See Robert Bellah, *Tokugawa Religion: The Values of Pre-Industrial Japan* (New York: Free Press, 1957); Reinhard Bendix, "A Case Study in Cultural and Educational Mobility: Japan and the Protestant Ethic." In Neil J. Smelser and Seymour Martin Lipset (eds.), *Social Structure and Mobility in Economic Development* (Chicago: Aldine, 1966), pp. 262–79; Horigome Yōzō, "Hakkagetsuburi no nihon" (Japan after eight months), *The Asahi* (5–7 March 1967).

2   The sketch here is based on Nakane Chie, " 'Ie' no kōzō" (the structure of *ie*). In Ōkochi Kazuo (ed.), *Tōkyō Daigaku Kōkaikoza 11: "Ie"* (Tokyo: Tōkyō Daigaku Shuppan Kai, 1968), pp. 3–27.

3   Ibid., p. 21.

4   Ibid., p. 7.

5   *Kenchi* was first put into practice under Toyotomi Hideyoshi immediately preceding the establishment of the Tokugawa regime.

6   Takeda Chōshū, *Nohonjin no "ie" to shūkyō* (*ie* of Japanese people and religion) (Tokyo: Hyoronshaw, 1976), p. 20f; Nakamura Kichiji, *Ie no rekishi* (the

history of *Ie*) (Tokyo: Nosangyoson bunka kyokai, 1978; originally published by Kadokawa shoten in 1967), pp. 132–39.

7   Nakane, ibid., p. 7f.

8   Ibid., pp. 24–26.

9   For a helpful study of changes in the legal status of the *ie* see Takeda, pp. 151–226.

10   Ibid., p. 45.

11   Ibid., pp. 38–41.

12   For a brief discussion of important aspects of *bushido* see Furukawa Tesshi, "The Individual in Japanese Ethics." In Charles Moor (ed.), *The Japanese Mind: Essentials of Japanese Philosophy and Culture* (Honolulu: East/West Center Press, University of Hawaii, 1967), pp. 228–44.

13   Important older examples of the *kakun* of merchant houses produced during the Takugawa period are collected in Yoshida Yutaka (ed.), *Shoka no kakun* (family instructions of merchant houses) (Tokyo: Tokuma shoten, 1973).

14   Ibid., p. 331.

15   Ibid., p. 124.

16   Ibid., p. 124.

17   Ibid., p. 82.

18   Ibid., p. 76.

19   Ibid., p. 337.

20   Ibid., pp. 90, 155, 186, 221.

21   Ibid., pp. 130, 178.

22   Ibid., pp. 137f., 275.

23   A great deal of emphasis is placed on early rising. Ibid., pp. 55, 235, 245, 302.

24   Ibid., pp. 54, 83, 235, 251f., 333f.

25   Ibid., p. 342.

26   Ibid., pp. 154f., 185.

27   Ibid., p. 260f.

28   The main source of this discussion is the series of eleven symposia on Japanese economic behavior organized and guided by Sumiya Mikio. The material was first published in *Shūkan Toyo Keizai* (a weekly magazine) and then collected into two volumes: Sumiya Mikio (ed.), *Nihonjin no keizaikōdō* (economic behavior of the Japanese people) (Tokyo: Toyokeizaishinpōsha, 1969).

29   Ibid., vol. 1, pp. 105–8.

30   Ibid., p. 113.

31   Ibid., p. 114.

32   Ibid., p. 115.

33   Ibid., p. 96.

34   Kamishima Jiro, *Nihonjin no kekkonkan* (the conception of marriage among Japanese people) (Tokyo: Chikuma shobō, 1968), pp. 1–132.

35   Okochi, p. 183.

36   Nakane Chie, *Tateshakai no ningenkankei* (human relations in vertical society) (Tokyo: Kodansha, 1967), 44ff.

37   Contemporary families, no longer organized as *ie,* have become the institution of consumption. The significance of the so-called my home ideology *(mai hōmu shugi)* should be understood in light of this development.

38   In addition to the most widely known *Tateshakai no ningenkankei,* I consulted its companion volume, Nakane Chie, *Tateshakai no rikigaku* (dynamics of vertical society) (Tokyo: Kōdansha, 1978). The English version of the first

work is available as *Japanese Society* (Berkeley and Los Angeles: University of California Press, 1972).

39 Max Weber, *The Religion of China: Confucianism and Taoism.* Trans. Hans H. Gerth (New York: Macmillan, 1951), p. 237.

40 Ibid.

41 I would like to thank James Robinson for his valuable editorial assistance in the preparation of this chapter.

8

Interrelationships of the Economic and Social Systems in Japan

Ron Napier

Japan's economic successes have become well known to the entire world. It is truly the story of the phoenix risen from the ashes and remains the unparalleled example of rapid economic development. Japan rewrote the book on economic development. Before Japan achieved its postwar record, development economics focused on the histories of countries like the United States, which marshalled abundant resources and grew at sustained rates of about 4 percent per year. Japan overcame a lack of resources, a low initial income level, and overpopulation problems, and churned out 10 percent annual growth for two decades.

It is tempting to look at Japanese success and assume that all its actions and institutional features must be good and highly positive factors. One can also look exclusively on the darker side and see many negative side effects that devotion to economic goals had on social values and welfare. I will attempt to address the issue of the interaction of economic development and the values, lifestyles, and attitudes of the Japanese people. This is a vast subject and only a cursory examination can be attempted here. The basic point of view developed here is that Japan's economic success story, given many poor initial conditions, required tremendous discipline, sacrifice, and fortuitous developments. The evolving economic system, due partly to the breathtaking growth rate and increases in income levels, put enormous pressures and strains on the social fabric. The Japanese have come through the experience well and have been amply rewarded for their efforts. However, it has not been either a costless or effortless journey.

Traditional Social Values

The Japanese social system developed gradually over the centuries. The social system was affected by Japan's inland status, centuries of isolation, and occasional bursts of borrowing from China, Korea, and more recently, the West. The idealized social values of traditional Japan include loyalty, filial piety, group harmony, *seishin* (literally spirit, but a concept which encompasses will, effort, perseverance, self-control, and attainment of skill in traditional Japanese arts and culture), and a strong sense of nationalism and identity (reflected in Japan's native religion Shinto and its imperial mythologies).

Traditional Japanese society was mostly rural with an overlay of an urban warrior-bureaucratic class and supporting artisans and merchants. The economy was organized with the twin function of generating necessary volumes of foodstuffs and collecting and spending taxation revenues. Traditional economies have small production units—the family being the most common. Most households were engaged in agricultural pursuits, with typical farm size of only two or three acres. The high man/land ratio made hard work and discipline necessary. Families were organized into villages for reasons of self-defense and interdependence. Villages were the building blocks of large feudal domains. During most of Japanese history all available land was in use, which meant that inheritance was the main vehicle of achieving economic security. This dependence on the previous generation enforced social values such as loyalty, filial piety, and group harmony. It also inculcated a sense of patience. The intergenerational relations of loyalty and filial devotion extend to Japan's system of ancestor worship. The tightness of supply and demand in foodstuffs reinforced fertility rites (many of Japan's festivals or *matsuri* are related to fertility and prosperity).

Traditional Japanese social and economic systems directly reflect each other. The traditional economy is agricultural, based on the family unit for production, and lacks avenues to increase markedly the scope of its activities because of land, technology, and capital constraints. The social system reflects the economic realities and reinforces the style of economic organization that has proven successful.

Traditional economic and social systems can evolve. In the Tokugawa period (1600–1868), agriculture became more commercialized, manufacturing spread into the countryside, and financial and commercial functions developed to a high degree. Social values evolved to make these economic structural changes more successful. Agricultural households became smaller, as smaller units can react to profit incentives better than larger ones. Despite the class ranking system imposed by the feudal government, the merchant class, which was ranked at the bottom, worked its way to prominence in terms of economic performance. However, even large merchant houses displayed traditional social values and structure. The legacy of the traditional economic structure and social values cast a long shadow on the modernization of Japan. Japan became the first non-Western country to modernize and has successfully developed its own unique social and economic institutions. These institutions reflect the policies, realities, and the traditional legacy.

Brief Summary of the Economic Record

The Japanese economy emerged from World War II in shambles. Under U.S. occupation, order was gradually achieved; by the end of the Korean War, the economy was nearly back to its prewar peak. The government set out to achieve the fastest possible growth, initially as a means of escaping from the extreme poverty it faced early in the postwar period.

The results were phenomenal. From 1954 to 1973 the economy averaged an unprecedented 10 percent growth rate of GNP. Per capita income soared and many Japanese households were able to fulfill their dreams of a single-family home filled with consumer electronics, with a car parked outside and memories of vacations in Europe or America. Japanese industry surged into world class status and has become a world leader in steel, motor vehicles, color television receivers, video tape recorders, sophisticated cameras, plain paper copiers, robotics, and shipbuilding. The political scene has been remarkably stable, the same party being in power since 1955. Inflation rates, especially for manufactured goods, have been among the lowest in the world, while unemployment rates rarely exceed 2 percent. Although economic growth has slowed significantly since the first oil shock of 1973 (only 4 percent per year), savings and productivity rates remain high, and Japan has recently been held up as the example to which the United States should aspire.

The government decided at an early time to design a progrowth policy. Social welfare concerns, defense, and other interests were downgraded in importance. In the tradition of supply-side economic analysis, Japan's economic growth was constrained by the shortage of capital stock and foreign exchange. To achieve rapid growth, the government sought to maximize investment and savings. Investment was aided by liberal depreciation allowances, especially for targeted industries, while savings was aided by large tax exemptions on interest, dividends, and capital gains earnings, as well as commodity taxes that tended to depress consumption. The government kept the taxation rate low on both corporations and individuals by limiting its activities to essential services and investments in infrastructure, and by minimizing expenditures on defense and social welfare. Low tax rates on individuals and publicly provided health care and public transportation helped keep wages down.

The government established direct control over the capital markets, steering capital mostly toward large corporations in industries it had identified as strategic. Public banks loaned large sums to infant industries at less than market rates. The government constrained individuals to place most of their savings in the banking system or postal savings at low interest rates and constrained the banks to loan most of their funds to large corporations at low interest rates. This compares to the focus on capital markets in the United States during most of the postwar period to provide adequate amounts of low-cost home mortgages. The government also kept foreign competition, in both import and direct investment forms, out of the country. It even supervised the ways that foreign firms could license their technologies and restricted the rates that could be paid for foreign technologies, thus ensuring access to cheap foreign technology.

The labor market also played a major role. Mandatory education was implemented in the late nineteenth century, thus ensuring near-total literacy by the postwar period. Overpopulation led to excess labor supply, which kept wages low. The labor market system that developed emphasized lifetime employment, which meant that the employer recouped the full investment in worker training and experienced no resistance to the introduction of new technologies. Weak union bargaining positions led to long work weeks, few strikes, hard work, willingness to delay significant portions of compensation to annual bonuses, and settling for one-year wage contracts, which allowed quick changes in wages in response to economic conditions. The Japanese domestic market is large. Import restrictions reserved it for Japanese producers and aided their development. Other factors include political stability (the ruling Liberal-Democratic Party has been in power since 1955), the talents of the trading companies, U.S. military spending in Asia, and the undervalued and fixed exchange rate (until 1971).

Economic factors such as those listed above do not occur in a vacuum; many have their ultimate basis in the nation's social fabric and traditions. The economic system owes a great deal to the initial social conditions. Henry Rosovsky has commented that one of the major lessons of the Japanese experience with economic growth was that a full century or more of institutional and social development appeared to be a major prerequisite —Japan's experience did not offer other countries a shortcut to economic growth. Although economic development depends on prior social conditions, the evolving economic system in turn will put pressure on and constrain that social system to change in ways that accommodate the modern industrial economy. In all developed countries, this has meant a more interdependent lifestyle, more urbanization, and gradual dissolution of the extended family and the family worker. We shall also see that economic development has brought about specific changes or pressures unique to the Japanese experience.

Japanese Hierarchies

One truism about postwar Japan is that it has been a shortage economy. Despite high savings rates, Japan was starved of capital stock, and needed raw materials beyond its ability to pay for them. This is particularly evident in the dualistic structure of the Japanese economy, which results in an extraordinary dichotomy of winners and losers. In a modern, unified economy such as that of the United States, there are small differentials among and within economic sectors in such entities as wages, capital invested per worker, output per worker, etc. In Japan we see no such unified structures, and differentials tend to be very wide. It is almost as if there were two economies existing side by side within Japan: one, a modern economy with high wage rates, capital intensities, and output per worker; the other, a more traditional economy with substantially lower values for these three variables. It is as if modern Japan had a Hong Kong or Korea on its doorstep. Why do market forces not wipe out the differences? The problem apparently lies in the insufficient level of capital stock in the country and the resilience of Japanese small firms. The modern sector of the Japanese economy began forming late in the nineteenth century. Modern firms require high levels of investment; modern technologies could not be achieved by simply raising the available capital per worker gradually for all workers. Instead, available capital was concentrated in a limited number of firms, and islands of modern industries formed, surrounded by a large traditional sector. Despite high rates of investment and very rapid growth, the modern sector has yet to grow sufficiently to absorb all the workers, which would eliminate the differentials. Until this happens, Japan will retain a dualistic structure.

The dualistic structure has extremely important implications for the social structure and values of Japan. Because larger corporations, banks, and the government make up the modern sector and offer substantially higher wages and salaries than are available in the rest of the economy, there is intense competition to be employed in the modern sector. Not only are wages higher, but job security is also better; and up to 1973, promotion opportunities were brighter. The question of where one works in Japan is fundamental; a job with a good firm or government ministry implies the good life and high status. Any other job does not measure up. The historical development of the dual structure has resulted in the classification of virtually all Japanese workers into a winner/loser set of categories.

That the economy would organize the labor force into distinct groupings is only natural for Japan. The individual in Japan is defined by membership in various, mostly functional, groups and by his position within the group. These are not trivial distinctions, since Japanese people will typically introduce themselves by their company or other affiliation in the same breath with their name. Nathan Glazer summarized the sociological position by stating: "The difference between Japan and the West: a difference exhibited in a net of obligations that binds individuals together and makes strong institutions of the family, principally, but by extension of the school and of the workplace."[1] Japanese society is viewed as nurturant; in exchange for accepting one's position in a complex hierarchy, one can expect good treatment. The Japanese speak of *amae*, the expectation of care and special consideration from a superior in exchange for one's efforts as an inferior.

The above can be interpreted as describing a smooth transition by the individual during his lifetime through the important hierarchies of Japanese society: family, school, and workplace. However, because of the limited number of students admitted to the better universities and the limited number of people employed in the modern sector, the Japanese escalator to success is a slippery one that, to shift metaphors, has been often described as the "narrow gate."[2] In the next several sections I will examine the selection and choice mechanisms of the workplace and educational systems to evaluate the equity of the social distribution of risks and rewards that result from the economic system Japan has evolved over the last thirty years.

Japan at Work

The government, through its progrowth economic policies, favored large firms. Progrowth policies required the rapid absorption of modern technologies, high level of investment in capital stock, and a strong capability of penetrating export markets. The government felt that large enterprises were most likely to accomplish these goals and designed policies to assist them. Capital markets were also established along dual structure lines, with large banks lending most of the funds to large corporations. Since large firms were more capital-intensive, they benefited most from accelerated depreciation tax incentives; and with their greater political clout, they were able to push for more permissive antitrust policies and inclusion on the strategic list of industries that received special favors, such as the rationalization depreciation tax incentive.[3]

The net result of dualistic development and postwar economic policies was to foster the growth of the modern sector of the dual structure. The rest of the economy was on its own. The differentials between the modern and traditional sectors that have persisted throughout the postwar era are well known to every citizen. The payoff of successful admission to the upper tier of the Japanese economic system of the labor force which employs about 30 percent is enormous. (The terms *large firms, modern sector, elite,* and *upper tier* are used interchangeably.) Therefore the effort, strain, and patience required to attain membership in the elite is justified in the minds of many.

The Nenkō System

The modern sector has evolved its own unique system of industrial relations. The system has two main pillars: permanent employment *(shūshin koyō),* in which the firm guarantees job security to its regular employees, and the seniority wage system *(nenkō joretsu),* which makes the number of years with the firm a major determinant of wages. Features of this system include the ideal of meeting all requirements for new employees directly from the "unsullied" new graduate pool, the incentives for both employer and employee to train the worker, and the lack of resistance to new technology due to the permanent employment guarantee. The employee sees his income rising steadily with seniority, which makes it less attractive to leave the firm as time goes by. The knowledge that commitment to the employer is a lifelong one generates long-term incentives. Japanese corporations typically postpone 30 percent of total compensation to semiannual bonuses, which are sensitive to profits and business conditions, giving the employee strong short-term incentives to work for the good of the firm. Employee incentives are not individual, and there is little incentive for the individual to work especially hard to increase his short-term compensation.

Although wages are higher than for most workers in the labor force, the employer receives a work force that is loyal, dedicated, unopposed to change, and has both the short- and long-term interests of the firm at heart. The employee receives job security and a steadily rising wage that is substantially higher than what prevails in the traditional sector. The permanent employment and seniority wage system has been acclaimed as a major contributor to the nation's economic growth. There are strong points to this system in comparison to the free-market, competitive systems that prevail in the traditional sector in Japan and in other countries including the United States. There are also some weaker points to the system that have a bearing on Japan's social conditions.

One of the common reactions to descriptions of the permanent employment system is the belief that it is not a work incentive system, but rather a work disincentive system. Wages depend more on seniority than ability, and once the employee has been given permanent status, there is little incentive to work hard. Bonus determination reflects companywide performance, and there is little the individual can do to alter his bonus significantly. The Japanese language has words *(madogiwa)* to describe workers who have succumbed to the job security of the system or who have at some stage in their careers given up on trying hard. The need to provide incentives within the system has gone so far as to create largely honorary positions for senior workers with little actual authority *(shikaki seido)*.

Perhaps the saddest casualty of Japan's economic slowdown has been those youths who graduated since 1973. A young man with a record similar to that of an older brother but who happened to enter the labor market after 1973, would receive far fewer good job offers and probably a lower salary. This had resulted in a breakdown between society's implicit promises and actual results. Although resignation and acceptance of one's fate are strong factors in Japanese behavior, there is resentment and disappointment that the system has not responded with appropriate results. One result of the shaky labor market status of many young people has been a delay in marriage and childrearing, and therefore a delay in the purchase of apartments, consumer durables, etc.

In summary, the rigidity of the lifetime employment system in collision with the economic slowdown has brought disappointment to young workers inside the better firms who cannot escape drudge work since they remain the low men on the seniority ladder, and for middle managers who have seen their chances for promotion evaporate. A more competitive labor market also exhibits many of the same characteristics, but at a lower level. The key difference between the Japanese system and a free labor market system is labor mobility.

Mobility in and out of the modern sector is extremely limited in Japan. By far the largest proportion of regular employees are hired soon after graduation. There are limited opportunities for older workers to join a large firm and even when this is the case, there remain disadvantages in terms of salaries and social relations. Employees within a Japanese firm identify themselves by stating which year they joined the firm; the "halfway worker," as the late transfer is called, has an entry year that does not match his age and experience. He also suffers from having had less opportunities to develop close personal ties with fellow workers and management.

Perhaps due to lack of job mobility, the early career of the young production worker or office worker is characterized by an extremely long incubation period which requires much patience. It is the practice of most large firms to take a group of new employees, train them, and set them to work. Since they have the same seniority, their salaries are virtually identical. Salaries are held at identical levels in some companies for ten or fifteen years as the employees must labor without tangible evidence of approbation from their managers. It is not until they reach their mid-thirties that individual salaries and responsibilities break ranks and rewards are given. It may be considered admirable that workers can put in sustained efforts for over a decade to show their loyalty and dedication; this feature has sometimes been discussed as one element of the "will and effort" that make up the "Japanese spirit" or *seishin*. However, the pressure on the young men who are locked into this seemingly interminable competition for recognition is enormous.

The Japanese firm does substantial amounts of training of its workers. Previous experience (the halfway worker) or graduate degrees are viewed with suspicion. "Relatively little stress is given to individual differences in innate ability. Perseverance and hard work in training are among the most important requisites for success. It is assumed that all beginners are more or less incompetent, and differences among them are not important. . . . The most important thing is to be teachable."[4] Since there is relatively little emphasis on the knowledge one brings to the job, Japanese workers tend to be talented generalists. Japanese corporations have well-defined rotation policies which result in most white-collar workers being exposed to many of the functions of the corporation.

Although the rotation system provides a wide view of corporate activities and helps develop a corporate memory, it fosters the development of highly general and somewhat superficial skills. Specialists do exist but are less numerous than in firms in the United States. This may become an increasingly important distinction as the level of business sophistication continues to rise.

Slow growth has brought numerous strains to the permanent employment-*nenkō* system. Unions have been consciously settling for lower wage increases in return for a continuation of the guarantees of the system. Any worker who has already acquired even a modest amount of seniority in the *nenkō* system has a vested interest in seeing it continue. However, corporations have been diluting the *nenkō* system in recent years. In 1980 for the first time wages peaked for men in the 45–50 age cohort instead of the usual 50–55. This partly reflects the trend to higher retirement ages (the average retirement age is gradually moving from 55 years to a new norm of 60). The trend to a higher retirement age would force firms to retain their highest paid workers for a longer time. As a result, seniority wage increases for more senior workers will probably continue to decline and the wage-age curve will continue to flatten out. With these changes, labor market practices by both employers and employees will evolve from current practices.

Discrimination

The permanent employment-*nenko* system is an important feature of the modern sector. It constrains the firm as it turns the cost of labor from being under corporate control to being largely a fixed cost. However, the benefits (and pressures) of this system are concentrated on regular, male employees. Women are explicitly excluded from the system. The historical mandatory retirement age for all but senior executives (currently 57 years on average) forces male employees out on their own with many years of life expectancy left (Japan has one of the highest longevities in the world). As a result, women, older workers, and workers in the traditional sector all face lower wage rates and job security than regular male workers in large corporations and the government.

Women have seen only modest improvement in their wage differentials with men in the postwar period. Women are expected to work from gradua-tion until marriage and then perhaps again when the children are grown. Their jobs range widely from production workers, to carpenters, to "office ladies" who serve tea for the male staff and guests. There are few promotion possibilities and virtually no seniority aspect to wages over the female worker's brief career.

If older workers are overpaid, as their postretirement wages suggest, the firm must compensate by underpaying young workers. This seems to be the case, as a recent university graduate can only expect to receive about 2.2 million yen ($10,000) as a starting annual salary including bonuses. There is virtually no difference in starting salaries between large and small firms. Workers must have low discount rates and be able to clearly see the future benefits of employment in a large firm to join one.

Perhaps the most surprising element of discrimination in Japan is the low level of concern with it. Resignation and acceptance of the status quo often typify those who are discriminated against. Other factors appear to include homogeneity of the Japanese people, lack of overt noneconomic discrimina-tion in terms of neighborhood organization or interpersonal behavior, and the belief in the power of perseverance, effort, and sheer will in accomplish-ing one's goals. Membership in the elite is decided by one's performance in an impersonal exam, and thus the outcome (except for sex discrimination) is in one's control.

Attitudes at Work

The Japanese employment system is being gradually affected by the intergenerational transition in attitudes. People old enough to remember World War II and the years immediately thereafter are said to have been permanently changed by the experience. They seek material rewards and work very hard to attain a secure position. They also retain the traditional standards of Japanese society. Younger people grew up in an increasingly affluent Japan heavily influenced by Western thought, customs, music, film, books. Ideas of individuality and lack of suffering have molded the younger generation into quite a different group in terms of attitudes. Surveys have traced the slow evolution of Japanese attitudes over the years and show increased modern content. One survey of middle managers showed that those over 40 years of age felt best in the morning with the day's work ahead of them and worst at night on their way home. Younger managers were just the opposite, feeling best when returning from work and worst in the morning. Although a limited amount of vacation is permitted, middle managers seldom take it, as it could be interpreted as a lack of devotion to the job.

The promotion process as suggested above is long and arduous. It can be viewed as a game of survivors, as those who make the fewest mistakes may be the ones to be promoted. The combination of this waiting game with the largest number of people who must be consulted before a decision can be reached tends to dampen entrepreneurial spirit and risk taking. Perhaps equally important as doing a good job and working hard is the cultivation of human relationships, especially with superiors. Eventually one may be accepted into a group within the firm and one's future is then directly connected to the power and influence of one's superiors. In this type of organizational structure, managers may be selected not just for their skill in making decisions and administer work, but also for their ability to carry out the human relations responsibilities required of managers and the corporation. Decision making in Japan is of the consensus form, and therefore requires much more time and participation than straightforward autocratic or voting styles. The first step in decision making is the examination of precedents. Managers are sought less for an aggressive ability to make decisions than for their ability to convince others and keep opposing factions happy.

The Educational System: Is Life Over at Eighteen?

The educational system is the midpoint of a backward chronological tracing of the three major "nets of obligation" that characterize Japanese society—the workplace, education, and the family. The dual structure and the wide differentials in wages and job security that prevail in Japan are the main motives for students—and their parents—to prefer employment in the government or a large firm. The modern sector not only restricts hiring to recent graduates, it also has strong preferences for graduates of better universities and high schools. National surveys have revealed a preponderance of graduates of a handful of universities (Tokyo, Kyoto, Hitotsubashi, Keio, and Waseda) in the top management and bureaucratic positions in the country. Every high school in the country is ranked in various popular magazines by its placement of graduates in prestigious universities. Thus the dual structure of employers directly translates into a dual structure for educational institutions, and payoffs in the labor market also translate into payoffs in education.

Admission into a school in Japan virtually guarantees graduation. In postwar Japan, despite the competitiveness of society, there is no tracking and no holding back or advancing of students from their current grade. This forms the first stable group of which the youngster becomes a part. The key to admission, stage by stage, is examinations plus minor checks into the student's previous background. It is all-important that the student do well on written examinations since other grades, extracurricular activities, leadership, social abilities, etc., have virtually no influence. As a result, "almost the entire secondary school system is oriented toward succeeding in these examinations."[5]

The pressure has backed up further and further into the system as admission into a good high school is largely settled by examinations (there are often residence requirements as well), which require attendance at a good junior high school, which in turn requires coming from a good elementary school, and ultimately a good nursery school. This is an example of uncontrolled and perhaps destructive competition where the willingness of even a small minority to up the ante forces everyone else to follow even if the bottom line (in this case admission to a prestigious university) is unchanged.

A direct result of the pressures on the educational system is the increased level of attendance in kindergartens. In 1960, only 29 percent of eligible children attended, but by 1978 the ratio had reached 64 percent. Schoolchildren's parents emphasize over and over again the importance of studying hard. Some mothers, known as *kyoiku mama* or "education mother," have become the virtual servants of their children to push forward their education at a faster clip. One traditional Japanese saying asserts that "if a schoolchild sleeps more than four hours a night, failure will result."[6]

Another manifestation of the pressure to succeed, which starts so young, is the importance of *juku,* which is a tutoring or after-school school. Much of the tutoring is done by university students, the rest by private schools sometimes manned by public school teachers in their spare hours. Enrollment in these schools has climbed steadily and can be a significant financial burden for parents. The pressure on the child begins early. Although there is little special treatment in school, the examinations that loom every few years cause both child and parents to focus on preparation.

Is Japanese Education Good?

Some observers have looked at the "examination hell" that Japanese students must go through and labeled the Japanese educational system as a rote learning system. This is an oversimplification, since Japanese students have performed well in international comparisons. The system must teach reading and writing of over 2,000 characters, six years of a foreign language, and still cover the many subjects that are fair game for the exam. The system develops habits of hard work, thoroughness, and the ability to quickly apply learned information to a problem. Students have to absorb and memorize vast amounts of information and devote much of their time to study. Perhaps the most unusual aspect of the educational system is that Japan spends so little on it. "Both in absolute terms and relative to national income, per capital Japanese investment is considerably lower for higher education than is that of other countries."[7] This shows up in many ways: teachers' pay is low, forcing many to take outside jobs (bribery has also been a problem), and class size is large (standards were 50 children per class in 1958, 45 in 1963, and 35 on average in 1969). However, if spending on tutoring, *juku,* supplementary books, musical instruments, etc., were added with direct public expenditures, the ratio is more in line with that of other countries.

Another unusual aspect of education to a Westerner is the unusual devotion of the student-teacher relationship. Teachers keep students after school for direct conversations and visit their homes. Japanese schools have few janitors or watchmen, because students and teachers fill these roles. School appears to be the site of the first nonfamily group-building exercise with teachers playing a very important role in the students' lives.

The examinations are in many ways great equalizers, as it does not matter who one's parents are or even which school one went to. However, in recent years income differences have begun to affect chances for admission to the best universities. More income buys better tutoring, which leads to better odds for admission. Many students from wealthier families, unwilling to accept their failure to gain admittance to a good university on the first round, try again by taking more tutoring and the examinations again the next year. These students are called *rōnin,* after the masterless samurai of Tokugawa Japan.

Is life over at eighteen? Due to the lack of labor mobility in Japan, there is a major fork in the road at eighteen years of age. The results of the examination process determine whether one will be allowed to join the upper 30 percent or will be relegated to the great mass of society. Once directed onto one of two paths, the course is largely irreversible. This contrasts to the American ideal that one can always become a success. Of course, some people turn small firms into giant ones, others become wealthy in any number of ways, but the widest and most general way to a guaranteed minimum level of success is to pass through the "narrow gate" guarded by the examination process. The competitive struggle is not over, as one's status within the upper tier is yet to be decided, but the arena in which the struggle will take place has been settled. Since the fate of the great majority of people has been irretrievably cast on one side or the other of the dual structure with its differential rewards, one can say that life in Japan is decided by age eighteen to an extent not seen in the United States. The system is a severe one which picks its champions through trial by fire, but in the process does not tolerate the random mistake or the late bloomer. This reduces the available supply of talent while emphasizing discipline and conformity.

On-the-Job Training

Large Japanese companies view the newly recruited employee as a blank board upon which the corporate way and training can be etched. The corporation expects to do substantial amounts of training of its employees. This is perhaps the reason why there has been little pressure on the universities to improve their product. Japanese universities are noted for low attendance, large class size, and virtually automatic graduation. Senior year is spent looking for a job. The government has had to intervene to forbid early recruiting by large corporations for the best graduates. Connections, known as *kone,* are important. Professors in the better universities often have personal quotas with the better companies to place their students. In an effort to impress, some students will sleep on the sidewalks overnight outside the front door of the companies for which they most want to work in order to be first in line when the doors open.

Once accepted by the firm, the new employees undergo a corporate training program of varying lengths. Throughout his career, the employee receives training. Much of the training comes informally from a "big brother" relationship known as *senpai-kōhai* (superior-inferior). There is also formal training in basic methodologies, technologies, languages, programming, often given by university professors or other outside consultants. "Even at national universities, 66 percent of those of professional rank and 53 percent of the assistant professors hold some job outside their home institution."[8] Although some may teach high school students in *juku* or work in research institutes, many provide tailor-made courses of instruction in corporations throughout Japan.

Graduate school is a minor feature in Japan. It is ironic to the Western observer that the "examination hell" may be forcing families to enroll their children in kindergartens, while few persons go on to graduate school. In 1970 Japan granted 13,000 graduate degrees compared to 238,000 in the United States in 1969.[9] These figures are misleading, since both law and medicine degrees in Japan are bachelor degrees. One businessman pointed out that the MBA (Master of Business Administration) degree is virtually useless in Japan, because no company would ever hire a recent graduate as a highly paid manager; one must instead work one's way up the seniority ladder with great diligence. In the area of the doctoral degree, the United States and Japan are closer, with Japan generating 4.5 degrees per 100,000 persons in 1967–68 and the United States 13.1 per 100,000. The main reasons for the lack of interest in graduate degrees in Japan besides the institutional ones given above is the fact that there is "little financial advantage to a graduate degree."[10] This may reflect the preference by large firms for the untrained but willing recruit that the firm can mold into a productive worker.

There is a theory in labor economics that education after a certain point may not be directly productive, but instead is a signal that a worker sends to prospective employers to indicate his qualities. This reduces the cost to the employer of finding suitable employees. In the United States this theory suggests that the acquisition of the Master's degree has become necessary more to differentiate the employee than to actually increase his productivity and value to the employer. In Japan, the rigid ranking of schools and colleges by the examination system provides the student with differentiation and the employer with an unambiguous way of ranking students. Thus the Japanese bachelor's degree distinctly conveys quality signals, making graduate degrees unnecessary except for certain professions. The alternative theory suggests that since the United States possesses more holders of advanced degrees, as the economy becomes increasingly complex the United States will be in a relatively strong position vis-à-vis Japan. No real proof exists for either theory, although one would have to note that thus far Japan's economic performance has been better than that of the United States.

Notes

1.   Nathan Glazer, "Social and Cultural Factors in Japanese Economic Growth." In Hugh Patrick and Henry Rosovsky (eds.), *Asia's New Giant* (Washington, D.C.: Brookings Institution, 1976), p. 816.
2.   Jon Woronoff, *Japan: The Coming Social Crisis* (Tokyo: Lotus Press, 1980), p. 130.
3.   Comptroller General of the United States, General Accounting Office, *United States-Japan Trade: Issues and Problems* (Washington, D.C.: U.S. Government Printing Office, 1979), p. 179.

4. Robert Frager and Thomas P. Rohlen, "The Future of a Tradition: Japanese Spirit in the 1980s." In Lewis Austin (ed.), *Japan: The Paradox of Progress* (New Haven, Conn.: Yale University Press, 1976), p. 261.
5. Glazer, p. 828.
6. Ibid., p. 829.
7. Ibid., p. 825.
8. Ibid., p. 825.
9. Ibid., p. 830.
10. Ibid., p. 830.

Part Five

NIGERIA

Introductory Essay

The Federal Republic of Nigeria is the most populous country in Black Africa and in terms of natural resources, the richest. Although it has a number of cities over 250,000—more than most African countries—only about one in five Nigerians live in an urban area, according to a 1980 World Bank estimate. The official language is English but there is a wide diversity of tribal groups that speak over 250 languages. The most numerous groups are the predominantly Moslem Hausa and Fulani in the North, the predominantly Catholic Ibo in the East, and the Yoruba in the West, who are almost equally divided between Moslems and Christians. Again very roughly, somewhat less than 50 percent of Nigerians are Moslem, 35 percent Christian, and 17 percent adhere to what have been termed traditional religions. Historically speaking, Islam and Christianity are latecomers to Nigeria, Islam coming only at the beginning of the nineteenth century and Christianity some thirty years later.

Christianity established the mission schools that provided, until recently, most of the education in the country. Although independent of the government, they received funds from the colonial authorities and, in turn, submitted to inspection of their curricula. Schools tended to give general support to colonialism that, in turn, advocated a laissez-faire economy and frowned on socialism and the nationalization of local industries. In teaching economics, there was a definable complex of ideas at once innovative and conservative. That school system has given way to a modern education system that proposes free, universal, and compulsory primary education by the state. But since Nigeria has been independent for only slightly over two decades, the most important posts in Nigeria are held by people educated in mission schools. This indicates one way that, during a particular historical period, religiously sponsored agencies transmitted sets of values into Nigerian society.

Nigeria is distinguished not only by its wealth and the size of its population, but by the fact that, in contrast to the Marxist or socialist regimes of other Black African countries, it has a markedly capitalist ethos. On small scale and large, the entrepreneur is a noticeable presence in the Nigerian economy. For many reasons, then, Nigeria offers a fertile field for the investigation of relations between religion and the economy. But the same reasons which make it promising also make it extremely difficult. It is probable that a variety of different approaches would be necessary to yield a completely satisfactory examination. One such approach, as Henry Bienen mentions, would be to concentrate on a small selected part of Nigeria and carry out a microanalysis that would focus on particular processes. The same approach could then be applied to other areas and processes.

Here Bienen has set himself a different task. Recognizing the formidable problems encountered in his approach, he has followed a line of investigation that others are finding attractive and useful. He attempts to relate economic change in Nigeria to underlying values of the society which may shape the many choices, attitudes, and decisions that are part of the economic process. As he points out, the effect of some religious values may have to be sought not directly in economic policies, but in political variables which in turn have an impact on the economy. To pursue this line of research, he must forego a number of other promising avenues, some of which he specifies.

His task is further complicated by a circumstance that plagues everyone who attempts a large-scale inquiry in Nigeria. There are very few dependable surveys on matters for which one would like reliable information. The data are frequently weak or spotty. The difficulties acknowledged, Bienen examines (1) the structure of the Nigerian economy; (2) specific aspects of the relation between religion and economics within that structure; 3) aspects of class, wealth, and poverty in Nigeria; and 4) equality and religion. He then draws the inferences his inquiry justifies and refines questions that need further inquiry.

Benjamin Ray, who also stresses the religious, ethnic, and linguistic pluralism of Nigeria focuses his study on a specific group—the Yoruba of Western Nigeria. Questioning whether it is possible to show that religion operates on a socially independent variable in critical matters, he works on the assumption that religious ideas contribute to social values which then generate or support various forms of economic behavior. He describes the traditional religion of the Yoruba, comparing and contrasting it with other African religions. Certain features of the traditional Yoruba religion are particularly pertinent to any discussion of that religion and economics. For example, he finds that concepts of destiny, judgment, and rebirth led to a disposition toward social achievement through personal effort and a desire to develop a high moral character. These and other religious features are seen as reinforcements of traits useful to an entrepreneur. Ray concludes, however, that specific entrepreneurial traits, having developed, may no longer depend on the religious traditions which fostered them.

Nigeria will remain for some time the rich, complex country that it is—a country of concern not only to other African countries, but to the United States as well. The kinds of investigations carried on by Bienen and Ray, in addition to those they mention but do not pursue, will be essential for those who wish to understand significant aspects of its political and economic behavior.

J.F.

9

Religion and Economic Change in Nigeria

Henry S. Bienen

When we explore the relationships between religion and economic structures and change in Nigeria, we are engaged in an extremely complex analytical and empirical undertaking. If we try to seek the impact of behavioral consequences of religion, we must be careful to distinguish the doctrinal aspects of religion, the practical religion (interaction between original doctrine and social, political, and economic conditions of the time), and the impact of religious organizations and structures acting as political and economic units themselves. The behavioral consequences have to do with individuals, groups, and very large categories called societies in which political culture can be examined.

The analytical problems we confront have been examined by Weber and the many commentators on his work.[1] Sociologists have long been concerned with elaborating complex models to try to understand the impact of religion, and these models include accounting for the growth of new religions in specific contexts. Religion can be understood as an outcome of social, political, and economic conditions as well as a cause of change. Where religious changes are produced or affected by political integration or economic growth, religious changes in turn have their influence. In Africa there have been many attempts to examine what Balandier has called the colonial condition,[2] to see the growth of new religions as a product of political relations, and anthropologists have studied "praying religions" and millennial cults with the aim of exploring industrialization and alterations in status as components of social change.[3]

The central theme of Weber and those who reacted to his work can be stated: To what extent does religion stabilize, change, or reformulate non-religious beliefs and actions?[4] Posing the question in this way implies that religious beliefs can be empirically isolated from wider attitudes associated with ethnic or national communities. In some ways Nigeria provides a good testing ground because Islam, Catholicism, and various Protestant denominations, including African churches, exist along with so-called traditional religions. However, it is not always possible to separate ethnicity from religion. Most Catholics in Nigeria are Ibo; most Hausa and Fulani are Moslem (although not all Moslems by any means are Hausa or Fulani or even from Northern Nigeria). The Yoruba have been seen as an extremely interesting group because they continue to have traditional believers and also divide roughly between Moslems and Christians. David Laitin, intending to examine the differential impact of Christianity and Islam (see Appendices for breakdown of population by religion) on Nigeria and wanting to control for nationality (or ethnicity), economy, numbers of generations in the presence of a world religion, motivations for conversion, and ecology—all of which are different in many Moslem and Christian areas in Nigeria—concentrates on a part of Yorubaland and is carrying out micro analysis on the historical process of conversion as well as on contemporary attitudes and behavior.[5] This is a sophisticated and sensible strategy.

My task is somewhat different. I want to try to relate economic changes in Nigeria to underlying values on which they may be based. The task is not easy. Few studies examine the import of religious values on economic change and ask whether religious values are consistent with or contradictory to economic change in Nigeria. Even the micro studies of entrepreneurship do not usually focus on religion. At a general level, there is more concern in the literature on Nigeria with religion and political integration than with religion and economic development. But religion's impact on economic policy may be a second-order effect which works through political variables. For example, one might conclude that Islamic values and institutions have not had direct impact on central economic policy, leaving aside for the moment their impact on individual behavior of investors and workers. But even so, Islam and Islamic institutions have had a major impact on politics and governmental structures in Northern Nigeria. The heated debate over a Sharia federal court of appeals during deliberations on the Constituent Assembly which was considering Nigeria's new Constitution made evident how important Sharia law remains to many Nigerian representatives from the North. Centralized institutions based on Sharia law, administrative modes tied to emirate structures, and a concern for central control, have limited opportunities for private entrepreneurship in the North. Islam has worked through political institutions to affect economic behavior and policies.[6]

Another example of indirect effects would be the conscious separation of church and state which motivated British colonial rulers in Southern Nigeria. This had the consequence of the British refusing to allow Christian education to be pushed in the North, as well as leading to a separation of church activity from direct governance in the South. One could go further and argue that the idea of a secular state is itself a religious value of sorts and that this idea had an impact in Nigeria. The British idea of a Protestant colonial state was consequential for the evolution of the Nigerian economy in the South. Christianity was introduced in Nigeria by economic liberals and thus the idea of an open economy was to some extent tied up with Christianity.[7]

The impact of world religions in Nigeria has to be seen historically, and often mediated through political administrations and values. Even so, it is not easy to describe what has occurred in the Nigerian economy over the last decades and to account for it in terms of religion and social change. Our conclusions depend on whether we focus on the decisions of policymakers at the center of the economy and on macroeconomic changes, or on the behavior of individuals and economic units. Moreover, religious institutions in Nigeria have themselves played economic roles. Churches and mosques, religious brotherhoods and orders are sometimes direct and sometimes indirect producers, consumers, and controllers of assets.[8]

Looking at the evolution of the Nigerian economy, some observers would put more emphasis on external variables of colonialism, trade, and the expansion of a world capitalist system, than on any factors indigenous to Nigeria. There are also peculiarly difficult problems in coming to grips with values in Nigeria. We have very few surveys of national or group attitudes. The society is extremely heterogenous by communal association, language, religion, ecology. Large-scale macroeconomic changes cannot easily be related to growth of world religions (which are relative latecomers to Nigeria) or national values. In the end, the complexity of factors, the uncertainty of data on attitudes, and gaps in our knowledge of behavior (how many people give according to *Zakat?* Are there biases towards size and capital intensity that can be traced to religious values?) force us back to some classic questions. We must again ask, for example, about entrepreneurship and about attitudes toward equality and organization, which must be understood in terms of individual as well as group behavior and about which we have some information. These matters have large consequences for the Nigerian economy and they can be translated into questions about the sociology of religion.

The structure of the Nigerian Economy

Nigeria is in many important respects an atypical African country. Its population of more than 85 million is much larger than that of most African countries. It has many more cities over 250,000 than most other African countries. Its revenues from oil are matched only by Libya and Algeria on the African continent. Because of its size and oil revenues, Nigeria's GDP is also large in African terms. Yet Nigeria is a poor country, its per capita income put by the World Bank at $560 per annum (1978), ranking it 53 out of 125 countries or at the low end of the middle-income countries. Nigeria has many features of poor African economies and societies. Its population grows at 2.5 percent per annum, at least. Its labor force is still 56 percent in agriculture, although this is a drop from 71 percent in 1960. Industry's share of the labor force has grown from 10 to 17 percent in 1960–78, while the service sector has grown from 19 to 27 percent during this time. The large service sector growth reflects the burgeoning informal sector which in turn is a function of Nigeria's high rate of urbanization of 4.9 percent in 1970–80. Nigeria's annual agricultural growth declined 1.5 percent in 1970–78, while GDP was growing 6.2 percent per annum.[9]

Nigeria shares many features of poor developing countries, although they are distorted by the oil boom. In the short run the oil boom worsened the distribution of Nigeria's income. Although there is no comprehensive nationwide household survey that would enable us to make authoritative pronouncements on the precise magnitude of income inequalities, there is evidence that the degree of inequality in the modern sector became greater in the 1970s, reaching a very high level around 1975–76 when the impact of massive new oil funds was felt.[10] These revenues overwhelmingly stayed in the urban areas through government spending policies. While oil made new revenues available, it also fueled inflationary fires in the Nigerian economy and gave the government more power to intervene in the Nigerian economy. Taxes were once raised and collected from millions of producers. Now, well over 80 percent of government revenues are derived from taxes, rents, royalties on oil companies, and from the direct operations of the Nigerian National Petroleum Company. The extension of the scope of the central government's authority and the development of stronger central institutions have been evident in many ways. In 1967 Nigeria moved from a federation of four regions to one of twelve states. In 1976 the number of states was increased to nineteen. These changes were a response to the complex ethnic-regional breakdowns in Nigeria and were designed to defuse ethnicity and regionalism. But it was also true that the creation of states meant more control for the center and less power for the no longer large state units.[11]

The Nigerian Constitution of 1979 and the return to civilian government through elections for president, Senate and House of Representatives, and state governors emphasized the federal nature of the Nigerian system. This federal system allows opposition parties political space at national, state, and local levels. But the new Constitution, for all its federal character, gives large powers to the central government and the list of concurrent powers is rather small.

Historically, two burning issues in Nigeria have been the share of revenues between the federal government and the regions and states and the formula for revenue allocation to go to individual states. Equity and distributional issues in Nigeria have largely been fought out in terms of ethnic and regional conflicts over revenue allocation and investments in the states rather than as conflicts over interpersonal income shares of various classes in Nigeria.[12] In 1981 Nigeria reverted to a pre–civilian rule formula which gives the federal government an even larger share of revenues. Very large resources remain in central hands. Also, while the Price Control Board was abolished under the new regime of Shehu Shagari, the government continues to issue price guidelines. Through wage and salary review commissions, it introduces income policy guidelines. And since mid-1974, Nigeria has operated with a uniform tax system.[13]

In Nigeria policies are an outcome of institutional and market forces. Pure market forces rarely obtain. Rewards for labor and prices for commodities are affected by productivity and supply and demand respectively, but they are also institutionally determined. Many features of the Nigerian economy obtained under the premilitary civilian regime of independent Nigeria during 1960–66 and can be traced to the colonial period.[14] In the past, large-scale government intervention was through marketing boards which extracted resources by taxing producers who were export-oriented. In the last few years, Nigeria's agricultural exports have all but disappeared. Once the largest groundnut exporter in the world, Nigeria now consumes all its groundnut production. Once a large palm oil exporter, Nigeria has now become a major importer of rice, wheat, and fish.[15] While a majority is still employed in agriculture, Nigeria's export revenues are no longer derived from agriculture and it has become a large food importer.

Before turning to the relationship between economic change and religious values, one further structural change in the Nigerian economy must be discussed—indigenization. Military and civil servant elites have been committed to centralizing power in Nigeria. These commitments were supported by ethnic minorities—the half of the Nigerian population that is not Hausa-Fulani, Ibo, or Yoruba, and who wanted to escape from the large regions dominated by the Ibos in the East and the Hausa-Fulani in the North. The military and civil service are situational more than class elites.

They depend on the expansion of the state for the expansion of their own power. The expansion of the educational system, parastatal corporations, the military and civil service, all can be seen as an expansion of the federal government and their own power.[16] These state elites advocated economic nationalism and were concerned to move the economy, which had been heavily penetrated by foreign corporations, more into the hands of Nigerians than it had been.[17]

In the industrial sector, a different story holds. Nigeria has long had significant private enterprise and, after independence, those who controlled the state wanted to develop private domestic producers and control foreign enterprise to enhance Nigerian ownership and control.[18]

Up to independence, Nigerian industrial production was characterized by diversity of ownership, specialization, capital intensity, technology. Foreign-owned industries were more capital-intensive and had higher technology than Nigerian-owned ones. To some extent, the diversity was locationally specific. A snapshot of Nigerian industrialization can be seen from the 1963 industrial survey. Of 649 establishments returning information, 59 percent employed 10–49 workers, 33 percent employed 50–299, and 8 percent employed 300 or more. Of the paid-up share capital of 321 limited companies, 68 percent was of foreign origin, 22 percent was Nigerian public, and 10 percent Nigerian private. Great Britain was the dominant foreign source.[19] While Nigerian-owned industrialization proceeded in the 1960s, the foreign component became more important with the growth of a high-technology oil industry.[20]

Business, land, labor, and ownership patterns are highly complex in Nigeria. An example can be given from Lagos itself. In Lagos, spatially, the inner city is dominated by native-born inhabitants who own land in the heart of the city. Certain families have owned land for generations and some of the largest skyscrapers and abodes of overseas trading corporations and multinationals rest on land owned by old Lagosian families. More recent urban migrants provide most of the skilled labor for the commercial and industrial sectors. These migrants settle on the outskirts of Lagos. The indigenous elements are overwhelmingly Moslem, and better-educated Christian and middle- to upper-class elements settle farthest away from the central business districts.[21]

The modernity of contemporary Lagos is built on a strong base of tradition; it is the most cosmopolitan of Nigerian cities but Lagos society is one of provincial groupings. The oldest and most cohesive urban community, the Lagosian Moslems, retains traditional characteristics of ethnic homogeneity.[22] In this context, private and communal interests are closely associated as are business and primary group relations. Contradictions inherent in Nigeria's social structure and the relationships of private to public ownership can only be touched on here. These contradictions also gave the indigenization policies embarked on by the government their own peculiar characteristics.

The Second Five-Year Plan of 1970–74 called for avoiding uncertainty and instability and building on national unity and the economic base provided by oil. Plans for growth were ambitious. While the goals of the Second Plan included "a just and egalitarian society" and a "land of bright and full opportunities for all citizens," its real thrust was to implement economic growth and nationalism even though in practice there were many compromises with foreign interests in this period. However, it is true that the Second Plan stated an increased emphasis on income distribution and the welfare of the common man.

As Sayre Schatz has pointed out, the Second Plan addressed the need to reduce areas of unearned income, broaden the social base of capital ownership in the economy, reduce the high degree of concentration of stock shareholdings, and enable Nigerians to share in the increasing profits generated. The means to achieve these goals were said to be a new national leadership that would be honest and dedicated, and an investment policy consistent with national goals.[23] Indigenization and Nigerianization were seen as a means to these ends, as well as good things in and of themselves. Schatz has called the Second Plan period one of "guided international nurture-capitalism with a welfare tendency."[24]

There was no direct assault on equity problems. Given the government's formula for economic development and the conditions of Nigerian political and economic life, such an assault would have been difficult to mount. The government was not about to attack private Nigerian accumulations either by helping to create new institutions designed to bring about redistribution through popular participation or by implementing policies from above for rapid income redistribution. Nor was the government's indigenization policy designed to cope primarily with distributional problems. Aboyade has argued that indigenization in 1972–74 worsened inequality.[25] As one critic of the program said, the idea was to create more entrepreneurial know-how and develop a better habit of saving and thrift so as to raise economic levels in the country.[26]

No doubt there were differences of opinion within the government on both the nationalization and indigenization programs. There is dispute as to whether the government's major aim was to support orderly indigenization through public purchase or whether the idea was to lessen private investment and be able to socialize wealth to deal with equity problems later on. The indigenization program, taken as a whole and especially in its later phase, is understandable more in terms of economic nationalism and a desire to expand the power of state officials in the economy than in terms of equity concerns. The idea of public control of corporations and resources is consistent with economic nationalism and public officials' own sense of identity with the state. Their sense of corporate and professional well-being is tied up with the expansion of state power, and their first order of motivation in Nigeria stemmed from the identity of public officials' interests and expansion of the state. This view receives support when we look at what outspoken civil servants said during the formulation and implementation phase of the Second Plan.[27]

Religion and Economics

The civil servants and military personnel committed to indigenization, as well as the businessmen who benefited from buying shares from foreign corporations, were from many ethnic groups and were overwhelmingly Moslems or Christians. There is little reason to suspect that religion distinguished these actors with respect to their economic nationalism. It is true that the northern part of Nigeria was less penetrated by foreign trade and investment than the South. It is also true that on most indices of modernization, the Moslem North lags behind the South, whether we measure education, income, or infrastructural development. The wealthy in Nigeria are concentrated in the Southwest and the oil-producing areas. The poorest are in remote areas of the country: Ibibio in the Southeast, Idoma, Tiv, and others in the Middle Belt, particularly those who are neither Moslem nor Christians. Among Moslems, Fulani and Kanuri in the North are poorer than Hausas.[28]

Modernization lags in Nigeria have been frequently attributed to the impact of Islam. Admittedly, agreements between British colonial authorities under Lord Lugard and the traditional Islamic rulers kept out Christian missionaries and their attendant schools, roads, and skills. Peter Kilby and others have asserted that the North and South differ in the intensity of their desire for modern consumer goods and that these differences can be accounted for by the conservative influence of religion and the sociopolitical system of Northern Nigeria. "Islam, the semi-feudal emirates, and the exclusion of western [missionary] education on religious grounds combined with a later and less intensive contact with the western world, have meant that in the north the whole process of modernization—changes in the way of living, values and skills, as well as directly material terms—has lagged behind that of the east and west."[29]

I am much more comfortable with the supply side of this argument than with the demand side of it. Relative lack of contact with external skills and technology did put the North at a disadvantage. And the political system of the North did hinder social mobility as compared to the West and East.

Ecology was also less favorable for much of the North. The non-Islamic North did not fare well.

How much of Northern conservatism should be attributed to Islam, rather than to the vested interests of ruling elites and the structures they built to maintain their political and economic control? It is quite possible that religion has been an important component of political control and the idea of state intervention in economic life in the North. The problem with focusing on Islam simply as a conservative religion has been much discussed. Many have pointed to the variety of entrepreneurial activities in Iran, Turkey, Pakistan, and Islamic Black Africa.[30] Hausas in Nigeria frequently say that *they* are the Jews of Africa in that they spread over much of West Africa and they stress their trade and merchant activities. If many Hausas went into trade rather than invested in business, so many Christian Ibos and Yorubas went into professions and gravitated to the civil service in the mid–twentieth century. It was characteristic of much of Africa for relatively educated people to work to obtain professional degrees or a place in the state hierarchy. But there were many reasons for the commitment to civil service, profession, and trade rather than to industrial enterprise. The structural bottlenecks to entrepreneurial activities have been widely discussed.[31] Outsiders with capital and access to broader markets had certain advantages over African businessmen starting small, although African traders had advantages of lower information costs. Still, by 1960 officials estimated that there were already more than one and a quarter million enterprises in Nigeria. As restraints were put on foreigners and as markets grew and Africans acquired skills and capital, large-scale entrepreneurial activity quickened.

It is thus hard to accept the view that either Islam or traditional religions were barriers to entrepreneurship in Nigeria, although Islamic political structures and educational developments may well have inhibited the growth of the private sector. It has been argued that traditional religions and culture caused Africans to be averse to risk because they attributed misfortune to malevolent personal interventions. Whether we should treat this belief, if it was widely held, as religious or cultural is a question. If it was held across religions, as most have argued, we must understand it in broad cultural terms. But how then can we account for rising entrepreneurial activities when structural conditions altered? Did the cultural beliefs change so rapidly too?

By the 1970s Nigerians were leaving the public sector to enter private business. Civil servants were using their contacts to form lucrative partnerships and smooth the way for foreigners in Nigeria. The civil service as a career had also become riskier after General Murtala Mohanned in 1976 purged civil servants appointed during and before the Gowon regime. Also, the private sector was booming, and for people with high education wages were higher there than in the public sector. Nigeria proved to be an unusual African country in that the private sector became a magnet for highly educated people. Public positions no longer dominated the aspirations of university graduates. Private and public sectors should not be seen as two ends of a scale in Nigeria in the 1970s, one going up as the other goes down. Rather, the public sector became a more vigorous actor as centralization proceeded and oil revenues grew. But private opportunities also increased and with greater national integration in the 1970s, private actors had a wider field on which to play.

Government policies and economic opportunities plus the growth of management skills appear to have been much more important in enhancing private activities than changes in religion and/or culture. But even scholars who have dealt with cultural variables as important elements in entrepreneurial activities have stressed the patterns of extended family and social mobility more than religious values. Kilby has argued that the roots of Nigerian entrepreneurial deficiencies may run deeper than lack of experience or training, and lie in the underlying disposition and attitudes of entrepreneurs. These attitudes in turn affect business ethics and the delegation of managerial authority. But Kilby does not single out religion as an independent variable nor does he isolate religious components of Nigerian culture. He emphasizes traditional sociocultural phenomena common to all Nigeria's ethnic groups[32] (and thus common to all religions). He argues that while Ibo and Yoruba patterns of status mobility based on achieved wealth provide a strong incentive to establish a business enterprise as a means of obtaining high social status, once established there are no antecedent roles conferring respect for efficient managerial performance.[33] Others have argued that the desire to get rich quick, willingness to channel resources to family, or engage in corrupt acts stem from traditional sociocultural patterns. But again, few have isolated the part of religious variables in these patterns.

It is not that analysts have been unaware of religion as a factor. But they have found that ethnicity, not religion, is critical in social and economic networks through which business is carried out. Cohen reports that Yoruba Moslems objected to Hausa Moslems' religious and economic separatism in Ibadan.[34] When analysts have tried to treat religion as an independent variable, they have had difficulties parceling religion out from ethnic subcultures. LeVine and others have speculated that individualism, childrearing, and individual achievement norms would be related to individualistic concepts of man's relation to God.[35] Ibos, however, are known as perhaps the most individualistic of Nigeria's ethnic groups and they are largely Catholic, whereas Catholicism stresses the individual's direct relation to

God less than does Protestantism. Commentators have emphasized elements in Ibo culture more than religion in accounting for Ibo desire for upward mobility. Individual initiative, not inherited position, establish an Ibo's place in the system. Willingness to innovate and a fluid world view structured as a marketplace characterize Ibo views. Religious views have not been seen as critical to commercial success.[36] Nor has traditional religion much affected agricultural practices, although certain ceremonies are performed by those who practice traditional religion in connection with their farming activities. The Smocks write that "the extent to which economic factors override religious traditions and sentiments can be seen in the gradual displacement of yams by cassava as the principal crop . . . the traditionally unchallenged significance of yams in the diet and the economy meant that yams were elevated to sacred status, and they continue to play a central role in religious ceremonies . . . [that] Cassava gives higher per acre yields, requires less work, and presents fewer storage problems is considered more significant than the religious status of the yam.[37]

Islam is often described as a religion of obedience and respect for authority and thus understood to discourage individualism and presumably to discourage achievement orientation. Yet Islam like Christianity involves individual, not group adherence to beliefs which are held as valid. In his study of Nigerian schoolboys, LeVine found among Hausas in his sample indications of lower frequency of a need for achievement—of what, following McClelland, is defined as a latent disposition to compete with a standard of excellence.[38] He found a strong positive association between Christianity and the percentage of his achievement imagery-dreamers for the same as a whole. Religion was almost completely confounded with ethnicity, since the ethnic groups with the highest percentages were Ibos and Southern Yoruba. The only ethnic group in his sample which had both Christians and Moslems was Northern Yoruba and here he found no significant association between Christianity and the frequency of achievement imagery.[39]

It is true that studies of Yoruba social mobility have shown a high percentage of Christians as compared to Moslems who attained political prominence during the Colonial period. For example town councilors in Lagos were overwhelmingly Yoruba and Christian between 1920 and 1947. During 1950–55 Christians still dominated, although many more Moslems appeared. From 1959 on, some Lagos wards elected Moslems overwhelmingly and these individuals came from a wide variety of occupations. A shift had occurred from political power resting on elite educational background to political power resting on communal ties and economic associations.[40] This shift occurred in Lagos in the mid- to late 1950s but not in all the Yoruba-speaking Western Region. In 1958 the Federal Executive Committee of the Action Group, the Yoruba-based ruling party in the Western

Region in the 1950s and early 1960s, had forty-five Christians, five Moslems, and twelve unknown in an area which by this time was about half Christian and half Moslem.[41] While some prominent Moslem Action Group politicians were educators, the Moslem Yoruba political elite tended to have backgrounds in business and trade rather than in education and law. Yoruba Christians used their education to become socially mobile and politically involved, but it is not clear that Yoruba Christians as compared to Moslems were more entrepreneurial or business-oriented in general. They were able to rise in bureaucratic organizations, both public and private, in which Western education was a key qualification.

In his examination of Moslem and Christian converts in Ile-Ife, Laitin notes that both religions took root there in the early years of this century. "Both won converts because their virtuosos had reputed healing powers, and because they were associated with progress and civilization (formal education and advanced technology for the Christians; associations with Lagos business life for the Moslems), and because neither religion presented itself initially as an exclusive alternative to the traditional religions." Laitin could find no discernible difference in occupation of the original converts to Islam or Christianity in Ile-Ife.[42]

To raise questions about entrepreneurship is to ask about the motivations for individual and family behavior and to operate at the micro level. Coming back to macro levels, one of the most interesting and difficult questions is that of the impact of religion on matters of equity in Nigeria. It is very hard to sort out the impact of ethnicity and religion on class consciousness, organizations, and on demands for equality. Before even trying to do this, it is essential to analyze how people understand class, wealth, and poverty in Nigeria.

Understanding Class, Wealth, and Poverty in Nigeria

Because Nigeria is a large heterogenous society with many culturally distinct groups and subgroups, we cannot expect that culturally associated views of wealth, poverty, and the way people are to be grouped will necessarily be the same throughout the country. For some areas we have extremely detailed data on the relationship of social values to social-structural variables such as patterns of landholding and stratification,[43] the relationship between fertility and attitudes,[44] and perceptions of inequality as they relate to occupational data.[45]

I want to present some vignettes culled on a selective basis from various authors who have done detailed studies in Nigeria. My aim is to show the variety of terms and their usage in the way people think about wealth, poverty, and equality in different parts of Nigeria. I also want to root understanding of inequality in the population's own context and vocabulary to avoid facile generalizations about class consciousness and class politics.[46] We should not deduce values from certain structural conditions, much less deduce political behavior from those conditions.

P.C. Lloyd argues that "tribally structured societies . . . tend to have a variety of terms with which to designate men of prestige, emphasizing variously their wealth, their moral standing, or their generosity. And these terms are applied to individuals and not groups."[47] Wealth itself is not an unambiguous concept. Students of fertility have been very conscious of the need to explore ideas about wealth. A.O. Okore tells us that "wealth, to an Ibo man, still consists of land, crops and livestock, children, money and other forms of material goods."[48] Ukaegbu notes that "numerous children are regarded as 'true wealth' and there is a tendency to regard couples who have large families as being rich or potentially so."[49] Caldwell says that four-fifths of all Yoruba hold that children are either better than wealth or are wealth.[50]

Studies of fertility in Nigeria and elsewhere indicate a sense of the variety of ideas about wealth in different societies. Ideas concerning children and wealth have to do with what we call "this-worldly income"—that children provide security, labor, and income. There are also considerations that have to do with maintenance of a family after the death of a couple and the ability of children to provide for the demands of the community at burial ceremonies. In rural Yoruba it is still taken as one of the immutable facts of existence that size of family, political strength, and affluence are not only interrelated but one and the same.[51]

Polly Hill insists that the Hausa informants of the Dorayi people near Kano City relate the concept of wealth specifically to economic well-being. They distinguish the economic from other factors. "The use of the word 'wealth' is meant to convey the importance of economic security." Wealth is separated from political power.[52] Hill goes on to argue that the concept of wealth, *arziki,* is a mysterious personal attribute necessary for success in this world. It is a gift which cannot be rationally explained in terms of inheritance, hard work, many sons, intelligence, or religious piety.[53]

It is important to know whether ideas of wealth are the same when applied to individuals and groups. In a work devoted to Yoruba perceptions of social inequality, Lloyd argues that distinctions should be made between how the Yoruba see themselves in society and how they view society. For example, equals of the same age are considered to be "class mates" rather than people of equal status or income.[54] According to Lloyd, answers to questions of social rank depend on differences in ethnic terms between "indigens" and "strangers," or between, for example, the Oyo or the Ekiti Yoruba. Lloyd says that his respondents made distinctions of wealth but to do this descriptively was not to raise questions of legitimacy or to attribute causal factors. People make distinctions between rich and poor but do not use class terms.[55] Lloyd also tells us that the Oyo and Ibadan Yoruba complained of not getting enough resources compared to other Yoruba; but these disparities between ethnic subgroups did not lead to distinctions in class terms. Distinctions between ethnic groups were made in terms of diet and speech.[56]

There are many places in Africa where differences between ethnic groups have come to be defined in terms of economic inequality. But the relationships between ethnic and class definitions are usually complex and sometimes the reverse of what might be expected. In some West African societies all herdsmen are called Fulani, an ethnic term. Occupations are given an ethnic identification. Lloyd, however, says that perhaps the Hausa language allows for the terminology of caste to be adapted to the terminology of class—for example, the terms *talakawa* (commoner) and *sarakuna* (officeholders and their kin) form categories into which the population may be divided. But while the stratified societies of the savanna have this terminology, Lloyd says that concepts of class are largely absent from West African vernacular languages.[57]

Equality and Religion

Having a sense of the ethnic and language complexities involved in understanding inequality should make us very careful as we approach the subject of inequality and religion. One can find highly egalitarian strands in Christianity and Islam, and depending on the social and historical milieus in which we look at the propagation and organization of these religions, we can find them acting as vehicles for egalitarian demands or as justifications for the status quo.

Laitin argues that Moslems have a rigid sense of social equality and that this is not just a doctrinal matter but observable in behavior. All members of the mosque have a moral responsibility to enforce community standards; modes of prayer are simple and dress is austere at the mosque; all prostrate themselves while praying and the floor is an equalizer. Laitin notes that Yoruba culture requires that young men prostrate, or at least lean, to elders or social superiors. While prostration does not go on in church, leaning does, but in the mosque norms require an equal bowing from the knees for all greeters.[58] The women of the mosque which Laitin visited, however, were consigned to dank rooms away from the men. There is no equality of sexes at the mosque, nor is there much at the churches in Yorubaland either.

So far, we have been talking about equality and the life of the mosque. But what about life outside the mosque? As many have pointed out, Islam demands of the rich that they give *zakat* or alms to the poor. It also requires that inheritance be spread among heirs. But there are varieties of land tenure and inheritance patterns among Moslems in Nigeria.

In his work on Ile-Ife, Laitin suggests that differences between mosque and church mean very little outside of them. The norms of Yoruba culture dominate.[59] Yorubas, Christian and Moslem, are hardly bent on income redistribution or on abolishing status and the hierarchy of traditional authorities. (The Yoruba-based Unity Party of Nigeria campaigned in the 1979 elections on a populist platform which stressed the delivery of services. It did not campaign for redistribution of income, and the party platform stated a commitment to freeing the private sector from regulations, although some UPN governors have taken over some private enterprises.) It may be that if one controls for wealth, Christians have fewer wives than Moslems (this appears to have been true in Ife), but polygamy is widespread among Christians, and Moslems have justified their own need to accumulate in terms of supporting large households and more wives.

In the North, Islam cuts different ways with regard to equality. Islamic Northern Nigeria is the most hierarchical part of the country. This is expressed in terms of relations between the sexes. Fewer women attend school in the Islamic North than in the South. Girls do not attend Koranic schools despite Nigeria's commitment to universal primary education. Women are channeled into a narrower range of occupations. Religion provides a rationale for the existing social order while providing an institutional framework through which women fulfill the economic and social roles assigned to them.[60] The wives of the Hausa ruling class experience seclusion in the husband's compound. Remy points out that better-off workers have begun to adopt the status symbols of the Moslem Hausa aristocracy, including the seclusion of women, which is justified in religious terms and which has important consequences for the development of a modern labor force in rural and urban areas. The gulf between commoners and royalty seems large in the Northern emirates. And Islam is used to justify status inequalities in both the political and economic realms. Class-based deprivation and criteria for leadership are likely to be mediated through an Islamic ideology, "less because of a deep religiosity, but more because, for uneducated workers, it is the only known and accepted standard of legitimacy."[61] Dorothy Remy tells us that the workers she interviewed in Zaria had both a clear perception of the status hierarchy within the factory and the realization that schooling was a prerequisite for higher-paying jobs. No one she interviewed thought it unfair that those in supervisory positions should receive an annual income four times as great as their own.[62] In Nigeria it is common that the status conferred by education justifies income differentials to workers. But there may be a special emphasis in the North whereby status and income differentials are justified in terms of ethnic values in which religion plays a part. Do Hausa owners who pay their workers low wages justify this in traditional and/or religious terms?

We must be careful not to see Islam simply as a component of an ideology which justifies inequality. For Islam in the North has acted powerfully as an integrative mechanism through which demands for equality are made. For example, observers of African trade unions and the working class have frequently argued that industrial trade unionized workers were forming a privileged labor aristocracy, as compared to the growing number of workers in the informal and nonunionized sector.[63] Paul Lubeck argues that formal and informal sector workers in Kano do not form two separate and distinct classes and that common backgrounds, including religious backgrounds, serve to integrate members of the occupationally differentiated sectors. "Because the urban workers in Kano emerge from the common inequality status of being a *talakawa* (commoner) before they became urban laborers and because marriage patterns, mutual aid, Islamic institutions, households, and community relationships integrate the formal and informal sector workers, there is no objective or subjective cleavage between them. . . . Members of the informal sector, by servicing the formal sector workers, participate in a redistribution of high income such that informal sector workers regard the formal sector workers as a political elite pursuing the class interests of the laboring population as a whole."[64]

A common language and set of symbols links managers and owners to workers. Workers in Kano see themselves as Hausa and as Moslems, like the owners of the processing industries in which they work or the managers they have contact with. When economically squeezed, they see a violation of Islamic norms and a repudiation of ethnic brotherhood. This intensifies ill feelings if redress is not made. In January 1971, when owners did not pay government-stipulated wage awards, known as the Abedo awards, as the Moslem festival of Idl Fitr approached, when gifts are given and celebrations made, traditional Islamic customs "interacted with industrial conflict so as to buttress the class solidarity of workers."[65] Islam integrated workers' demands and when Islamic norms were seen to be violated, because gifts were not given, the gulf between owners and workers was widened. In this case, Islam provided a language and values through which to express egalitarian demands.

Currently in Nigerian politics, the most radical demands and implementation of policies have come from a splinter faction of the People's Redemption Party (PRP) which has controlled the governorship of two states: Kano and Kaduna. The PRP is led by Aminu Kano, who had been the populist leader of the old Northern Element's Progressive Union based in the Middle Belt areas of the North and in Aminu Kano's home areas of Kano city and emirate. NEPU did use the language of class struggle as it contended with the Northern Peoples' Congress in the pre-1966 civilian-led Nigeria. But NEPU's appeals were very heterogeneous and made to leaders of tribal unions in the Middle Belt, Moslem Northerners of the *Ma'aikata* class such as teachers, native administration workers, and ex-servicemen.[66] Amino Kano, the leader of NEPU and the PRP was a *mallam,* a Moslem teacher.[67] After Nigeria returned to party politics in the late 1970s, Aminu Kano was able to gather support of some major trade union leaders and, with traditional support plus workers' support, was able to carry Kano State in the presidential election.

The PRP's manifesto called for the state to take command of the economy and was more socialist in orientation than the other parties' platforms, although many PRP ideas remained highly general. When two PRP governors won (although in Kaduna State the legislature remained in the hands of the National Party of Nigeria),[68] they embarked on a radical program. They abolished head and cattle taxes and pushed to democratize local government procedures and reform land tenure systems. They made common cause with governors from parties other than the NPN and were expelled from their own PRP. Eventually the governor of Kaduna State, Alhaji Balarabe Musa, was impeached by the state assembly in 1981.

The point of retelling these stories is that it has been in the Moslem North, especially in Kaduna and Kano City, the largest urban concentrations in Northern Nigeria, that radical and conservative forces have faced each other directly. The expelled PRP governors and their supporters see both the NPN and the established PRP as oligarchic and reactionary. They are viewed in turn as dangerous radicals. Very different economic and social interests and programs are developed in a context of struggle between traditional emirate authority and secular leaders; different religious and traditional authorities with bases in Kano and Sokoto also contend with each other; and different Moslem movements and sects operate in the fluid political and religious milieu of Nigeria's North.

In December 1980 large-scale rioting in Kano City led to the death of 1,000–10,000 people as a sect led by Muhammudu Marwa Maitatsine fought pitched battles with Nigerian police and army. Marwa appears to have been a leader of the Yan Izala sect whose stated aim is to strike against materialism and privilege and purify Islamic practice. The sect has been supported by refugees from Chad and Niger, as well as by recent rural migrants to Kano City. Police and army put down the rioting with great violence and it may have been that the perception of the sect as heretical led to the lack of restraint by army and police.

In July 1981 riots again broke out in Kano. The governor of Kano State, Alhaji Abubakar Rimi, sent to the traditional ruler, the emir of Kano, a letter in which he charged the emir with disrespect to the secular authority. The emir's supporters in turn took the governor's letter to be disrespectful and unacceptable. State government offices were sacked and the governor's political advisor was killed.

Thus parts of Northern Nigeria continue to be roiled by the movements of Islamic sects calling for reform and purification and by conflict between secular and traditional-religious authorities. The North, like other areas of Nigeria, continues to have syncretistic mixtures of world religions and ethnic cultures. There is a complicated history of reforms as purification, modernization, Westernization, and secularization in the North and in Kano particularly.[69] Islam in the North has developed through brotherhood communities that "reflect" ethnic, geographic, and generational factors, all of which intersect with underlying economic patterns (such as urbanization and division of labor). The brotherhoods also create transethnic loyalties in Nigeria. The brotherhoods in Nigeria, as in other parts of Africa and especially in Senegal, engage in direct economic activities.[70]

While the Islamic brotherhoods link political and economic actors and achievement-oriented bureaucrats, in Iboland ethnic unions facilitated accommodation between tradition and modernity and have harnessed elements in the traditional political culture that have been conducive to political development.[71] There were many values in Ibo traditional society that were compatible with rapid development. But the traditional Ibo villages were isolated and not integrated into a wider community. As Smock describes the process, the ethnic unions, not religious groups or religious values, emerge as the critical transforming factors. "By transforming religious facets of traditional culture into expressions of communal loyalty, the unions prevented communities from fragmenting as they went through the process of Christianization."[72] Interestingly, Smock does not describe the process of Christianization as itself an integrative one for Ibos. She stresses the limited role of the Catholic Church in the areas studied. The church was predominant and filled a vital role in community life. But most priests were Irish, not Nigerian, well after Nigeria's independence, and the Nigerians did not come from Eastern Region, and were therefore not involved in local disputes. Smock also argues that conversion to Christianity effected limited change in the convert: "Membership in the church did not preclude participation in other rites, since former pagan festivals were transformed to celebrate the secular unity of the community, rather than the beneficence of a deity."[73]

It may be that Catholicism in Iboland like Islam in Northern Nigeria affected attitudes toward political authority more than attitudes toward economic activities. Perhaps Catholicism played a role as Ibos came more to accept centralization of political authority.[74] Similarly, as political modernization and integration proceeded in Northern Nigeria, reformist movements in Islam were important. Paden suggests that strands in Islamic political thought of repairing and holism have been merged with an accent on the former.[75] If this is the case, it may suggest possibilities for reform rather than change being necessary in the core values and structures of society with all the political implications this entails.

Conclusion

No one concerned with the economic and political history of Nigeria could ignore the impact of Islam and Christianity. No one concerned with Nigerian culture and values could ignore these religions and the continued impact of pre-Colonial traditional religions. Having said this, it is still difficult to isolate the effects of religion and especially to distinguish the importance of religion from a wider set of ethnic and cultural attitudes, values, and structures when we look at entrepreneurship, attitudes toward equality, or commitments to indigenization of the economy.

This is not to say that religion has not been important in affecting economic changes. Sometimes religious values and institutions have affected more directly political values and institutions and these in turn have been consequential for the relationship between, for example, private and public sectors in Northern Nigeria and perhaps for a concern with state control.

Religion, acting on social structures and the formation of groups, and itself often an outgrowth of fundamental social, economic, and demographic changes, is a critical component for the analysis of economic and social change. There is a broad agenda for research on religion in Nigeria and a great deal of work needs to be done on the interrelationship of religion and economic change and development in Nigeria. For example, we need much more work on the economic activities of religious institutions such as has been done in Senegal.[76] This would entail work on Islamic brotherhoods in Nigeria and an examination of the economic activities of Christian churches. We also need more interviewing of public officials to try to understand how general attitudes about economic matters relate to religious beliefs and whether diffuse attitudes translate into specific policies.

We have a better understanding of the ways that politicians both mobilize constituents through appeals to religion and use communal institutions to further political ends and organizations than we have of the relationship between religion and economy. A wide research agenda looms before students of Nigerian society. Historical and contemporary work needs to be undertaken at the level of individuals, firms, and government agencies. No one with even a passing acquaintance of Nigeria would deny the historical and present importance of religious movements and the interaction of world religions with African religious beliefs and institutions that existed before the spread of world religions and coexisted with them. The need now is to understand the impact of world religions. It is especially important to examine these in the context of a rapidly changing society, an economy that retains many old features while manifesting important new ones associated with an oil economy, foreign financial and industrial interventions, and growing connections in trade and investment with the rest of Africa and the world.

APPENDIX 1

NIGERIA: Religious Affiliation by Region, 1952 and 1963

Region	Percent Muslim		Percent Christian		Percent Other	
	1952	1963	1952	1963	1952	1963
North	73.0	71.7	2.7	9.7	24.3	18.6
West	32.8	43.4	36.9	48.7	30.3	7.9
East	.6	.3	46.2	77.2	50.2	22.5
Lagos	41.0	44.3	53.0	54.6	2.0*	1.1
Mid-West	--	4.2	--	54.9	--	40.9
TOTAL	44.4	49	22.0	34	33.6	17

*Plus 4 percent other.
Source: Nigerian Census, 1952; Nigeria Yearbook, 1969 (Lagos: Times Press, 1970), p. 193. As found in J.N. Paden, *Religion and Political Culture in Kano* (Berkeley: University of California Press, 1973), p. 44, table 4.

APPENDIX 2

NIGERIA: Percent of Moslems in States and Party Votes (1979)

	State	Moslem	%NPN*	%GNPP*	%PRP*	%UPN	%NNP
1.	Sokoto	97.6	66.5	26.1	3.3	2.5	.9
2.	Kano	97.4	19.9	1.5	76.4	1.2	.9
3.	Borno	93.1	34.7	54.0	6.5	3.4	1.4
4.	Bauchi	80.6	62.5	15.4	14.3	3.0	4.7
5.	Kwara	75.2	53.6	5.7	.7	39.5	.5
6.	Oyo	62.4	12.8	.6	.3	85.8	.6
7.	Niger	59.7	74.9	16.5	4.0	3.7	1.1
8.	Kaduna	56.4	53.1	13.8	31.7	6.7	4.7
9.	Ogun	54.3	6.2	.5	6.2	92.1	.3
10.	Lagos	44.3	7.2	.5	.5	82.3	9.6
11.	Gongola	34.1	35.5	34.1	4.3	21.7	4.4
12.	Plateau	25.7	34.7	6.8	4.0	5.3	49.2
13.	Ondo	12.3	4.2	.3	.2	94.5	.9
14.	Benue	11.3	76.4	7.9	1.4	2.6	11.7
15.	Bendel	7.4	36.2	1.2	.7	53.2	8.6
16.	Rivers	0.2	72.7	2.2	.5	10.3	14.4
17.	Cross RIvers	.1	64.4	15.1	1.0	11.8	7.7
18.	Imo	.1	8.8	3.0	.9	.6	86.7
19.	Anambra	.6	13.5	1.7	1.2	.8	82.9

*Presidential candidate was Moslem
*NPN - Alhaji Shehu Shagari
*GNPP - Alhaji Waziri Ibrahim
*PRP - Alhaji Aminu Kano

Notes

1. For an interesting analysis of religion and political culture see David Laitin, "Religion, Political Culture, and the Weberian Tradition," *World Politics* 30 (July 1978): 563–92.
2. George Balandier, *Sociologie actuelle de l'Afrique Noire* (Paris: Presses Universitaires de France, 1955).
3. For a major study of the adoption of Aladura Christianity and the development of the Christ Apostolic Church and the Cherubim and Seraphim in Yorubaland see, J.D.Y. Peel, *Aladura: A Religious Movement among the Yoruba* (London: Oxford University Press, 1968). Peel describes the members of the Aladura churches as "the middling men," the "industrious sort of people and recent immigrants to the town," (p. 228) as Walzer and Hill have written of adherents to Puritanism. Michael Walzer, *The Revolution of the Saints* (London, 1966); C. Hill, *Religion and Puritanism in Pre-Revolutionary England* (London, 1964). Peel is concerned to explain the fundamental character of a religion of industrialization in the Yoruba context as a new morality of obeying rules (p. 299). The difficulty with picking out individuals who themselves seek out a religion like the Aladura churches and then arguing that the religion has a particular impact is that the religion may be sought precisely for its compatibility with values and attitudes the individual already has. Peel is aware of this and does not hold that economic behavior stems from religious beliefs. He argues that the doctrine held by Aladura believers was determined by a particular world view they held (p. 298). This world view, as a system of ideas, seems to give rise both to church membership and to economic traits.
4. Laitin, p. 591.
5. David Laitin, "Conversion and Political Change: A Study of (Anglican) Christianity and Islam among the Yorubas of Ile-Ife." Paper delivered at the Annual Meeting of the American Political Science Association (Washington, 28–31 August 1980).
6. I am indebted to Larry Frank of Sarah Lawrence College for these insights.
7. I am indebted to Graham Irwin of Columbia University for these insights.
8. I am not going to deal with the direct economic roles of religious institutions.
9. These figures are from *World Development Report, 1980* (Washington: World Bank, August 1980).
10. V.P. Diejomaoh and E.C. Anusionwu, "The Structure of Income Inequality in Nigeria: A Macro Analysis." In Henry Bienen and V.P. Diejomaoh (eds.), *The Political Economy of Income Distribution in Nigeria* (New York: Holmes & Meier, 1981), p. 115. They conclude that the Gini coefficient increased from .55 in 1970 to about .7 in 1976.
11. For a discussion of the creation of states see Keith Panter-Brick (ed.), *Soldiers and Oil: The Transformation of Nigerian Politics* (London: Cass, 1968); *Federal Military Government Views on the Report of the Panel on Creation of States* (Lagos: Federal Ministry of Information, 1976).
12. For a review of revenue allocation see Douglas Rimmer, "Development in Nigeria: An Overview." In Bienen and Diejomaoh, pp. 29–88. For a discussion of class and ethnicity in Nigeria see Henry Bienen, "The Politics of Distribution: Institutions, Class, and Ethnicity." In Bienen and Diejomaoh, pp. 129–72.
13. For an analysis of the Nigerian tax system see P. Ada Omorogiuwa, "Personal

Income Taxation and Income Distribution in Nigeria." In Bienen and Diejo-maoh, pp. 421–53.

14. For a review of Nigerian economic history see Rimmer; Sayre P. Schatz, *Nigerian Capitalism* (Berkeley and Los Angeles: University of California Press, 1978); Carl Eicher and Carl Liedholm (eds.), *Growth and Development of the Nigerian Economy* (East Lansing: Michigan State University Press, 1970); Adebayo Adediji, *Nigerian Federal Finance* (London: Hutchinson Educational, 1969); Gerald Helleiner, *Peasant Agriculture, Government, and Economic Growth in Nigeria* (Homewood, Ill.: Irwin, 1966); Wolfgang Stolper, *Planning without Facts: Lessons in Resource Allocation from Nigeria's Development* (Cambridge: Harvard University Press, 1966). There are various World Bank studies of the Nigerian economy and the various Nigerian plans and guidelines to plans. The *Nigerian Journal of Economic and Social Studies* is a major source for analysis of the Nigerian economy; *West Africa* (London) provides good coverage of current economic events.

15. Various estimates of projected grain supply and demand indicate a cereal grain equivalent of twenty million tons deficit by 1990.

16. These centralizing institutions have had a disproportionate share of minorities in key roles. In the federal civil service, significant positions among permanent secretaries and principal assistant secretaries have been held by people from Bendel State. Military officers frequently came from the old Middle Belt areas (Tiv, Angas, Idoma, Birom, and others); enlisted men and noncommissioned officers from these areas have been prevalent too. While the number of Yorubas increased markedly in the army in 1967–71, as the army itself expanded tenfold from 20,000 troups, it was striking that many Yoruba officers came from what is now Kwara State (Northern Yorubaland) rather than from the Yoruba core areas.

17. Peter Kilby, *Industrialization in an Open Economy: Nigeria, 1945–1977* (London: Cambridge University Press, 1969).

18. Schatz, p. 5.

19. *Industrial Survey of Nigeria, 1963* (Lagos: Federal Office of Statistics, 1966), as reported in Kilby, pp 19–20.

20. For a discussion of the impact of multinational corporations in Nigeria see Thomas Biersteker, *Distortion or Development* (Cambridge: MIT Press, 1976).

21. Pauline Baker, *Urbanization and Political Change: The Politics of Lagos, 1917–1967* (Berkeley: University of California Press, 1974), p. 45.

22. Ibid.

23. Schatz, p. 23.

24. Ibid., p. 24.

25. O. Aboyade, "Closing Remarks." In *Nigeria's Indigenization Policy: Proceedings of the 1974 Symposium,* organized by the Nigerian Economic Society (Ibadan: University of Ibadan, Department of Economics), pp. 77–78.

26. Omafume F. Onoge, "The Indigenization Decree and Economic Independence: Another Case of Bourgeois Utopianism." In ibid., p. 61.

27. The following publications contain accounts of high-level Nigerian civil servants who have spoken their minds. Mahmud Tukur (ed.), *Administrative and Political Development: Prospects for Nigeria* (Kaduna: Baraka, 1971); A.A. Ayida, "The Nigerian Revolution, 1966–1976." Address to the Nigerian Economic Society Annual Meeting (Enugu, 1973). In 1972 a conference was held at Ahmadu Bello University in Zaria at which permanent secretaries addressed

the questions of institutional and administrative perspectives for national development. A number of papers were subsequently published in the *New Nigerian* (Kaduna), especially in the 25 November 1972 issue.

28. See Donald Morrison, "Inequalities of Social Rewards: Realities and Perceptions in Nigeria." In Bienen and Diejomaoh, pp. 173–92.

29. Kilby, p. 32.

30. For one study which insists that Moslems have been encouraged by their religion to make profits, see Maxime Rodinson, *Islam and Capitalism* (New York: Panther, 1974).

31. Among studies of entrepreneurship in Nigeria see Schatz, pp. 77–97; E.O. Akeredolu-Ake, "Some Thoughts on the Indigenization Process and the Quality of Nigerian Capitalism." In *Nigeria's Indigenization Policies;* Kilby; John Harris, "Industrial Entrepreneurship in Nigeria." Ph.D. thesis (Evanston, Ill.: Northwestern University, 1967); E. Wayne Nafziger, "Nigerian Enterpreneurship: A Study of Indigenous Businessmen in the Footwear Industry." Ph.D. thesis (Urbana: University of Illinois, 1967); Peter Kilby, *African Enterprise: The Nigerian Bread Industry* (Stanford: Hoover Institution, 1965); Peter Marris, "Social Barriers to Entrepreneurship," *Journal of Development Studies* (October 1968); E.O. Akeredolu-Ake, "Values, Motivations, and History in the Development of Private Indigenous Entrepreneurship: Lessons from Nigeria's Experience, 1946–1966," *Nigerian Journal of Economic and Social Studies* 13 (July 1971): 195–220; E. Wayne Nafziger, "The Effect of the Nigerian Extended Family on Entrepreneurial Activity," *Economic Development and Cultural Change* (October 1969).

32. Kilby, *Industrialization in an Open Economy,* pp. 341–42.

33. Ibid.

34. Abner Cohen, "The Politics of the Kola Trade." In Edith Whetham and Jean Currie (eds.), *Readings in the Applied Economics of Africa.* Vol. 1, *Micro Economics* (London: Cambridge University Press, 1967).

35. Robert A. LeVine, *Dreams and Deeds: Achievement Motivation in Nigeria* (Chicago: University of Chicago Press, 1966).

36. Audrey C. Smock, *Ibo Politics: The Role of Ethnic Unions in Eastern Nigeria* (Cambridge: Harvard University Press), pp. 16, 30. For studies of Ibo culture see Victor Uchendu, *The Ibo of Southeast Nigeria* (New York: Holt, Rinehart & Winston, 1965); K. Onwuka Dike, *Trade and Politics in the Niger Delta, 1830–1885* (London: Oxford University Press, 1956).

37. David R. Smock and Audrey C. Smock, *Cultural and Political Aspects of Rural Transformation: A Case Study of Eastern Nigeria* (New York: Praeger, 1972) p. 95.

38. See David McClelland, *The Achieving Society* (Princeton: Van Nostrand, 1961).

39. LeVine, p. 58.

40. Baker, Appendices on socioeconomic and political profiles of Lagos town councilors, pp. 286–306.

41. Richard Sklar, *Nigerian Political Parties* (Princeton: Princeton University Press, 1963) p. 484.

42. Laitin, "Conversion and Political Change," pp. 5–6.

43. See Polly Hill, *Population, Prosperity, and Poverty: Rural Kano 1900 and 1970* (Cambridge: Cambridge University Press, 1977).

44. A.A. Okore, "The Ibos of Arochukwu in Imo State, Nigeria." In John C.

Caldwell (ed.), *The Persistence of High Fertility,* part 1 (Canberra: Australian National University, 1976).

45. See Oshoma Imoagene, *Social Mobility in Emergent Society: A Study of the New Elite in Western Nigeria* (Canberra: Australian National University, 1976); P.C. Lloyd, *Power and Independence: Urban African Perceptions of Social Inequality* (London: Routledge & Kegan Paul, 1974).

46. As J.D.Y. Peel says when he examines the Yoruba concepts of development, "the linguistic vehicles of central concepts enable particular experiences, solitary or shared, to be linked into something of a unified interpretation of a collective historical experience." J.D.Y. Peel, "Olaju: A Yoruba Concept of Development," *Journal of Development Studies* 14 (January 1976).

47. P.C. Lloyd, *Africa in Social Change* (Baltimore: Penguin, 1967).

48. Okore, p. 316.

49. Alfred Ukaegbu, "The Practice of Traditional Birth Control and Attitudes toward Family Planning in Rural Eastern Nigeria" (in press), cited in Caldwell.

50. John C. Caldwell, "Towards a Restatement of Demographic Transition Theory." In ibid., p. 75.

51. Ibid.

52. Hill, pp. 110–13.

53. Ibid., p. 155.

54. Lloyd, *Power and Independence,* p. 140.

55. Ibid., p. 168.

56. Ibid., p. 177.

57. Lloyd, *Africa in Social Change,* p. 314.

58. Laitin, "Conversion and Political Change," p. 18.

59. Peel makes the same point when he says that "Yoruba Moslems have been tolerant and Yoruba before they are Moslems, except for the most orthodox." Peel, *Aladura,* p. 4. See also J.S. Trimingham, *Islam in West Africa* (London, 1959).

60. Dorothy Remy, "Underdevelopment and the Experience of Women: A Nigerian Case Study." In Gavin Williams (ed.), *Nigeria: Economy and Society* (London: Collings, 1976) p. 124.

61. Paul Lubeck, "Unions, Workers, and Consciousness in Kano, Nigeria: A View from Below." In Richard Sandbrook and R. Cohen (eds.), *The Development of an African Working Class* (Toronto: University of Toronto Press, 1976) p. 158.

62. Dorothy Remy, "Economic Security and Industrial Unionism: A Nigerian Case Study." In Sandbrook and Cohen, p. 169.

63. For arguments concerning labor aristocracies see John S. Saul, "The Labor Aristocracy Thesis Reconsidered." In ibid., pp. 303–10; Adrian Peace, "The Lagos Proletariat: Labour Aristocrats or Populist Militants." In ibid; Peter Waterman, "Communist Theory in the Nigerian Trade Union Movement," *Politics and Society* 3 (Spring 1973).

64. Paul Lubeck, "Contrast and Continuity in a Dependent City: Kano, Nigeria." In Janet Abu-Lughod and Richard Hay (eds.), *Third World Urbanization* (Chicago: Maaroufa, 1971) p. 289.

65. Lubeck, "Unions, Workers," p. 152.

66. See Billy Dudley, *Parties and Politics in Northern Nigeria* (London: Cass, 1968), p. 169.

67. For a biography of this interesting political figure see Alan Feinstein, *African*

Revolutionary: The Life and Times of Nigeria's Aminu Kano (New York: Quadrangle, 1973).

68. The NPN was also seen as a Hausa-Fulani and a Moslem party, the lineal descendant of the Northern Peoples Congress. But the NPN had the broadest base of support of all parties in the 1979 elections. It came in first or second in all but six of the ninety-five Senate seats. It won more than a third of the vote in Gongola and Bendel states, which do not have significant Hausa-Fulani voters. It won more votes than the Hausa-Fulani share of the population in Niger and Kwara states. The NPN did not do well among Yoruba Moslems who voted for the Yourba-led Unity Party, voting for ethnicity, not religion.

69. For the most detailed treatment see John N. Paden, *Religion and Political Culture in Kano* (Berkeley: University of California Press, 1973). For a review see Laitin, "Religion and Political Culture."

70. Paden argues that the *mallam* or teacher class was a natural link between political and economic classes in Kano and that the reformed brotherhoods facilitated social mobility in Kano. Paden, p. 392. It would be interesting to know if Christian ministers filled similar functions. Laitin ("Conversion and Political Change," pp. 11–12) says that there was a clear functional specification of roles in the Christian missionary tradition as opposed to role diffusion among Moslems: "While the Christian missionaries saw the clear linking of trade, military might and religious conversion, they almost universally refused to take a direct role in the first two functions." The missionaries, as Laitin points out, supported the growth of cash crops, farming, and trade. Subsequently, church figures did play roles in party politics and appear to have been figures linking economic and political actors. Since the emphasis in this chapter is on religious values and economics, I am not dealing directly with the economic undertakings of religious institutions.

71. Smock, p. 237.

72. Ibid., p. 238.

73. Ibid., p. 140.

74. Christianity led to division in Iboland as well as to integration, because it caused splits between pagans and Christians and later, as different missionary societies competed for converts, new sectarian differences divided communities. See Smock and Smock, p. 56.

75. Paden, p. 386.

76. Lucy Behrman, "Muslim Politics and Development in Senegal," *Journal of Modern African Studies* 15 (June 1977): 261–77. Donal B. O'Brien, *Saints and Politicans: Essays in the Organization of Senegalese Peasant Society* (London: Cambridge University Press, 1975). L.B. Venema, *The Wolof of Saloum: Social Structures and Rural Development in Senegal* (Wagenigen: Center for Agricultural Publishing and Documentation, 1978).

10

Economic Values and Traditional Religion among the Yoruba of Nigeria

Benjamin C. Ray

This chapter assumes that religion is one of the many factors contributing to a society's economic patterns. Following Max Weber, I have tried to identify certain religious conceptions which seem to reinforce certain kinds of economic behavior.[1] While I do not think religion acts as a critical independent factor, except sometimes at the personal level, I believe religious ideas contribute to social values and personal attitudes which motivate general forms of economic behavior. I have identified those religious conceptions which seem to have the closest affinity with a set of recognized economic behavior traits, especially among the Yoruba of Western Nigeria.

Analysis of this kind is considerably complicated by the fact that in Nigeria there exists both religious and ethnic pluralism. Unlike post-Reformation Europe, which was the subject of part of Weber's study, contemporary Nigeria does not possess a common (or even dominant) religious ideology nor ethnic constituency. This kind of pluralism means that generalizations about Nigeria are meaningless unless they are tied to specific ethnic groups and religious contexts. I have concentrated here on a single ethnic group, the Yoruba, with some comparative references to the Ibo of Eastern Nigeria. The Yoruba live in the western part of the country and are prominently involved in all aspects of Nigerian political, economic, and cultural life. Like the rest of Nigeria, the Yoruba are about equally divided between Christians and Moslems, while a small proportion continues to practice the traditional religion.

It is widely recognized that the most apparent religious influence on the contemporary Nigerian economy must be seen in the greater Westerniza-

229

tion of the Christian members of the population as contrasted to Moslems and traditionalists. This is largely due to the educational system originally established by Christian missionaries and which, until recently, was controlled by the churches. Moslems and traditionalists were excluded from these schools, with the result that the Christians acquired more Western skills and were more exposed to the economic motivations associated with modernization. Colonial authorities also attempted to isolate the Moslems, concentrated in the northern part of the country, from modernizing influences spreading from the Christian South.

As Henry Bienen rightly argues, it is difficult to accept the view that either Islam or the traditional religions were the main barrier to entrepreneurship or that Christianity was a chief cause.[2] Once colonial administration ended and indigenization of the political, educational, and economic structures began, entrepreneurial activity rose among all religious groups. As Bienen notes, most analysts have found that ethnicity, not religion, is the crucial factor in explaining differentiation in economic activity.

This being true, analysts have not, however, sufficiently recognized that ethnicity is fundamentally bound up with a set of values originally shaped by the traditional religious systems. As anthropological studies increasingly show, local cultural patterns in Africa were originally defined and legitimized by mythological and ritual forms. If ethnicity is the key to economic behavior in Nigeria, traditional religious ideas and practices (along with sociological ones) should be regarded as major factors in explaining ethnically differentiated economic patterns. This means that analysis must reach below the overlay of Christian and Moslem ideas and institutions to the level of the indigenous religion and its world view where the effective ethnic value systems were originally created and still live on.

In *The Protestant Ethic and the Spirit of Capitalism* Weber concentrated on theological doctrines of salvation. In the Calvinist tradition he saw the rational pursuit of capitalist goals flowing from spiritual norms which had to be fulfilled to ensure salvation. Among the Yoruba the situation is both strikingly similar and different. In certain respects the Yoruba may be compared with the Ibo of Eastern Nigeria who are sociologically different but share similar economic and religious characteristics.

Both the Yoruba and the Ibo are highly achievement-oriented and both ethnic groups dominate the public and private sectors of the Nigerian economy. Much of this can be attributed to the presence of oil in both regions, but at a different level it also derives from the early Westernization and Christianization of these two groups. However, as LeVine has argued, the achievement orientation of these two groups lies more fundamentally in their ethnic make-up, especially their social structure. Equally significant for our purposes, the social structure of both the Yoruba and Ibo was fundamentally imbedded in indigenous religious ideology.

Yoruba traditional religion followed the general pattern shared by other African religions,[3] with certain important exceptions. These contrasts will be useful in focusing on the unique features of Yoruba traditional religion. Like other traditional religions in Africa, Yoruba religion had a dual mono-theistic/polytheistic character. The notion of a supreme being was widely known in Africa and existed prior to the coming of Islam and Christianity. The concept of supreme being expressed the element of transcendence or ultimacy common to most African religions. As the ultimate principle behind things, the supreme being had no cult, images, temple, or priesthood. The supreme being transcended all reciprocal relationships with human beings on which the lesser gods depended. When the supreme being acted, it was unilaterally for reasons which were only partially known. As the supreme source of life and ultimate arbiter, the supreme being was not involved in everyday life. He was called upon only in moments of personal and collective crisis, when recourse to other powers had failed. The Yoruba supreme god was called Lord of the Sky (Olorun) or Almighty (Olodu-mare), and the lesser gods were known collectively as the *orisha.* Yoruba religion was hierarchically organized, like Yoruba social order, and it dis-played all the complexities of a professionalized ecclesiastic system.

Fundamental to African traditional religions is the notion of the flawed nature of human existence. Almost every African society had a creation myth which explained the origins of the human condition. According to this myth, the world was once a perfect place and the first human beings were immortal; there was no suffering, sickness, toil, or death. This paradisiacal situation came to an end, either as the result of a divine or human misdeed or as the result of an accident. The Yoruba say that originally the sky was close to the earth and that people could take their food from the heavens until some greedy people took too much or until a woman soiled the sky with her hands, whereupon the sky withdrew and people had to toil for their food. Death was said to have come into the world only after the killing of the mother and of the god of death; and human physical deformities were said to have been caused by the drunkenness of the demiurge Obatala. Whatever the specific causes, the point of these myths was to explain the flawed condition of humankind.

The corollary to this idea was the notion that the imperfections of humanity can be temporarily alleviated through ritual action. There was no promise of ultimate salvation in the next world or of the transformation of this world at some future time. The promise of African religions was more limited. It was the promise of periodic redemption of human affairs through the procedures of collective ritual, of a this-worldly salvation. Although life was imperfect, the assumption was that there were ritual means of making it temporarily better. Misfortunes might be overcome, sicknesses might be removed, death might be put off. In general, what ought not to be might be transformed into what ought to be, at least temporarily. This required recourse to ritual, mainly animal sacrifice and spirit possession, through which the world of the sacred was brought into the human realm to "save" it.

Among the Yoruba, the concept of destiny, one's allotted portion *(ipin)*, explained both misfortune and fortune at the personal level.[4] The rites of divination which gave access to one's destiny prescribed the ritual remedy for all life's problems. According to the mythology, a person chose his destiny before birth, without knowing whether it was good or bad. During the course of people's lives, they frequently consulted their destinies to ensure that (however good or bad their destiny might be) they would have the best life possible. In the Yoruba view destiny determined the general outline of a person's life: occupation, spouses, children, successes, failures, and time of death. The details of this pattern might be altered significantly for better or worse by the individual, depending on how conscientiously he manipulated the forces affecting his destiny by ritual procedures. This required constant recourse to divination, which could disclose the content of one's destiny, and it required the formulation of responsible, goal-oriented plans of action. Only in this way could the individual marshall the assistance of the gods and of his own "inner head" *(ori)* to further the path of his destiny.

The divination system, called Ifa, required the individual to be self-reflective and acutely aware of his situation. The client never told the diviner the problem for which he was seeking the solution. The matter lay squarely in his own hands. After the divining chain had been cast, the diviner recited a series of poems which told of real-life problems experienced by the gods and ancestors in the past, and he prescribed the appropriate remedies. The client himself had to choose the poem which best fitted his own situation, after carefully considering the various alternatives. Then he inquired further by asking more questions, until at length he discovered all the potential dangers and benefits which his destiny held forth, together with means for ensuring the best possible outcome. In doing so he also gained the psychological satisfaction of knowing that the gods and ancestors were in support of his plan. From the perspective of Ifa, the gods and the rest of the religious system were primarily relevant to the degree that their actions fitted into a person's destiny. What mattered was the person's cultivation of his own "inner head" *(ori)* or alter ego to which destiny was attached. Other African systems of divination were either public in character or enabled the diviner to manipulate the process in light of the client's problem, thus thwarting individual reflection and initiative. As a sophisticated ritual technique, Ifa divination provided the individual with a supreme "science" by which he himself could contact the ultimate source of things and rationally govern his life.

In contrast to this "egocentric," almost atheistic element was the powerful theistic dimension of Yoruba religion. As in other African religions, the lesser gods and ancestor spirits may be viewed as aspects of the collective unconscious, as powerful images of fundamental psychological and sociological forces which had to be attended to in everyday life. Depending on the society in question, relationships with the gods and spirits were viewed either positively or negatively. The gods and spirits were either cultivated for their beneficial powers or cast out and kept at a safe distance because of their destructive effects. Every Yoruba was a devotee of a particular god which was his personal guardian or savior. At times worshipper identification with the god was so close that he became "possessed" by the god during ceremonies. The gods, who were formerly human beings, had definite personalities. During possession, the devotee became identified with the god and thereby expressed certain unconscious aspects of himself, thus balancing and integrating unrealized aspects of his total personality. On the psychological level, the *orisha* cult was a kind of collective psychodrama filled with therapeutic possibilities. This was the sphere of intensely moral and spiritual relationships.

The gods punished sin and rewarded devotion, thus marking out a clear moral path for the believer. Although one could never achieve perfection in the eyes of the gods, one could achieve the conviction of divine favor, of "chosenness," and experience the closeness of divinity amounting to mystical identification with the god himself. Another feature, rarely present in other African religions, was the concept of final judgment. After death, the individual appeared before the supreme god and was judged. If the person had led a good life, he would be reborn into this world; otherwise, the person was condemned for eternity to the realm of broken potsherds. A contemporary Yoruba playright has taken this idea and adapted a medieval Christian morality play, *Everyman,* to show the redeeming effect of the traditional Yoruba notion of final judgment upon a Yoruba king. The play begins with a praise song to the supreme god: "You, only, decide whether we may return to challenge fate [destiny] once more on earth or whether—our characters beyond repair—we'll be condemned to the heaven of potsherds."[5]

Traditional Yoruba religion did not promise salvation in the afterlife but rebirth in this life, and this was regarded as desirable. A prosperous life was not a sign of the god's favor, for the individual chose his own destiny, and the course it took depended on him alone. Ideally, the individual had to work both at fostering his destiny, which controlled his material success, and at improving his own moral character,[6] which would result in his salvation through rebirth. A disposition toward social achievement through personal effort and a desire to cultivate moral character were built into the traditional culture theologically through the concepts of destiny, judgment, and rebirth.

The concept of personal destiny also lies behind the strong achievement motivation of the Ibo of Eastern Nigeria. Early in a child's life, the parents discovered through divination what kind of destiny had been assigned to their child by the supreme god Chukwu. This destiny, called *chi*, belonged to an ancestor and determined the abilities, successes, and failures the person would have in life. Because each destiny was different, every young man was expected to prove what kind of destiny he possessed through various economic and social activities.[7] Even if one's destiny were small or inauspicious, this inadequacy might be made up by constant ritual activity, especially sacrifices to the ancestors, so that one could finish life more successfully than destiny originally intended. Every individual was also regarded as a reborn ancestor. Since only good persons were believed to be reincarnated, everyone knew that they had formerly been exemplary individuals in their lineage. Traditionally, Ibo society encouraged the emergence of responsible and successful individuals by rewarding them with a number of status titles, because such individuals ensured the preservation of the community. The Ozo title accorded the highest political and social status, and the rituals of the Ozo title organization were regarded as the chief religious means of achieving the prosperity of the community. As LeVine has shown, the Ibo status system provided strong achievement motivation which, he theorizes, made the Ibo among the most successful entrepreneurs in Nigeria.[8] But behind the status system lay the notion of personal destiny and the imperative for young men to demonstrate the kind of destiny accorded them, the best being one which led to membership in the title associations.

David McClelland has suggested that Weber's thesis about the influence of Protestantism on the rise of modern capitalism is but a special instance of a more general influence of "need achievement" on entrepreneurial activity.[9] According to McClelland, the key religious feature involved here is a Weberian-like "institutionalized individualistic approach to God (represented usually by some strain of positive mysticism)."[10] This, he claims, engenders an attitude of personal responsibility for decisions in which "the individual is 'on his toes' in the same sense that the believer is in individualistic religions."[11] McClelland rightly avoids attempting to say whether achievement motivation is rooted in certain religious ideas or vice versa. Rather, he argues that individualistic approaches to deity are significantly

correlated with high achievement motivation and high levels of entrepreneurial activity in both Western and non-Western cultures. Using
McClelland's same achievement standards, LeVine's study of Ibo and
Yoruba also found a high correlation between entrepreneurial activity and
achievement motivation which he believes is rooted in the social status
system.[12]

While these studies have sought to avoid imposing Western value concepts on non-Western ones, this has inevitably, though not seriously, occurred. The original Weberian thesis has also been significantly modified to
suit non-Christian contexts. Where Weber examined the relation between
Protestantism and modern Western capitalism, economic motivational
studies in non-Christian societies have looked at the relation between general achievement values (as seen in religious doctrines, myths, folktales, and
dreams) and general entrepreneurial characteristics. Such a correlation
seems to exist among both the Yoruba and the Ibo, as LeVine has argued.
My purpose here has been to discover (in Weberian fashion) whether any
individualistic and rationalistic religious ideas are also present at the fundamental ethnic level among these groups and how they operate, especially
among the Yoruba.

While obviously speculative, it does not seem misleading to interpret the
Yoruba practice of divination and its related concepts of destiny, final
judgment, and rebirth as involving an individualized and rationalized relation to the divine. Nor does it seem illegitimate to regard these religious
features as positive reinforcements, together with certain sociological and
historical factors, of entrepreneurial behavioral traits. As defined by
McClelland, these traits are: moderate risk taking, energetic and/or novel
instrumental activity, individual responsibility, knowledge of the results of
decisions, and anticipation of future possibilities.

Without much distortion, the Yoruba divination system can be viewed
as developing each of these traits in the individual. While everyone knew
that he had a specific destiny, no one knew what the outcome of that destiny
would be. In a sense one's personal destiny was an unknown risk, and it was
the individual's responsibility to try and make it come out well. To do this
required careful attention to one's destiny through divination, so that one's
path of destiny might be fulfilled in the best possible way. Traditionally, no
important decision was made and no venture undertaken without recourse
to divination. During the seance the individual had to consider his own
situation in light of divination verses recited by the diviner which told how
the gods and ancestors had been advised to act in similar situations in the
past. The client, reflecting on his own problem, chose the divination verse
which best applied to himself; here there was room for interpretation and
originality. Once the client investigated all the possibilities, he followed the

prescribed procedures in strict conformity to instructions. Success was not guaranteed. The aim was to maximize one's advantages within the context of complex and conflicting forces: the gods, the witches, and one's destiny. Not without reason did the Yoruba liken personal destiny to the market-place into which there were various roads. As the outcome of one's fortunes in the market were uncertain, so was the outcome of one's destiny in life. Risk taking, decision making, practical activity, and individual responsibility were the key to success in both spheres.

For the Yoruba the marketplace was also perceived to involve a high degree of change and potential conflict. The Yoruba god of the marketplace was Eshu. Eshu was both a trickster, a creator of confusion and conflict, and a messenger of the gods, a facilitator of transactions with the source of things. As Eshu presided over the marketplace, so, together with Orunmila, the god of divination, Eshu presided over a person's negotiations with his destiny in this world. "The world is a market, the market is the world," says a Yoruba proverb. Belasco has pointed out that this equation between the world and the marketplace helped equip the Yoruba not only with entrepreneurial habits but also with "preadaptations" to capitalism before the end of the Colonial period.[13]

Traditionally, accumulation of wealth was not sought as a private end in itself. A man's wealth was consumed in the prestigeful acquisition of wives, children, and slaves; and it was shared out among his kinsmen in the large family compound. Accumulation of wealth carried social and moral obligations and these were communal and worldly in nature. This differs markedly from the ideal of moneymaking for its own sake, which Weber saw at the root of Western capitalism. The Calvinist could not indulge in displays of worldly success and had to keep his money growing productively. Only in this way could he be sure that he was fulfilling his economic "calling." The Yoruba "salvational" scheme was different and was based upon communal morality and this-worldly values. Here the goal was rebirth in this world through the development of good character based on collective moral values. Thus while reinforcing entrepreneurial behavior, Yoruba traditional ethics emphasized different economic goals from those associated with classic Western capitalism.

By comparison with other African religions, Yoruba religion was highly professionalized and contained a considerable amount of specialized and rationalized knowledge. It has not been seriously eroded by the conversion of large numbers of people to Christianity and Islam, and it has attempted to adapt both these religions to its own ritualistic mode. Yoruba traditional religion is an emerging "world religion" whose boundaries reach beyond the ethnic Yoruba in Nigeria to millions of Afro-Americans of Yoruba descent in the Caribbean, Brazil, and the United States. The effects of the African

diaspora and of Westernization on Yoruba society have been to transform
Yoruba traditional religion into a more encompassing system, something
like Hinduism in India, with the potential of synthesizing traditional, Christian, and Islamic deities and ritual practices within itself and developing a
broadened philosophical framework. By contrast, many other more localized and less sophisticated religions in Africa have largely succumbed to
Christianity and Islam.

The concept of supreme being and the moral/instrumental character of
traditional ritual made African religions fertile ground for Christianity and
Islam, which extended these features to a more universal level. But Yoruba
religion like Hinduism and Buddhism, developed the personal, philosophical, and institutional aspects somewhat further in directions which
matched those of Christianity and Islam. Yoruba novelists and playwrights
of today show how skillfully the Yoruba can draw from the West and from
their own heritage and create innovative yet characteristically Yoruba literary achievements. This talent for intellectual synthesis occurs only at the
individual level, but its roots lie in the culture and perhaps in the religious
sphere.

Yoruba religion was somewhat exceptional, although structurally similar to other African religions. It viewed human existence as imperfect and
imperfectible. Human life and people's destinies were generally flawed;
ritual was the primary instrument for coping with suffering and death. The
salvational schemes of Christianity and Islam, together with the social and
political opportunities associated with both these religions, have attracted
millions of converts, freeing them from what has appeared to be a closed
ideological and social system.

Yet there was considerable openness and inherent versatility with the
Yoruba religious system, making it maximally adaptable. An example of
this is the transformation of the divinity Ogun, the ancient god of hunting,
war, and iron. Today Ogun is as vital a reality in the modern city as he was
in the rural village, and his cult flourishes.[14] As the protector (savior) of
those who work with iron, he is the patron deity of taxi drivers, truck
drivers, and industrial workers, as he is of rural farmers who use steel
machetes to harvest their crops. Linked to the personal unconscious, the
Yoruba concept of divinity is as appropriate to the denizens of the industrial
city as to those of the agricultural village. The African city may erode
locally based kinship ties on which much of traditional religion depends
(e.g. the sphere of the lineage ancestors), but it creates even more intense
psychological problems about which the traditional gods have much to say
(through their priests). Ogun not only protects his devotees from the dangers of mechanized labor, he advises them on how to succeed in the new
industrial professions. Ogun both protects and destroys, and he personifies

the conflict, struggle, and will it takes to live as a member of the proletariat in the city. Even nominal Christians acknowledge the reality of Ogun, as do New World Africans who identify him with Saint George, the bearer of the iron sword, and with Saint Peter, the holder of the iron keys to heaven.

Sociologically, an important factor is the urban experience of the Yoruba prior to Western contact. Yoruba religion was both the religion of the centralized city-state and of the lineage groups of which the state was composed. The Yoruba city produced specialized classes of palace officials, *orisha* priests, craft guilds, and tradesmen, all of whom had their gods and rituals. Contact with other Yoruba cities and with different ethnic groups expanded cultural horizons and created a pluralistic setting. This contrasts strongly with the small-scale, stateless societies whose kinship-based political structure and localized religious systems gave easy way to the impact of Christianity and Islam.

The specific sources of Yoruba capitalism may now no longer be relevant. Weber maintained that the spirit of Western capitalism was no longer connected with any specific world view and "no longer needs the support of religious forces." If this is true, the same could be said about Yoruba capitalism, that it is no longer attached to ethnic religious ideas. What Weber attempted to identify was the religious sources of a new character type specifically suited to the development of modern industrial capitalism. I have attempted to identify the religious sources of an ethnic character type which seems specifically suited to the development of entrepreneurial and industrial leadership in Nigeria.

Notes

1. Max Weber, *The Protestant Ethic and the Spirit of Capitalism.* Trans. Talcott Parsons (New York: Scribner's), 1958.
2. Henry Bienen, "Religion and Economic Change in Nigeria" (draft, August 1981), p. 19.
3. Benjamin C. Ray, *African Religions* (Englewood Cliffs N.J.: Prentice-Hall, 1976).
4. 'Wanda Abimola, *Ifá: An Exposition of Ifá Literary Corpus* (Ibadan: Oxford University Press, 1976).
5. Obotunde Ijimere, *Everyman.* In idem, *The Imprisonment of Obatala and Other Plays* (London: Heineman Educational Books, 1971), p. 47.
6. E. Bolaji Idowu, *Olódùmarè: God in Yoruba Belief* (London: Longmans, 1962), p. 186ff.
7. Edmund Ilogu, *Christianity and Igbo Culture* (New York: Nok, 1962), p. 36ff.
8. Robert A. LeVine, *Dreams and Deeds: Achievement Motivation in Nigeria* (Chicago: University of Chicago Press, 1966), ch. 8.
9. David C. McClelland, *The Achieving Society* (Princeton: Van Nostrand, 1961), p. 48.

10. Ibid.,p.370.
11. Ibid., p. 372.
12. LeVine.
13. Bernard I. Belasco, *The Entrepreneur as Culture Hero: Preadaptations in Nigerian Economic Development* (New York: Praeger, 1980).
14. Sandra I. Barnes, *Ogun: An Old God for a New Age* (Philadelphia: Institute for the Study of Human Issues, 1980).

About the Contributors

William O. Beeman is a member of the Department of Anthropology, Brown University. He has published widely in both scholarly and popular publications. He has special interests in the relationship of sociocultural needs to planning priorities in development. His specific area interests include the Persian Gulf region, particularly Iran.

Douglas C. Bennett was educated at Haverford College (B.A.) and Yale University (M.Phil., Ph.D.). He is currently associate professor of political science and director of the Institute for Public Policy Studies at Temple University. His articles on the state and transnational corporations in Mexico have appeared in *World Politics, Comparative Politics,* and *International Organization.* He is particularly interested in the intersection between questions of political economy and values.

Henry S. Bienen is William Stewart Tod Professor of Politics and International Affairs, Princeton University, and Director of Woodrow Wilson School's Research Program in Development Studies at Princeton University. A prolific author, he has published articles in many scholarly journals. His most recent book, of which he is editor and coauthor with Vremudia P. Diejomaoh, is *The Political Economy of Income Distribution in Nigeria.*

Ralph Buultjens is professor at Pace University (Graduate School) and at Maryknoll Graduate School. He teaches international politics at the New School for Social Research in New York City. He is chairman of the International Development Forum and is the author of several books and other publications on politics, economics, and sociocultural topics with a special focus on Asia.

James Finn is editor of *Freedom at Issue* for Freedom House in New York. He was for many years editor of *Worldview* and, before that, of *Commonweal.* Author and editor of a number of books, he has written and lectured widely on the relation of religion to politics and culture.

Francine R. Frankel is a professor in the Department of Political Science, University of Pennsylvania. She has worked and studied intermittently in India over a number of years. She has written widely on India, her most recent book being *India's Political Economy, 1947–77: The Gradual Revolution.*

Ron Napier is vice-president of Data Resources in charge of Japan and Asian economic analysis and forecasting. His specialties include the Japanese labor market and modeling the Japanese economy. Napier has been a lecturer in the Economics Department at Harvard University and a visiting research fellow at Hitotsubashi University near Tokyo. He received his Ph.D. in economics from Harvard.

Claude Pomerleau is director of the Latin American Area Studies Program at the Helen Kellogg Institute for International Studies, University of Notre Dame. He is a priest of the Congregation of Holy Cross. He specializes in the study of the role of ideology and ritual in political systems. He has published articles in the *Review of Politics* and *The Americas,* and has a forthcoming book on the politics and organization of the Mexican Catholic Church.

Benjamin C. Ray is an associate professor in the Department of Religious Studies at the University of Virginia. He has done field work in Uganda and is the author of *African Religions: Symbol, Ritual, and Community.*

R.K. Ramazani is Edward R. Stettinius Professor of Government and Foreign Affairs at the University of Virginia where he has taught since 1954. He is a native of Tehran and an American citizen. He has authored eight books, including the prize-winning *The Foreign Policy of Iran, 1500–1941,* and recently *The Persian Gulf and the Strait of Hormuz.* He has contributed to twenty other books and published numerous articles. Ramazani is a former vice-president of the American Institute of Iranian Studies. He has been a consultant to the U.S. government, the Rockefeller Foundation, and the United Nations.

Koichi Shinohara is a member of the Department of Religion, McMaster University, Ontario, Canada. A graduate of the University of Tokyo and Columbia University, he has published in a number of journals in this country and in Japan. He has a special interest in applying concepts of Max Weber to religion in China and Japan.

Study Group Participants

Each of the participants attended one or more of the study group sessions. The contributors to this volume were able to use many of the valuable and often astute critiques and suggestions offered in these sessions.

Beeman, William O.
Department of
Anthropology
Brown University
Bekker, Konrad
Foreign Service Officer
(retired)
Bennett, Douglas C.
Director
Institute for Public Policy
Studies
Department of Political
Science
Temple University
Berger, Peter
Department of Sociology
Boston University
Bienen, Henry S.
William Stewart Tod
Professor of
Politics and International
Affairs
Director
Woodrow Wilson School
Research Program

in Development Studies
Princeton University
Buultjens, Ralph
Department of
International Politics
The New School for Social
Research
Carman, John B.
Director
Center for the Study of
World Religions
Harvard University
Chadda, Maya
Department of Political
Science
William Patterson College
Chittaee, Azize
Formerly with National
Iranian Radio
& Television
Chittaee, Linda
Carnegie Endowment for
International Peace
Former resident of Iran

Danso, Justin
Society for Missions in
Africa

Dzidzienyo, Anani
Department of
African-American
Studies
Brown University

Embree, Ainslee
Department of History
Columbia University

Farrar, Curtis
Deputy Assistant
Administrator for Research
Bureau for Science &
Technology
Agency for International
Development

Finn, James
Project Director
Council on Religion and
International
Affairs

Frank, Lawrence
NEH Fellow
Sarah Lawrence College

Frankel, Francine R.
Department of Political
Science
University of Pennsylvania

Gannon, Frank
Director
Department of Public
Information
Advisor to the Secretary
General
Organization of American
States

Greene, James
Executive Director
The Conference Board

New York City

Heinz, Susan
Director of Corporate
Policy
The Asia Society

Hettinger, Cynthia
Latin American Specialist
on Liberation Theology

Heugel, John
Missionary
Overseas Ministries Study
Center

Horner, Norman
Associate Director
Overseas Ministries Study
Center

Irwin, Graham
Institute of African Studies
Columbia University

Johnson, Donald
Director of International
Education
Department of Social
Studies
New York University

Kazemi, Hardad
Department of Political
Science
New York University

Lloyd, Robert J.
Regional Director
Catholic Foreign Mission
Society of America
(Maryknoll)

Miller, Norman
Professor of Community &
Family Medicine
Dartmouth Medical School

Mortimer, Edward
Senior Associate
Carnegie Endowment for
International Peace

Myers, Robert J.
President
Council on Religion &
International Affairs

Napier, Ron
Vice President
Data Resources
Manager: Japanese, Asian,
Latin American,
Macroeconomic & Energy
Services

Novak, Jeremiah
Economic Journalist
The Asia Mail

Patrick, Hugh
Economic Growth Center
Yale University

Pomerleau, Claude
Director
Latin American Area
Studies Program
Helen Kellogg Institute
for International Studies
University of Notre Dame

Ramazani, R.K.
Chairman
Woodrow Wilson
Department of Government
& Foreign Affairs
University of Virginia

Ray, Benjamin
Department of Religious
Studies
University of Virginia

Ryerson, Charles
Assistant Professor of the
History of Religion
Princeton Theological
Seminary

Shinohara, Koichi
Department of Religious
Studies
McMaster University

Sudhir, Sen
United Nations
Development Program
Author-Member of UN
Correspondence
Association

Swai, Nsilo
United Nations Secretariat

Thompson, Kenneth W.
Director
White Burkett Miller
Center of Public Affairs &
Commonwealth
Department of Government
& Foreign Affairs
University of Virginia

Tith, Naranhkiri
School for Advanced
International Studies
The Johns Hopkins
University

Valliere, Paul
Department of Religion
Columbia University

Wriggins, Howard
Institute of War & Peace
Columbia University

Index

Agni (Aryan god), 18

Agnosticism, in Nehru's worldview, 26

Agriculture: economic assistance to, in India, 46–47; growth in production, 55; in Gandhian vision, 21; in India, 11, 30, 40, 41, 42, 43, 44, 46, 55, 61; in Iran, 81, 90, 91, 92, 94, 98; in Japan, 171, 180; in Mexico, 131, 133, 135; in Nehruvian vision, 25, 49–50; in Nigeria, 204, 205, 211, 237; research in, 42. *See also* Farmers; Farming; Agriculturists

Agriculturists: and domestic savings, 44; and employment, 44; "farm lobby" in Indian politics, 52–53; labor-investment projects, 53. *See also* Agriculture; Farmers; Farming

Ahimsa (noninjury), 38

al-Afghani, Jamal al-Din, 87

al-e-Almad, Jalal, 136

Alemán, Miguel, 151

America: and Japan, 181, 186, 187, 192; and Mexico, 122, 126, 130–39, 145; approach to Middle East and Southeast Asia, 116–17; comparative attitude toward college degrees in U.S. and Japan, 193; economy compared with Japan, 163–64; hostages in Iran, 69; interest of, in Iran, 89, 106, 107, 111, 114; secular philosophy of, 145; trade with Mexico, 130; view of Mexican development, 122. *See also* CIA, United States

Amouzegar, Jamshid, 95

Ancestors: in Ibo tradition, 234; in Japan, 169–71, 180, services in honor of, 171;

spirits in Yoruba tradition, 233; worship of, 170, 180

Anglo-Iranian Oil Company, basis for industrialization of Iran, 87

Anglo-Russian partition of Iran, 76

Anticlericalism in Mexico, 125, 127–30, 137–38, 143–44, 146, 152

Anticlerical laws in Mexico, 152

Aquinas, Saint Thomas, 155

Arab conquest of Iran, 76

Aristotle, 136

Arms buildup in Persian Gulf states, 115–17

Aryans, 18

Augustine, Saint, 154

Authority: authoritarian regime in Mexico, 121, 126; rejection of temporal authority by Sunni Islam, 110; religious vs. secular in Iran, 78, 83–84, 86, 87, 88, 105; religious vs. secular in Mexico, 148; religious vs. secular in Nigeria, 218; resistance of tribal Khans in Iran, 88. *See also* Cristero rebellion

Azerbaijan, attempted Soviet annexation of, 76

Aztecs: and Roman Catholicism, 127–28; influence of on modern Mexico, 153

Babur (emperor), 18

Baghdad, 76

Bahrain, 110

Bani-Sadr (president), 107

Banking: in Iran, 83, 86, 93; in Japan, 181–82; in Mexico, 131–33

Bateson, M.C., 75

Bazaar (Iran): and new banking regulations, 93; benefits from Reza Shah rule, 88; conservative nature of, 82; independence of, 82

Behbehani, Sayyed 'Abdullah (Iranian religious leader, 1905–11), 105

Behrangi, Samad (Iranian writer), 94

Belgian, development and communications in Iran, 85

Bellah, Robert, 5

Bhakti (popular Hindu religious movement), 35

Bihar, underdevelopment linked to caste system, 51; Kosi Irrigation Project, 51

Bolshevik Revolution, 131

Bonih, water distribution system in Iran, 81–82. *See also* Irrigation; *Ganat*

Bose, Subbas Chandra, 22–23

Bourgeoisie, in Mexico, 132

Brazil, 236

Brahmin (caste) 36–37

British: colonialism in Nigeria, 203, 208; communications and development concessions in Iran, 85; conflicts in Iran, 90; empire in India, 19; oil concessions in Iran, 87; Tobacco Rebellion (1890–92), 86–87; trade with Mexico, 130

Buddhism: and politics, 2; in modern Japan, 169; registration of *ie,* 169; Bon Festival, 170

Bushido (warrior ethic of Japan), 171

Calles, Plutarco Elías (1924–28), 130, 144, 148, 149, 151; determination of, to crush the church in Mexico, 149, 153

Calvinism, and capitalism, 230; and money, 236; qualities of and economics, 2

Camacho, Manuel Avila, 130

Camarillas (political families of Mexico), 152–53

Capitalism: and religious ethic, 2, 24; and social morality, 37; influenced by Protestantism, 2; in Japan, 172, 182; in Mexico, 121–22, 125–26, 130–35, 139; in Nigeria, 198, 203, 230, 234, 235, 236, 238; preadaptation to, among Yoruba, 236, 238; predatory nature of, 24

Cárdenas, Lázaro, 133, 149, 151, 153

Carter, Jimmy, 116

Caste system: abolition of untouchability, 39; among Nigerians, 213–14; and experimentation in cultivation methodology, 55; as an obstacle to progress, 57–58; conflict between Forward and Backward castes, 57, 61–62; differences accentuated by modernization, 57–58; economic implications of, 33, 51–53; explained by Mahatma Gandhi, 36; four castes named, 36; in India today, 27, 38, 51; not dispelled by education in India, 27; values of which impede political behavior, 33, 55

Catholicism, *see* Roman Catholic Church; Christianity

Censorship, under Mexican Constitution (1824), 128

Centralization, of authority: in Iran, 89, 93; in Mexico, 128; in Nigeria, 210

Central Planning Commission of India, under Indira Gandhi, 25

Chad, support of Yan Izala sect in Nigeria, 217

Chador, outlawed in Iran, 88

China, agricultural growth compared to India, 11

Christianity: and achievement orientation in Nigeria, 211–12; and open economy, 203; and technology, 212; educational role of in Nigeria, 197, 229–30; in India, 11; in Japan 169; in Nigerian government, 211–12; limited effects of conversion to, 218; Nigerian acceptance of, 202, 208. *See also* Roman Catholic Church; Protestantism; Religion

CIA, intervention in Iran, 116. *See also* United States; America

Civic policy and religious belief, 19

"Civil Religion," in Mexico, 146, 150, 153–54

Civil War, in Mexico, 131

Class consciousness: accentuated by modernization, 57–58, 61–62; among Yoruba, 213–14; and Hindu caste system, 55; impact of religion and ethnicization on, 212–13; Indian society and, 55, 56, 57, 58; Nigerian understanding of, 212–14

Coalition, domination of Mexico, 125–26

Colonialism: in India, 19; in Mexico, 215–16, 220; in Nigeria, 197, 201, 203, 205, 230

Communications: development of in Iran, 84, 85, 87; ineffectiveness of in India, 49; disrupted by Civil War in Mexico, 131

Communism: in India, 31, 60; in Iran, 90–91, 98, 110, 116

Conference of Mexican Bishops (1980–82), 143

Confucius, teachings of, 165, 167–68, 171; effect on Japanese institution of *ie,* 171

Congress Party of India: and family planning issue, 29; challenge to modernist vision of Nehru and Indira Gandhi, 26; defeated by Janata Party, 29; dissension in, 28; preservation of, 39

Conservative Party of Mexico, 147–48

Constitution of Nigeria (1979), 204–5

Constitution of Mexico, 125, 128, 129, 130, 131, 138, 143, 152

Constitutional Revolution of Iran (1905–11), 105, 107

Corporations, in Japan, 173–74, 185, 187; *ie*-like character of in Japan, 173–74

Cortés, Hernán, 127

Crime rate, lowered in Japan, 163

Cristero rebellion (1926–29), 130, 135, 148, 152

Culture: contrasting principles of Iranian, 74–78; festivals of Japan, 170; traditional religious culture and agricultural practice in Nigeria, 211; samurai of Japan, 169, 170, 172; societal values of Nigerian, 198, 202–3, 229, 230; values in Japanese, 180–81; women's place in Iranian, 88

Dal, Janata-Lok, 23

D'Arcy, oil concession in Iran (1901), 87

Delhi, 18

Democracy: in India, 25, 41; in Mexico, 139

Depression, effect on Mexican manufacturing, 133

Desai, Morarji, 28–29

Destiny (personal): and divination, 232, 235; and economic striving, 232, 234; in Ibo tradition, 234; in Yoruba tradition,

232, 233, 235, 237; Ifa (system of divination), 232

Development: and distribution of resources, 3–4; and religion, 4, 41; and traditional values in Ibo society, 218; models of, 4; obstacles to Mexican progress in, 146

Díaz, Porfirio, 125, 127, 130, 144, 147

Diego, Juan, 128

Diezma, 128

Discrimination: against Shi'i Moslems (Iran), 113; in Japanese work force, 187–88

Dorayi people (Nigeria), 213–14

Dualism, secular and sacred, 154

Ecology: and nomadic tribal life in Iran, 80; in Northern Nigeria, 208–9

Economics: and religion, 12, 156–57, 219; changes in, 219; development in Iran, 89–91, 111; development in Mexico, 131, 136–37, 145; development in Nigeria, 203–8; discontinued aid to Iran, 111; Nehruvian vision of, 24–25; Westernization and modernization of, 163

Education: and Christianity, 128, 212, 229–30; and caste system, 56; and economic development, 26; and tradition, 26–27; church control of, in Mexico, 128; exclusion of in universities, 146; in Japan, 164–65, 182, 189–90; in Nigeria, 197, 208, 209–10, 212, 215; modern education and economic development in India, 32; religious, 30, 88–89, 93; rural elementary schools in Mexico, 149; university enrollment in India, 32; women and, 88, 215

Egypt, 111, 114

Ejido (Mexican communal landholding), 133

Elections in Mexico, 153

Elite: economic in Japan, 188; elitist politics, 149, military and civil servant elites of Nigeria, 205, 209; religious in Islam, 78–79; revolutionary in Mexico, 150–51; ruling elites, 115, 145, 148, 153, 208–9

Emergency Rule (India, 1975–77), 41, 46, 59, 60

Employment: creation of jobs in Mexico, 135; Employment Guarantee Scheme (1975), 48; Food for Work Program, 46; handicaps of in India, 46, 49; in Iran, 91; permanent, in Japan, 185–86; systems in Japan, 188–89

Enlightenment: influence of, in Mexico, 128, 144–45, 147; influence on Jawaharlal Nehru, 23

Enterprise, private, 37. *See also* Capitalism

Entrepreneurship: as consequence of Ibo religious tradition, 234, 235, 236; in India, 52; Islamic, 209; Mexican, 126, 132, 133–34; Nigerian, 198, 210, 212, 230, 234, 235, 236; relation to individualistic approaches to God, 324–25; skills lacking in India, 49

Eshu (Yoruba god of the marketplace), 235 –36

Ethics, in Japanese institution of *ie*, 171

Exploitation of Mexican laborers, 130

Faith, traditional vs. revolutionary, 151

Family: disintegration of life of, 37; in Japan, 164–65; planning, 29–30

Farmers: and credit, 95; exploitation of, in Mexico, 130; failure of special programs for small and marginal, 48–49, 61; *ie* of, in Japan, 172, 180; Indian, 11, 30, 40, 41, 42, 43, 46; insistence on land reform in Mexico, 133; political expression of, 52–53; special programs for, 46; system of land/labor in Iran, 80–81; under Iranian development plans, 92. *See also* Agriculture; Agriculturists

Fascism, 22

Festivals, religious, 170–71, 180

Five-Year Plans (India), 26–27, 40, 45, 49, 50

Food For Work Program (India), 46–48

Foreign Investments: in India, 42; in Iran, 85; in Japan, 182; in Mexico, 130, 132; in Nigeria, 206, 208–9

France: anticlericalism in, 146; secular philosophy of, 145; trade with Mexico, 130; development programs of, in Iran 85

Fulani, 197, 202, 205, 208, 214

Ganat, 81. *See also* Irrigation

Gangetic Plain, underdevelopment linked to religious attitudes, 51

Gandhi, Indira, 13, 20, 24, 29, 41, 57, 58, 60; "Abolish Poverty" Program of, 46; acceptance of Nehru vision for India, 23–24; campaign against Janata Party, 29; defeat of Congress Party, 29; Emergency Rule, 41, 46; family-planning policy of, 29; future casting of political role of, 32–33; return to power (1980), 30; sociopolitical concepts of, 20; vendetta against, 30; vision contrasted with Mahatma Gandhi's, 24

Gandhi, Mahatma, 12, 19–21, 36, 4, 50; and the Untouchables, 36; assassination of, 23, 39; compared with Nehru, 25; contrasted with Nehru–Indira Gandhi, 27–28; economic plans of, 36, 41; in Indian liberation movement, 20–21, 35; possible resurrection of Gandhian vision, 41, 50; rejection of Gandhian vision by intelligentsia, 36; vision of, 20, 21, 36

Garibi Hatao (Abolish Poverty), 46

Geertz, Clifford, 73

GNP, 34, 45

Government: and social mobility in Nigeria, 211; relations with sheiks and khans in Iran, 77, 80, 88; stability in Mexico, 145

Grant, James (president, Overseas Development Council), 54

Great Kings, 19

Greek conquest of Iran, 76

Guadalupe, Virgin of, 128, 138, 151

Gulf, Persian, 114–17

Harijans (Children of God), 35

Haryana (province in Northern India), 47: agricultural transformation of, 47; growth of, 51, 52–53; technology in, 55

Hausas, 208, 209, 210, 215

Hidalgo, Miguel, 128, 147, 149, 155

Hindi, 32

Hinduism, 11, 12, 20, 32, 33; as obstacle to national development, 39, 50; and Westernization, 237; destruction of by modern secularism of Indira Gandhi's government, 29; vision of morality in, 21–22

Holy wars, 18
Hosein, Imam, 76–77
Hoveyda, Amir Abbas (prime minister, Iran), 95, 111
Humanism, in Nehruvian vision, 26
Hydrocarbon, 138

Ibadan, 210, 214
Ibibio, 208
Ibo: attitude toward wealth, 213, 234; Catholic tribe of Eastern Nigeria, 197, 202, 205, 206, 209; compared with Yoruba, 230–31, 234–35; ethnicity and religion of, 210–11; personal destiny in tradition of, 234; status mobility of, 210, 213, 234; trade unions among, 216; villages, 218
Ideology of Iranian society, 74–78. *See also* Culture; Religion; Tradition
Idoma, 208
Ie: authority in, 168–69; and the Japanese religious tradition, 169–73; continuation of lineage in, 164–65, 168–69; ethics and, 170–71; industry of, 173–74; interlacing of consanguinal and economic lineage in, 168–69; place of women in, 168
Ifa (Yoruba divination system), 232–33
Ile Ifa, 212, 215
Imams, 74, 79
Independence: in India, 38, 41, 54, 57, 58, 61; in Mexico, 125–28, 144–47, 150; in Nigeria, 206
India: 11–65; agriculture in, 11, 30, 40, 41, 42, 43, 44, 46, 55, 61; Aryan migration into, 18; Aryan gods in, 18; Bihar, 51, 52, 62; Bose, Subbas Chandra, 22, 23; Brahmin caste, 36, 51, 52, 58; British empire in, 19; Buddhism, 11; capitalism in Nehru vision, 24; caste system, 21, 27, 33, 36, 38, 51, 55; Christians in, 11; class consciousness, 55, 56, 57, 58; communications, 49; Communism, 60; Congress Party, 26, 39, 57, 58, 61; conquest by Islamic Moghuls, 18; democracy in, 24, 27; Delhi, 18, 19; Desai, Morarji, 28, 29; education, 27, 30, 32, 42, 56; Emergency Rule (1975–77), 41, 59, 60; Employment Guarantee Scheme, 48; employment handicaps, 49; exports, 42;

farmers, 44, 46, 53, 59; Five-Year Plans, 40, 45, 49; Food For Work Program, 46, 48; foreign investments in, 42; Gandhi, Indira, 13, 20, 24, 29, 41, 46, 57, 58, 60; Gandhi, Mohandas K., 12, 19–21, 36, 41, 50; Ganges Plain, 51; *Garibi Hatao* (Abolish Poverty) 46, 57, 61; Haryana, 47, 51, 52, 54, 55; Hindi, 32; Hinduism, 11, 12, 20, 32, 33, 39, 50; history of, 17; Independence, 38, 41, 54, 57, 58, 61; Indian National Congress, 21; Industrialization of, 11, 27, 30, 40, 41, 43, 49, 59; influence of European Enlightenment, 23; influence of religion on economic progress of, 33; international credit rating, 42; Islam, 11; Janata-Lok Dal, 28; Janata Party, 29, 46–47; 59; Jats (caste), 51, 54, 55; Jeffersonian economics and Indian policies, 20; Kerala, 60, 61; Kshatriya (caste), 36, 37, 52; Kosi Irrigation Project, 51; lack of confidence in democracy, 41; land distribution, 60, 61; liberation of, 19; Lok Sabha, 26, 40; maharajas, 19; Maharashtra, 48, 51; Marxism, 25, 31, 36, 60; modernization, 25, 37, 56, 59, 62; Moslems, 62; nationalism, 11, 20, 35; Narayan, Jayaprakash, 28, 39, 41; Nehru, Jawaharlal, 13, 20, 23, 24, 37, 38, 39, 40, 46, 49; New Delhi, 19; nonviolence, 19, 38, 39, 40; nuclear power, 42; oil, 42; Panchayats (councils), 26, 40, 54; passive resistance, 19; partition of, 39; politics in modern times, 56–59; population, 28, 30, 43, 49; poverty, 27, 43, 45, 49, 59, 61; Punjab, 47, 50, 52, 54, 55; Rajputs ("twice-born" caste), 52; religion, 11, 40, 50; Republic of, 11; revolution, 41; Rig Veda, 18; Rockefeller Foundation, 42; Shastri, Lal Bahadur, 28; Sikh, 11; Singh, Charan, 28, 29, 46, 50, 54; Sixth Five-Year Plan, 45, 47; Small Farmer Development Agencies (SFDA), 46; socialism, 24, 36, 37, 38; Sudra (caste), 36, 37, 51, 52, 56, 57, 59; technology, 46, 49, 55; underdevelopment of India linked to religious attitudes, 41, 50; unemployment, 41, 43, 46; universities, 42; untouchability, abolition of, 56; Uttar Pradesh, 47, 51, 52,

54; Vaishya (caste), 36, 37; villages, 36, 38, 54, 57, 59, 60; West Bengal, 60, 61; Zamindari Abolition, 57

Indian National Congress, 21

Indigenization, 205, 207, 219

Indra (Aryan god), 18

Industrialism, 3

Industrialization: and D'Arcy oil concession in Iran (1901), 87; and Japanese ie, 173–74; as impetus to change in India, 40; expansion of, 43, 181; Indian, 11, 27, 30, 40, 41, 43, 49, 59; Iranian, 89, 91, 93, 97, 111; Japanese, 173, 181; Mexican, 133, 135; Nigerian, 201, 206

Industry: aid to Indian, 47; and clergy of Iran, 93–94; and foreign capital in Iran, 93; and Japanese institution of ie, 173; Gandhian vision of, 36; growth of, in India, 30–31, 41, 47; in Mexican development, 133–34; in Nehru vision, 25; in Nigeria, 204, 206; in postwar Japan, 181; investments for, in India, 41–42; labor force for, 42, 131, 137, 139, 183–84, 215–16; problems of, in India, 45–46

Inflation: control of, in Iran, 83; control of, in Mexico, 132, 143; low, in Japan, 163, 181–82; oil and, in Nigeria, 204

Innovation: difficulties with, in Iran, 83; Ibo willingness for, in Nigeria, 211

Institutional Revolutionary Party (PRI, Mexico), 121, 131, 135, 137, 151, 152

Investments, see Foreign investments

Iran, 67–117; Abbas (shah), 79; Abbot, K.E., 84; agriculture, 81, 90, 91, 92, 94, 98; al Afghani, Jamal al-Din, 86–87; Allied occupation of, 76; Amad, Jalal al-e, 94; American hostages in, 69; American interest in, 89, 106, 107, 111, 114; Amouzegar, Jamshid (prime minister), 95; Anglo-Iranian Oil Company, 87, 107; Anglo-Russian partition (1907), 76; Anti-Americanism, 69, 107, 114, 116; Azerbaijan, 76; Baghdad, 76; Bahrain, 110; baten (esoteric knowledge), 76; Behbehani, Sayyed 'Abdullah, 105; Belgians, 85; bonihs (cooperative labor groups), 81; British, 85, 87, 107; centralization, 89, 93; church/state conflicts, 88, 93, 96; CIA intervention, 116; communications, 84, 85, 87; Communism,

90, 91, 98, 110, 116; Constitutional Revolution (1905–11), 105, 107; crimes of Mohammed Reza Pahlavi, 96–97, 106; differentiation in Iranian society, 77; economic development, 89, 90, 91; education in, 88, 89, 111; Egypt, 114; employment, 91; engineering, 94; farmers, see Agriculture; First Plan (1949), 90; Fourth Plan (1968–72), 92; foreign domination of, 76, 93; foreign investments in, 70, 93; French, 85; ganat system, 81, 92; GNP, 90, 91, 92, 94, 95, 111; Grand Mosque (Mecca), attack on, 112; Greek conquest of, 76; Hoveyda, Amir Abbas (prime minister), 95–111; Hosein, Imam, 76–77; Imam (descendant of prophet Mohammed), 73, 79, 87, 108, 111; immorality (alleged consequence of modernization), 70, 75; industrialization, 89, 91, 93, 97, 111; inflation, 95; internal/external conflict in Iranian society, 75; Iraq, 87; Islam, 69, 70, 111, 112; Islamic Republic, 70; Ithna'Ashari (Twelver), 73; Kasem, Musa al-, 78; Kashani, Sayyed Abulqasem, 105; Kerbala, 76; khans, 77, 80, 88; Khomeini, Ayatollah, 69, 96, 105–11; Kurdistan, 76; landholding, 81, 83, 88, 91, 92; land reforms, 81, 91, 93, 97; Mahdi (Master of the Ages), 79, 108, 111; materialism (alleged consequence of modernization), 70; Millspaugh, A.C., 87; modernization, 70, 83, 85, 86, 88, 93, 111, 112; Mohammed, 73, 76, 78; Mohammed Mossadeq, 90; Mohammed Reza Shah, see Pahlavi, Mohammed Reza; Mongol, 76; Moslems, 69; Mullah, 79; Mujtahid (Islamic wiseman), 79, 87; Naser od-Din Shah, 85, 94; nationalism, 111; Nationalist Movement (1951–53), 105; Nuri, Shaikh Fazlullah, 105; oil, 89, 92, 93, 94, 117; OPEC, 94; Ottoman Empire, 79; Pahlavi, Mohammed Reza, 69, 83, 84, 89–97, 105–6, 109, 116; Persian Gulf, 69; population increase, 80; Qajar Period, 79, 82–86, 88; Qom (holy shrine city), 96, 105; Qur'an, 76; religious education, 93; religious opposition to modernization, 86; religious practice in, 73, 76;

revolution, 69, 70, 73, 75, 84, 87, 105, 106, 110, 111, 113, 114; Russia, 84–87, 107; Sadeq, Ja'far al-, 78; Sa'edi, Gholam Hossein, 94; Safavids (1501–1722), 78, 79; Salar, Hajji Mirza Hosein Sipah, 85–86; Saudi Arabia, 112–13, 117; Second Plan (1955–62), 90; secularization, 70; Shah, see Pahlavi, Mohammed Reza; sharecroppers, 80; Shari'a (Islamic religious law), 69; Shi'a Islam, 69, 73, 75, 76, 79, 106, 108, 109, 110; social interaction in, 77–78; society, ideological basis of, 74–78; Soviet, 76; spirituality of Islam, 75; Sufism, 75, 78; Sunni Islam, 69, 79, 108, 110; Tabataba'i, Sayyed Mohammed, 105; Tabataba'i, Allamah, 76; Tabriz, 87; taxation, 89; Tehran, 89, 95, 96, 116; Third Plan (1962–67), 90, 91; Tobacco Rebellion (1890–92), 86; transportation, 84, 90; trans-Iranian railway, 89; Twelver, Shi'ism (Ithna'Ashari) 73, 78; ulema (Islamic leaders), 79, 86–87, 89, 105, 106, 110, 112; urban migration, 91, 111; Westernization, 70, "Westoxication" (essay by Jalal'al-e Almad), 94, 97; "White Revolution," 91; women, status of, 88; World War II, 76, 87, 89, 112; zaher (esoteric knowledge), 75; Yazid (caliph of Damascus), 76

Iraq, 110, 115

Irrigation, 81, 92. See also Qanat

Islam: and entrepreneurship, 209, 211; and Iranian Revolution, 73; brotherhoods of, 218; comparison of Iranian with other Islamic states, 73–74; in India, 11; in Iran, 69–70, 73, 76, 86, 106, 108, 109, 110, 111, 112; in Nigeria, 197, 202, 208–9, 211, 212, 214, 218, 219, 231, 237; in the Persian Gulf, 69; justification of political and economic inequalities in, 215–16; law of, 98; purification of, 73, 76, 86, 217; resurgence of, 112; Shi'ism, 69, 73, 75, 76, 79, 106, 108, 109, 110; Sunni, 69, 79, 108, 110. See also Mohammed; Moslems; Mullah; Mujtahid; Qom; Qur'an; Shari'a

Islamic Black Africa, 209

Ithna' Ashari Shi'ism, See Twelver

Janata-Lok Dal (India, 1977–79), 23

Janata Party, 28, 29, 46, 47

Jan Sangh, 28

Japan, 161–94; agriculture, 171, 180; ancestor worship, 169, 170, 171, 180; banks, 182; Buddhism, 165, 167–68, 170; Bushido, 171; capitalism, 172, 182; China, 180; Christianity, 169; classes of society, 180; Confucianism, 165, 167–68, 171; corporations 173–74, 185, 187; decision making, 189; discrimination in labor force, 187; economic development, 163, 165, 179, 181–83; economic rationalism, 172, 176; education 182, 184, 189–93; employment, permanent, 185–86; entrepreneurship, 189; export markets, 184; farmers, see Agriculture; festivals, 170; foreign investment, 182; GNP, 163, 181; ie, 165, 168, 169, 170, 173; industrialization, 173, 181; industrial relations, 184–87; inflation, 163, 181; investment 181, 183–84; Kamishma, Jiro, 173; Korea, 180; Kyoto Period, 169; labor, organization of, 184; Meiji Restoration (1868), 168; modernization, 163, 168, 173; Nenko system, 185–87; "nets of obligation," 189; oil, 181; population, 164, 182; recession, 165; religion and economics, relation between, 164, 167–68, 170, 176, 180; samurai, 169, 170, 172; seishin (Japanese spirit), 187; seniority wage system, 185; Shinto, 165, 168, 180; society, structure of, 174–75; Soviet Union, 163; technology, 182–83; Tokugawa Period, 169, 171, 173, 180, 191; tradition, 172; unemployment, 163, 181; universities, 189–93; urbanization, 182; and United States, 181, 186, 187, 192; values, traditional social, 180–81; villages, 180; Weber, Max, 167, 172, 175, 176; Westernization of, 163; women, place of, 188; work incentives, lack of, 185–87; workplace, importance of, 164–65, 184; World War II, 165, 169, 181; yoshi, 169

Jats (Indian caste), 51, 54, 55

Jesuits, 155

Jews, 134

John Paul II (pope), 125, 138

Johnson administration, 111
Juárez, Benito (president of Mexico), 129

Kaduna State, 216–18
Kano, Aminu, 216
Kano City, 213, 216
Kashani, Sayyed Abulqasem, 105
Keddie, Nikki, 86
Kennedy administration, 91, 116
Kerbala (holy city of Iran), 76, 79
Khans, 77, 80
Khomeini, Ayatollah, 32, 69, 96, 105–8
Kissinger, Henry, 115
Koran, see Qur'an
Korean War, 181
Kosi (irrigation project), 51
Kripalani, Acharya, 28
Kshatriya (Hindu caste), 36, 37
Kufa (shrine city of Iran), 79
Kurdistan, attempted Soviet annexation of, 76
Kuwait, 110, 114, 115
Kyoto Period, 169

Labor: division of, in Hindu system, 36; labor force in India, 42; and the Mexican Revolution, 131, 137; organization in Japan, 183–84; rights of, in Mexico, 139
Lagos, 206, 211
Land: distribution and tenure in India, 54, 56; distribution of, in Mexico, 121–22, 128–29, 139; ejidos (communal landholding in Mexico), 133; for farms in Iran, 80–81; landholding customs and abuses in Iran, 82; landholdings of Roman Catholic Church in Mexico, 128–29; land reform in India, 49–50, 59–60; land reform in Iran, 81, 91–92; land reform in Mexico, 133; seizure of church lands in Mexico (1859), 128–29
Landlord, in Iranian village life, 82
Las Casas, Bartolomé de, 155
Leo XIII (pope), Rerum Novarum encyclical (1891), 130
Ley Lerdo (1856), 129
Liberalism, 125–28, 138, 145, 147–48
Liberation: modern equivalent for "contemplative life," 155–56; of India, 19–20; theology of, 150, 155–56

Liberty, religious, 5
Libya, 204
Limantour, José Ives, 130
Literature, Yoruba, 237
Loans, foreign, 132
Lok Sabha, 26, 40
Lugard (lord), 208

Madero, Francisco, 131
Maharashtra, 48
Mahdi (the Twelfth Imam), 79, 108, 111
Maitatsine, Muhammudu Marwa, 217
Manual labor, in Gandhian economics, 21
Manufacturing, see Industry; Industrialization
Maritain, Jacques, 1
Martyrdom, Iranian ideal of, 76–77
Marx, Karl, 126
Marxism, 24, 31, 37, 60, 151, 155
Maximilian (archduke), 129
Mecca, uprising in, 112
Meiji Constitution (1898), 169
Meiji Restoration (1868), 169
Merchants: benefits under rule of Reza Shah, 88; imprisoned in Iran, 95; ie, 171–72. See also Bazaar.
Mexico, 119–60; agriculture, 131, 133, 135; anticlericalism, 125, 127–30, 137–38, 143–44, 146, 152; Aztec Indians, 127, 153; banking, 132, 133; Britain, trade with, 130; Calles, Plutarco Elías, 130, 144, 148, 149, 151, 153; Camacho, Manuel Avila, 130; capitalism, 121, 122, 125, 126, 130–35, 139; Catholic Church, see Roman Catholic Church; Catholic Social Action Movement, 130; Catholicism, doctrine and practice, 126, 127–30, 135, 138, 153–57; Cárdenas, Lázaro, 133, 149, 151, 153; centralization of authority, 128; científicos, 129, 130; "civil religion," 146, 154; Civil War, 131; colonialism, 215–16, 220; communications, 131; Conference of Mexican Bishops (1980–82), 143; Constitution, 125, 128, 129, 130, 131, 138, 143, 152; Cristero rebellion (1926–29), 130, 135, 148, 152; democracy, 125; depression, 133; development, 126–27, 156–57; Díaz, Porfirio, 125, 127, 130, 144, 147; Diego, Juan, 128; diezma

(tithes), 128; economic growth, 121, 126, 129, 135, 146; economic reconstruction, 131; education, 125, 146, 157; Enlightenment, influence, 128, 145, 147; entrepreneurship, 126, 132, 133, 134; European influence on, 126; farmers, *see* Agriculture; foreign investments, 130, 134; foreign loans, 132; France, 130, 145, 146; government, 145; Guadalupe, Virgin of, 128, 138, 151; *hacendados,* 128, 129; hydrocarbon, discovery of, 138; Hidalgo, Miguel, 128, 147; immigrants, 134; Independence, 125, 126, 128, 144, 145, 146, 147, 150; industrialization, 133, 135; inflation, 132; Institutional Revolutionary Party (PRI), 121, 131, 135, 137, 151, 152; Juárez, Benito, 129; *Labyrinth of Solitude, The* (Octavio Paz), 125; laissez-faire, 128; land distribution, 125, 128, 129; land reform, 126, 129, 133; Ley Lerdo (1856), 129; liberalism, 126, 127, 129; liberation theology, 150, 156; Limantour, José Ives, 130; Madero, Francisco, 131; manufacturing, 131; Marx, Karl, 126; Marxist analysis, 155; Mexico City, 129, 146; mining, 131; Monterrey Group, 134; Morelos, José María, 128; National Catholic Labor Confederation, 149; nationalism, 136, 138, 147; New Spain, 128, 147, 151; Obregón, Alvaro, 148, 149; oil, 122, 134, 135; organic-statist tradition, 136; Paz, Octavio, 125, 127, 153; petroleum, *see* Oil; political economy and religious values, 135–36; Pope John Paul II, 122, 125, 138; Pope Leo XIII, 130; Porfiriato, 133; positivism, 126, 127, 129, 130; PRI, *see* Institutional Revolutionary Party; Puebla Conference of Latin American Bishops (1979), 154; railway construction, 130; *Rerum Novarum* (1891), 130; revolution, 121, 122, 125, 126, 131, 138, 145, 148, 150, 151; Revolutionary Coalition, 131; Rockefeller Foundation, 42; Roman Catholic Church, 122, 125, 136, 147–48, 156–57; separation of church and state, 126; social consciousness, 121; Spain, trade with, 130; Spanish Conquest, 144, 150; *técnicos,* 133; theocracy, 128, 145, 148; Tonantzin (Aztec mother of gods), 128; transportation, 131; Triple Alliance, 144; United States and, 122, 126, 130–39, 145; Villa, Pancho, 131, 133; Vasconcelos, José, 149; Vatican Council, Second (1962–65), 144, 153, 155; World War II, 133; Zapata, Emiliano, 131, 133

Mexico City, 121, 146–47
Middle Belt (Nigeria), 208
Migration, tribal, in Iran, 80
Military, 26
Millspaugh, A.C., 87
Modernization: in India, 25, 37, 56, 59, 62; in Iran, 70, 83, 85, 86, 88, 93, 111, 112; in Japan, 163, 165, 168, 173, 181, 183; in Nigeria, 208, 218, 230; synonymous with Westernization, 163; viewed as a mixed package, 4
Moghuls, Islamic, 18
Mohanned, Murtala, 209
Monarchies, 111
Mongol conquest of Iran, 76
Monterrey Group, 134
Moral base of society, 6
Morelos, José María, 128, 149
Moslems, 62, 69, 197, 202, 206, 208, 211, 214, 216, 222, 229, 230; cultural barriers between Hindus and Moslems, 58; fundamentalists and revolution, 114; resurgence of Islam, 111–12. *See also* Islam
Mosque, Grand of Mecca, 112
Mossadeq, Mohammed (prime minister), 89–90
Mujtahid (Islamic wisemen), 79; Shiraz Mujtahid and the Tobacco Rebellion (1890–92), 86–87
Mullah, 79
Musa al-Kazem, 78
Myrdal, Gunnar: *Asian Drama* (1968), 3, 5, 40, 41, 50, 51, 59, 60; on irrational religious beliefs and cultural patters, 40–50; on revolution vs. evolution, 41
Myths (Yoruba), 231–32

Najaf (shrine city of Iran), 79
Narayan, Jayaprakash, 28, 39, 41
National Catholic Labor Confederation, 149

National Party of Nigeria, 217
National Revolutionary Party, 151
Nationalist Movement of Iran (1951–53), 105
Nationalism: and martyrdom, 76; in India, 11, 20, 35; in Iran, 90; in Mexico, 136, 138, 147; in Nigeria, 207–8
Nehru, Jawaharlal: blamed by Charan Singh for India's modern problems, 46; commitment to nonviolence, 39; compared and contrasted with Mahatma Gandhi, 23–25; death of, 40; first prime minister of India, 20; Five-Year Plans, 41; influenced by European Enlightenment, 23; influence of, on Indira Gandhi, 24; modernization of India under, 13, 38; Nehruvian strategy, 49; vision of India, 20, 23, 24, 37
Nenko system, 185–87
New Spain, 128, 147, 151
Niger, 217
Nigeria, 195–39; agriculture, 204, 205, 211, 237; Algeria, 204; British in, 203, 206; capitalism, 198, 203, 230, 234, 235, 236, 238; centralization, 210; Chad, 217; Chukwu (Ibo supreme god), 234; Christianity, 197, 203, 208, 211, 214, 218, 219, 229, 230, 231, 237, see also Roman Catholicism; church/state separation, 203; class consciousness, 212–14, 216–17; colonialism, 197, 201, 203, 205, 230; Constitution (1979), 205; corporations, foreign, in, 206; destiny (personal), 198, 232, 234, 235; divination, Yoruba, see Ifa; Dorayi, 213; ecology, 209; economic change and religion, 203; economy, 197, 203; economy, structure of, 204–8; education, 197, 203, 206, 208, 298, 210, 215, 230; entrepreneurship, 198–99, 202 –3, 207–10, 212, 219, 230, 234, 235, 236; Eshu (Yoruba god), 236; ethnicity, as critical factor in economic change, 210– 14, 230; foreign trade and investment, 206, 208, 209; Fulani, 197, 202, 205, 208, 214; GDP, 204; Hausa, 197, 202, 205, 208, 209, 213, 215; Ibadan, 210; Ibo, 197, 202, 209, 210–11, 213, 218, 230, 234; Ifa (Yoruba divination system), 232, 235; Ile-Ife, 212, 215; imports/exports, 205; Independence, 206;

indigenization, 205, 207, 219; industrialization, 201, 206; Islam, 197, 202, 208, 209, 211, 212, 214, 216, 218, 219, 231, 237; judgment (personal), 198, 234, 235; Kaduna, 216; Kano, Aminu, 216–17; Kano City, 213, 216, 217; Kanuri, 208; labor force, 204; Lagos, 206, 211, 212; Libya, 204; Maitatsine, Muhammudu Marwa, 217; Marxism, 198; military, 206; modernization, 208, 218, 230; Moslems, 197, 202, 206, 208, 211, 214, 216, 222, 229, 230; Musa, Alhaji Balarabe, 217; myths, religious, 231, 232, 233; nationalism, 207–8; National Party of Nigeria (NPN), 217; Niger, 217; Nigerian National Petroleum Company, 204; Northern Element's Progressive Union, 216; Ogun (Yoruba god), 237; oil, 204, 207, 208, 210; Orunmila (Yoruba god), 236; People's Redemption Party (PRP), 216–17; politics, 202; poverty, 208, 212–14; private enterprise, 206; Protestantism, 202, 203, 211, 234, 235; rebirth (personal), 198, 234, 235, 236; religious affiliation by region (table), 221; religion and economics, 208– 12, 218, 229; religion, behavioral consequences of, 201; religions, traditional, 197, 202, 209, 211, 212, 219, 229–30, 233; Rimi, Alhaji Abubakar, 217; ritual, place of in Nigerian culture, 231–32, 233; Roman Catholicism, 202, 210, 218; schools, see Education; Second Five-Year Plan (1970–74), 207; secularization, 218; Senegal, 218; Shagari, Shehu, 205; Shari'a (Islamic law), 202; Socialism, 198; technology, 206; trade, 203, 209; universities, see Education; urbanization, 197, 204; values, societal, 198, 202–3, 229, 230; wealth, people's understanding of, 212–14, 236; Weber, Max, 229, 230, 234; Westernization, 218, 229 –30, 237; women, place of, 215; World Bank, 204; zakat, 203, 215; Yan Izala (sect of Islam), 217; Yoruba, 197, 198, 202, 205, 209, 210, 211, 213, 214, 215, 229, 230
Nigerian Constitution (1979), 205
Nonalignment in Indian politics, 24
Nonviolence, 19, 38, 39, 40

Northern Element's Progressive Union of Nigeria, 216
Nuclear Energy, 42
Nuri, Shaikh Fazullah (1905–11), 105

Obregón, Alvaro, 148–49
od-Din, Naser Shah, 85, 94
Ogun (Yoruba god), 237
Oil: Anglo-Iranian Oil Company, 87; and Indian economy, 41–42; in Iran, 89, 92–94, 117; in Japan, 181; in Mexico, 122, 134, 135; in Nigeria, 204, 207, 208, 210; OPEC, 94–96
Organic State tradition, 136–37
Ottoman Empire, 79
Oyo Yoruba, 213
Ozo tithe, 234

Pahlavi, Mohammed Reza: and CIA intervention (1953), 116; crimes of, 140–42, 155, 161, 96–97; economic program of, 89–90; opposition to, 70; prosperity of Iran and, 83–84; purchase of military equipment by, 115–16
Pahlavi Dynasty, 73. *See also* Pahlavi, Mohammed Reza; Iran; Reza Shah Period
Pakistan, 209
Panchayat (village councils in India), 26, 40, 54
Parliamentary liberalism, 24
Partition of India, 39
Paz, Octavio, 125, 127, 153
Peasants: and the failure of land reforms in Iran, 91; displacement of, in Mexico, 129, 143; in Gandhi's vision, 36; oppression of, by landlords, in Iran, 82; represented in PRI (Mexico), 131; support of Mexican Revolution by, 137, 148–49. *See also* Agriculture; Agriculturists; Farmers
People's Redemption Party (PRP), 216–17
Persian Gulf, 114–17
Petroleum, *see* Oil
Poland, 1, 2, 4
Politics, place of, in modern India, 27
Population: in India, 22, 25, 28–30, 43, 49; density in Japan, 164, 182; growth of, in Iran, 80
Porfiriato, 133
Portillo, José López, 138

Positivism, 126, 127, 129, 130, 131
Poverty: corruption of relief programs in India, 48–49; elimination of, under Indira Gandhi, 25, 45–46, 47; in Gulf societies, 113; in India, 22, 27; perpetuated by religious and cultural attitudes, 51–52
PRI (Institutional Revolutionary Party), 121, 131, 135, 137, 151, 152
Protestantism, 53, 175, 202, 203, 211, 234, 235
Puebla Conference of Latin American Bishops (1979), 154
Punjab, 47, 50, 52, 54

Qom (shrine city of Iran), 96, 105
Quiroga, Vasco de, 155
Qur'an, 76

Railway: Mexican, 130; trans-Iranian, 89
Ram, Jagjivan, 28
Rationalism, economic 176
Rebirth: in Ibo tradition, 234; in Yoruba tradition, 233, 234, 236
Recession, 165
Religion: ancestor worship in Japan, 169–70; and economic change in Nigeria, 211, 219; and Revolution in Iran, 69–70; as component of political control in Nigeria, 208–9; as force of inertia and irrationality, 3; breakdown of Iranian religion, customs and ideals, 86; Buddhism, 11, 165, 170–71, 180; Catholicism, 126, 127–30, 135, 138, 153–57, 169; Christianity, 11, 197, 203, 208, 211, 214–19, 229, 230–31, 237; Confucianism, 165, 167–68, 171; doctrine of, as core symbols of society, 74; exclusion of, from public life in Mexico, 146; force of, in India, 40; in colonial Mexico, 147; in Japan, 165, 168, 170, 171, 180; internal focus of religious practice, 75; Islam, 69, 70, 75, 78, 79, 108, 110, 111, 112; losses of, under Reza Shah, 88–89; martyrdom and suffering, a component of, 76; participation of, in public life of Mexico, 146–47; political economy and religious values in Mexico, 135–36; practice of Islam in prerevolutionary Iran, 73–74; Protestantism, 202–3, 211,

234–35; relationship between religion and economics in Japan, 164, 167–68, 170, 176, 180; religious attitudes and underdevelopment in India, 33, 41, 50; religious philosophy in Iran, 74–76; religious tradition and economic development, 12, 51, 155–57, 164, 167, 215–18; restrictions against the study of, 146; Shinto, 165, 168, 180; weakening of, in India, 40

Religious education, 30, 88–89, 93–94
Religious liberty, 5
Religious reforms, 150
Rerum Novarum (1891), 130
Reuter, Julius de, 86
Reza Shah Period, 88–136
Revolution: and religion in Iran, 1, 69–70; agitation by Moslem fundamentalists, 114; as product and process, 106–7; call for total revolution in India, 41; demands of, in Mexico, 126; expression of anti-Americanism in Iran, 107; goals of, in Mexico, 151; Mexican, 125, 129, 131, 137, 138–39, 145, 148, 150, 151; vs. evolution, 41
Revolutionary Coalition (Mexico), 131
Rice, 47
Rig Veda, 18
Rim, Alhaji Abubakar, 217–18
Ritual: adaptations of Christianity and Islam, 236–37; as instrument for coping with suffering and death, 237; Ifa (rites of divination), 232–35; Yoruba, 231–37
Rockefeller Foundation, 42
Roman Catholic Church: and social justice, 150; and state in modern Mexico, 126, 128, 135, 137–38, 144, 146–47; anti-clericalism in Mexico, 125–26; "closed to future," 125; condemnation of Mexican Constitution (1857) by, 128–29; Conference of Mexican Bishops, 143; conversion of Aztecs, 127–28; in Mexico, 122, 125, 127–28, 136, 147–48, 156–57; in Nigeria, 202, 210, 218; landholdings of, in Mexico, 128–29; religious reforms of, 150; restrictions on, by Mexican government, 128–30; role of, in Mexican struggle for independence, 128; seizure of church land, 128
Roman law, 136

Ronin, 191
Rudra (Aryan god), 18
Russia: British-Russian partition of Iran (1907), 87; development programs of, in Iran, 85–86; financial obligations of Iran to, 87; seeking control of Iran, 87; target of hostility in Iran, 107–8

Sa'edi, Ghlam Hossein, 94
Safavids (1501–1722), 79
Saikaki, 172
Salar, Hajji Mirza Hosein Sipah, 85
Samarra (shrine city of Iran), 79
Samurai, 169, 171, 172, 191
Samarkand, 18
Saudi Arabia: compared with Iran, 112, 115, 116–17; Five-Year Plan of, 1980–85), 113; military buildup in, 116; Shi'i Moslem uprising in (1979), 113; U.S. policy toward, 116–17
Science, in Nehru vision, 26
Schools: creation of rural elementary schools in Mexico, 148–49; introduction of primary schools in India, 40. *See also* Education
Second Five-Year Plan (Nigeria, 1970–74), 207
Second Vatican Council (1962–65), 144, 153, 155
Secularism, 24
Secularization, 4, 5
Senegal, 218
Shagari, Shehu, 205
Shah, Mohammed Reza, *see* Pahlavi
Sharecroppers: in India, 53, 59; in Iran, 80–81, 91–92
Shari'a (Islamic religious law), 69–70, 202–3
Shastri, Lal Bahadur (premier), (1964–66), 23, 28
Sheiks, in opposition to government, 80
Shi'is: conflict between Sunni Islam and Shi'is, 108–9; ethics of, 108–9; foundations of Iranian Islam, 73–74; Moslems, 69, 110; uprising at al-Qatif (1979), 113
Shinto, 164–65, 180
Sikh, 11
Singh, Charan, 28, 29, 46, 50, 54
Sixth Five-Year Plan (India), 45
Smuggling, 45

Solidarity, 155
Soviet Union: attempts to annex Azerbaijan
 and Kurdistan, 76; compared with In-
 dia, 11, 42; model of socialism for Indi-
 an intellectuals, 36; rank of, with Japan,
 economically, 163
Spain, 128, 130
Spirituality: in Hindu teaching, 21–22; in
 Islam, 75; place of martyrdom and suf-
 fering in, 76–77. See also Religious edu-
 cation; Religion
Sri Lanka, 2
Structures, as limitations on human choice,
 126–27
Suárez, 155
Sudra (Hindu caste), 36
Suffrage, in India, 61–62
Sufism: mystical enlightenment, 75–76, 78;
 persecution of, 78–79
Sunni Islam: 69, 78–79, 108–9, 110
Surya (Aryan god), 18
Syria, 114

Tabatab'i, Allamah, 76
Tabataba'i, Sayyed Myhammed, 105
Tagore, Rabindranath, 22
Tamerlane, 18
Taxation, policy of Reza Shah, 89
Technology: in India, 3, 46, 49, 55; in Iran,
 70, 81; in Japan, 182–84; in Mexico,
 133; in Nigeria, 206, 208, 212
Tehran, 89
Theocracy, 126, 128, 145, 147
Theology, 226. See also Liberation theology
Third World, 41
Timur, see Tamerlane
Tobacco Rebellion (1890–92), 86
Tokugawa Period, 169, 171, 173, 180, 191
Tradition: and ie in Japan, 169–72; and Jap-
 anese economic culture, 164; Nehru's
 appreciation of, 26; of Islam and class
 solidarity, 216; reassertion of, in Iran,
 97–98; religious, in Mexico, 145; tradi-
 tional religions of Africa, 210, 231–34;
 traditional social values of Japan, 237–
 38; vs. modernity, 25; Yoruba tradition,
 231–34
Triple Alliance, 144
Turkey, 208
Twelver (sect of Islam), 73, 78, 79

Ulema (Islamic leaders), 79, 86–87, 89, 105,
 106, 110, 112
Underemployment: 44, 45, 53, 54
Unemployment: 41, 43, 46, 163, 181
United States, 41. See also America; CIA
Universities: Indian, 42; Japanese, 189;
 Mexican 146
Untouchability, abolition of, 39
Urban life, in modern Japan, 173
Utaiba, Juhayman al-, 112
Uttar Pradesh, 47, 51, 52, 54

Vaishya (Hindu caste), 36–37
Values: Ibo values and development in Nigeria, 218; influence of religious values
 in Mexico, 135–36, 139, 144; Islamic,
 111–12, 216; Japanese, 172, 180, 181;
 place of wealth in Yoruba traditional
 value system, 236; rejection of religious
 values in Mexico, 146–49; religious values and economic values, 32–38, 149–50
Varnashramadnarma, 36
Vasconcelos, José, 149
Villa, Pancho, 131, 133
Village: council's authority in India, 38;
 cultic organization of Japanese, 170,
 180; emphasis in Gandhian political
 philosophy, 36, 38; glorification of in
 India, 38; in Ibo society, 218; in India
 after Independence, 36, 37; life of, in
 Iran, 81–82, 92; redevelopment projects
 in Iranian, 97–98

Weber, Max, 2
Westernization, 70, 163
"Westoxication," 94, 97
"White Revolution," 91
Women: and institution of ie in Japan, 188;
 changing status of, in Iran, 88; discrimi-
 nation against, 187–89, 215; education
 of, in Nigeria, 215; place of in Yoruba
 religious practices, 214–15
Work, sacred quality of, 22
Workplace, importance of, in Japan, 164,
 183–84
World Council of Churches, 2
World War II, 3, 89–90, 133–34, 165, 169

Yoruba: as emerging world religion, 236;
 class consciousness among, 211–12, 213

–15; compared with Ibo, 230–31, 234–35; effects of Westernization on, 236–37; ethnicity and religion of, 197, 210–12; inequality among the sexes, 214–15; myths of, 231–32; place of wealth in tradition of, 236; religious practices of, 214, 231–33; social mobility among, 211–12; traditions of, 231–34

Yoshi (adopted son in *ie* tradition), 169

Youth, 143

Zapata, Emiliano, 131, 133

Zaria, workers of, 215

Zimbabwe, 2